Instant Pot Cookbook

550 Delicious, Easy-to-Remember and Quick-to-Make Instant Pot Recipes for Beginners and Advanced Users

By: Amelia Jackson

(What this book is all about:)

1. 550 Effortless, Easy and Yummy Recipes for your Instant Pot Pressure Cooker

2. It contains complete Instant Pot beginner's guide

3. Start cooking immediately, no need to have any experience with your instant pot.

4. Everything is done a lot faster and it will taste delicious.

5. Common and Tasty Ingredients for no-fuss meals

6. Big variety of recipes for any taste to surprise your friends and guests

7. Easy-to-follow steps to make cooking sound like a child's play -funny and carefree

8. You will enrich your daily life with tasty and nice-looking dishes.

TABLE OF CONTENTS

Introduction

In today's fast-paced world, many people opt to eat out because they don't have time to prepare their own food. While this is convenient, the caveat to eating out constantly is the lack of variety and nutrition. This is the reason why metabolic syndromes and diseases are rampant because people are no longer spending time in the kitchen making conscious efforts while preparing their food. While it is ideal to go back to the old days when you have to prepare your own, you just can't find enough time to slave in the kitchen. Well, worry no more! This book will teach you how to cook delicious meals every single day with a single device!

The Instant Pot is revolutionary device! You can cook virtually anything - from meats and main courses to rice, potatoes, vegetables of every description, dessert to even yogurt. Better yet, pressure cooking allows you to prepare foods up to 70 % faster, on average, than conventional cooking methods do, which means you save energy in addition to your precious time!

You no need to be an expert chef. No need to have all evening to yourself. You don't even need much money! These delicious and simple recipes are easy for anyone to pull off, and you will not miss your old fast food and microwave lifestyle. So, whether you are a busy family, a working professional, or a student, the instant pot will be your kitchen friend for many years to come

Enjoy a culinary adventure using recipes based on meat, seafood, vegetarian ingredients! Discover desserts that are easier and more delicious than you thought possible. Whether working and living a busy life, entertaining friends and family, you're sure to find a great many uses for the recipes in this book. Convenience and diversity of ingredients, quick cooking or slow cooking for home cooked meals basically cook themselves, there is much to find and delight in here!

You can forget about long hours in the kitchen, about using hundreds of pots and pans. Forget about complex cooking methods and energy consumption. All you have to do is to purchase your ingredients and cook them in your instant pot. The best thing about these marvelous pots is that they allow you to cook so many different dishes in just minutes and they all taste amazing

Each recipes is accompanied with the basic cooking instructions, ingredients, time and servings. The recipes are specially tried and hand-picked in our kitchen to give you maximum satisfaction and near possible results. All the recipes contained in this book are fresh, foolproof and easy that anyone can cook without breaking a sweat.

Nutritious meals

Pressure cooking, slow cooking, and steaming foods keep in flavor and nutrients and create delicious and moist dishes. The recipes in my book use all of these functions

Save time and energy

Using the Instant Pot saves you a lot of time. You can eat healthy at home, without spending the time you don't have, prepping and then cooking your meals. And fast cooking = energy saving. Cooking with your Instant pot is fast and efficient, cutting down your electricity bill by cooking in less time than you would on the stovetop or in the oven.

No more mad-rush cooking

How often have you had no time at all to even think about what you're making for dinner? Those days of panic are over. Your Instant Pot is there for you! There are some fast and easy meals included in the recipe book that in just minutes help you get a fantastic dinner on the table

Hot breakfast!

Tired of waking up to cold cereal as your only breakfast option? Your Instant Pot can make hot oatmeal in minutes. Or make breakfast in your Instant Pot the night before and just heat up in the morning.

Cook perfect rice every time!

Make rice in your electric pressure cooker, and you'll never go back to making it stove-top again. White, brown, or basmati – some people would say the Instant Pot was made for rice

Time your meals

Because of the Instant Pot cooks so fast, use the Delay Start function to time your meals, so they're ready when you get home. Many of my recipes let you prep your food the night before and then put them in the Instant Pot on the timer, cooking them to perfection every time.

The handy "Keep Warm" function

Most Instant Pot models will have a Keep Warm function. When cooking is done, Keep Warm will turn on, so your meal is ready, warm, and waiting for whenever you're ready to sit down and eat

Effortless cooking

Instant Pot provides you with flavorful cuisines in an effortless manner. It cooks food in an ideal method to make it tastier and healthier. It's simple to use with automatic cooking functions, and it is easy to clean also for a completely effortless cooking experience.

Kills harmful micro-organism

Instant Pot saves your body from many harmful bacteria and viruses by killing them in high-temperature cooking. Many cereals, vegetable, and pulses are prone to contain bacteria and fungus, even after washing them. Such bacteria and viruses get killed during the cooking process in Instant Pot

Manual / Pressure Buttons:

This is probably going to be the buttons you use most on the Instant Pot. It will allow you to pressure cook and manually select the time you want – rather than the preset buttons (such as Soup/Stew or Meat buttons). You can adjust the pressure, temperature and time by selecting the "+/- "buttons

Poultry:

Make your favorite chicken recipes with the "Poultry" button with the Instant Pot. It will default to a High Pressure for 15 minutes. You can adjust for "More" to High Pressure for 30 minutes or "Less" for High Pressure for 5 minutes

Bean / Chili:

One of my favorite things to make in the Instant Pot is beans. It's so much faster (and tastier) with the Instant Pot. When you use the "Bean / Chili" button, it will default to a High Pressure for 30 minutes. You can adjust for "More" to High Pressure for 40 minutes or "Less" for High Pressure for 25 minutes.

Meat / Stew:

Make your favorite stew or meat dish in the Instant Pot. Adjust the settings depending on the texture you want. For instance, the "More" setting is better for fall-off-the-bone cooking.

It will default to a High Pressure for 35 minutes. You can adjust for "More" to High Pressure for 45 minutes or "Less" for High Pressure for 20 minutes

Sauté Button:

The "Sauté" Button is the second most used function with my Instant Pot. You can do that and basically cook up anything as you would in a skillet or pan. You don't need the 1 cup of liquid. Just press the "Sauté" button, add some cooking oil to the inner pot and add food you want to cook like a skillet or pan.

Soup:

Use the "Soup" button to make broth, stock or soup. The Instant Pot will control the pressure and temperature so that the liquid doesn't heavily boil. You can adjust the cooking time as needed, typically between 20-40 minutes, and the pressure to either low or high

Slow Cook Button:

Use your Instant Pot like a slower cooker with this option. Just add food as you normally would to a slow cooker, close the lid and then press the "Slow Cook" button.

It will default to a 4-hour slow cook time. You can use "+/- "buttons to adjust the cook time.

Porridge:

Use the "Porridge" button to make rice porridge (congee) and other grains (not regular white or brown rice). It will default to a High Pressure for 20 minutes, which is best for rice porridge. You can adjust for "More" to High Pressure for 30 minutes or "Less" for High Pressure for 15 minutes

After the porridge is finished, do not use the Quick Release handle. Because it has a high starch content, using the Quick Release will splatter the porridge through the steam release vent. Use the Natural Release.

Multigrain:

The "Multigrain" button is best for cooking brown rice and wild rice, which typically takes longer than white rice to cook. Cook brown rice to a 1:1.25 ratio rice to water and wild rice to a 1:3 ratio rice to water for 22-30 minutes.

It will default at the "Normal" setting is 40 minutes of pressure cooking time. Adjust as needed for the "Less" setting is 20 minutes of pressure cooking time, or "More" at 45 minutes of warm water soaking and 60 minutes of pressure cooking

Rice:

You can cook rice in the Instant Pot in nearly half the time as a conventional rice cooker. White rice, short grain, Jasmine and Basmati rice can all be cooked on this setting in about 4 to 8 minutes. In general, you'll need a 1:1 ratio of rice to water (Basmati is a 1:1.5 ratio).

When you choose the "Rice" button, the cooking duration automatically adjusts depending on how much food you put into the unit and cook on low pressure. Be sure to add about 10-12 minutes to the total cooking time to allow the Instant Pot to come to pressure

Steam:

Use the "Steam" button to steam vegetables, seafood or reheat food (it's a great alternative to the microwave). Be sure to use the steam rack included with the Instant Pot, otherwise food may burn and stick to the bottom of the inner pot

Timer Button:

Use the Timer button to delay the cooking start time for the Instant Pot. This works for both pressure cooking and slow cook options.

To use this feature, just press the Timer button with 10 seconds of pressing either the Pressure / Manual button or Slow Cook button. Use "+/- "buttons to adjust the delayed hours, then wait a second and press Timer again to set delayed minutes. You can cancel the Timer anytime by pressing the Keep Warm / Cancel button

Cancel Button:

At any time, you can cancel cooking and return to standby mode by pressing the "Keep Warm" / "Cancel" button. This is a great option if you selected the wrong time for pressure cooking and need to stop to make adjustments to the pressure or time

Keep Warm Button:

When pressure cooking is done, the Instant Pot will beep and automatically go into the "Keep Warm" function. It will display an "L" in front of a number to indicate how long it's been warm – e.g. "L0:30" for 30 minutes. It's a great feature to keep food warm for up to 99 hours, 50 minutes. It's perfect for pot lucks.

How Natural Release Works and When to Use It.

Natural release works exactly the way it sounds. Using this method, there's really nothing you have to depressurize your pressure cooker. Once the cooking is finished, the pressure will automatically slowly drop inside the electric pressure cooker. Because of this slow drop in pressure and heat, when using natural release, food continues cooking even though active cooking is complete

Use this method when cooking meat, foods that increase in volume or foam [like dried beans and legumes], soups, or any other foods that are primarily liquid.

How Quick Release Works and When to Use It.

Quick release works by turning the valve once active cooking is complete. This process takes an extra degree of care, as a loud burst of steam is released from the valve. Rapid release takes no more than a minute or two, and works best with foods, like eggs, vegetables, or delicate ingredients that don't benefit from any extra cook time. This method is also helpful when you need to check the doneness of food or add additional ingredients to the pressure cooker, as you might with a stew

It's best to avoid using Quick release when cooking foods that increase in volume, froth, or foam, like legumes, or those that are mostly liquid, like soup, as the liquid can boil up and vent through the release valve

Note:

1. Use Quick release when adding additional ingredients to the pot [like with a stew], or cooking eggs, vegetables, delicate foods, or ingredients that don't benefit from additional cook time

2. Use natural release when cooking meat, dried beans and legumes, rice, soup, and other foods that are mostly liquid

As with any cooking appliance, keeping your Instant Pot Mini clean is very important. A clean Instant Pot is one that lasts a long time and continues producing great meals every time. Before cleaning, always unplug the Instant Pot and let it cool if you just used it. There are four parts you need to concern yourself with: the outside of the pot, the removable inner pot, the exhaust valve, and the gasket/silicone ring

The outside

Cleaning the outside of the Instant Pot is easy. It can get grimy and dusty, so just dampen a paper towel or rag and wipe it down. A shiny clean Instant Pot is more than just an attractive appliance on your counter; keeping it clean keeps bugs and bacteria at bay

The inner pot

Made of stainless steel, this pot can be removed and run through the dishwasher. You can also wash it by hand, but be sure to use a soft sponge since abrasive ones will scratch the surface. Regular dish soap and hot water is all you need

The exhaust valve

Turn over the lid to your Instant Pot, and you'll see a little "hat" with holes fitted to the inside. This is the exhaust valve cap, and food can get stuck in it and the valve itself. Pop off the cap (don't twist) and rinse it out well. Clean out the hole to the valve with something sharp and non-breakable, like a needle

The gasket/silicone ring

The official name of the airtight silicone sealing ring is the gasket, so if you see that written anywhere, it's referring to the ring. This holds on to a lot of odors, so you want to clean it out at least every two to three meals you make. Like the inner pot, it is dishwasher-safe

If you make something with tomato, fish, onion, or a lot of spices, you'll probably want to soak it in a mixture of water, vinegar, and baking soda. Rinse and dry it well. When it starts to get discolored and you can't seem to get rid of the odors, it's time to replace it. You should also replace the ring when it starts to feel loose in the lid

Other maintenance tips

When storing your Instant Pot, keep the lid off the pot. This lets it air out, so odors aren't trapped. It also lets the Instant Pot dry out completely if there's any water from cleanup leftover. If you want your Instant Pot to last as long as possible, we recommend hand-washing over using the dishwasher. It can be a pain, yes, but it's gentler on the cooker parts

Like with all cooking appliances, there is a right way and a wrong way to use your instant pot. By keeping an eye on what you are doing you can make sure that your instant pot is safe, quick to use, and lasts a very long time

Watch out about overfilling. Your instant pot should not be completely filled. Ever! You need space for pressure and/or steam to build up. Whether you are filling it with food or fluid, always make sure there is plenty of space from the top

Experiment with the functions. Your instant pot does so many things, don't just use it for pressure cooking and get other pots and gadgets for the rest. Otherwise what's the point in having it? Use it to shallow fry, boil, steam, bake, etc. The possibilities are plentiful

Measure your liquids carefully. Your instant pot has two different limits: the pressure limit and the slow cooker limit. Do not exceed the fluid amount for either! Always count things that liquefy, like gelatine or sugar, as a liquid.

Clean it well after each use. Your instant pot will not last if it ends up with a built up film of fat or layer of burnt and sticky food in it. Besides, that is unhealthy. Even if you have "only" used it to steam, remember that steam carries fat particles and creates a greasy film, so it still needs cleaning.

Do not leave the house when it is on. Unlike with a traditional slow cooker, the instant pot reaches high temperatures, can carry a high voltage, and involves literal pressure

Be careful handling steam. Steam and pressure are nothing to joke around with! Never put your hand right in the steam, and always release the pressure according to the instructions manual. Always seal your instant pot properly before building pressure. Always open it when it is ready

Don't Try and force it open. Again: intense pressure. Forcing it open could cause a seriously painful blast.

Don't Use quick release unless specified. The pressure that can build up in your instant pot is intense. If you release it too fast you could get hurt. Only use quick release when a recipe specifically calls for it.

Don't Put things in in huge pieces. Even cooking is important, and big pieces do not respond as well to pressure or quick cooking. Leave the whole chickens for slow cooking only

Don't Fill it with hot oil. This is not a deep fat fryer! Filling it with oil is dangerous and could cause a grease fire. At the very least, you will break your instant pot

This is section is designed for the interest of every reader who has chosen to use this book in place of other instant pot manuals and for necessity purposes, I believe it is important for me to give a brief review of the basic parts of the instant pot, as it may come in handy to most of us who love the usage of the instant pot and also to some of us who hardly go through the manuals that come with the instant pot. It may also serve as a Reminder, for any of us who may have forgotten the use of some of the functionalities available on the instant pot

The Instant Pot Lid:

the lid is the cover of the pot; it is the uppermost part of your instant pot which is used to seal the cooker when cooking. In other words, it is used in either sealing or opening the cooker at will. To open the lid after cooking, it is a must that you release the pressure from pot using the quick release method or using the natural release method

Trivet & Steam Basket:

These two, the trivet and the steam basket help to keep the food above the pressure cookers bottom so as to prevent the intense heat of the pot from reaching the food, prevent the nutrient from leaching into the liquid and to prevent the food from burning. Such types of food include; egg, vegetables etc

Silicone Sealing Ring:

this is sometimes referred to as the gasket, it is a sealing ring inside the lid of the cooker which helps to keep the steam inside the pot. For safety purposes, the gasket or silicon sealing ring should be cleaned immediately after cooking and should be replaced when cold

Steam Release Valve:

the valve is used for releasing pressure from the Instant pot when it is high, it is also useful when all you intend to do is to add more COOKING ITEMS to the pot or check if the food is properly cooked. The knob located on the lid and the direction in which it is turned determines if it used for venting or to completely seal the cooker

Pressure Indicator:

The pressure indicator, is usually located on the cover of the instant cooker. It's a small pin situated right at the top of the cover and would normally stay up when the pressure cooker is at its maximum pressure point. The pin stays down when the pressure is low and this indicates when the pot is safe or unsafe to open

Steam Condensation Collector:

the steam condensation collector is a plastic container, which is located on the side of the cooker to help collect extra condensation

Troubleshooting

1. Silicon Sealing Ring Retains Odors

The sealing ring of the pressure cooker can pick up odors from previous meals cooked. The odors can be removed by soaking the ring in denture cleaner solution or washing the sealing ring with dishwasher. You can buy an additional sealing ring to use separately when cooking desserts or sweets

2. Steam Escaping from Sides of the Lid

You have to push down the lid and ensure that the lid is sealed or turn off the Instant Pot by pressing the Keep Warm/Cancel button. Open the lid to check the sealing ring and make sure that the sealing ring is secured.

3. Instant Pot Not Coming to Pressure

Check the pressure valve to ensure that it is closed to the sealing position. Also, check the sealing ring and press the Keep Warm/Cancel button. Open the lid to check the sealing ring and ensure that the sealing ring is secured. In a situation that your inner pot is too full or filled to the brim, it can take a longer time to come to pressure

4. Instant Pot Beeping with an Error Code

The pressure will not come to pressure on time if you are cooking with tomato based sauces or thicker cream bases. The thick liquids can burn to the bottom of the pot and not come to pressure properly. Ensure to add equal parts of water to sauce ratio

You can thicken the sauce in the sauté mode after the cooking time has completed. When you are in the middle of cooking, ensure that you turn off the pot and mix in more water to prevent burning at the bottom of the cooking pot

5. The sealing ring can loosen up from the heat of back to back cooking

Carefully place the ring under cold water or place in freezer for a while to shrink the ring back to size. I will recommend you to purchase a backup sealing ring to keep on hand

How do I return to the cooker's default setting?

To return to the factory default setting for a specific cooking program, return the cooker to Standby' mode displaying OFF; then, press and hold the cooking program key until the cooker beeps

For a full reset of all cooking programs and system settings, return the cooker to standby mode displaying OFF, then press and hold the Cancel key until the cooker beeps

Does the instant pot really speed up the cooking process?

Cooking in any pressure cooker is almost always faster. It may not be noticeable for some foods like broccoli or shrimps. However, tender and juicy pulled pork can be done in under 90 minutes, when it usually takes 2 - 4 hours to make in the oven

Why does the keep warm setting have a maximum time of 24 hours?

The Keep Warm will automatically shut off after 24 hours for safety and energy consumption reasons.

The steam release handle is loose, is this normal?

Yes, the Steam Release handle should not lock tightly into the lid, it must fit loosely

Why does the stainless steel inner pot have a rainbow like stain after washing?

The discoloration on the stainless steel cooking pot is called "rainbowing" which can be caused by exposure to high heat, cooking starchy food (e.g. rice, pasta) or even detergent staining after hand or machine wash. This is common and normal in all stainless steel cookware

Can I use the instant pot for pressure frying?

Please don't attempt to pressure fry in any electric pressure cookers. The splattering oil may melt the gasket. KFC uses a commercial pressure fryer (modern ones operate at 5 PSI) specially made to fry chickens. The Chicken recipes in this book is probably as close as it gets

How do I know if I should use natural pressure release or quick release?

Start by referring to the recipe. The Quick Release method is used for delicate dishes such as custards and fresh vegetables and the Natural Release method is used for meats, soups and grains

Poultry Recipes

Chicken Adobo Recipe

(Prep + Cook Time: 40 minutes | **Serves:** 3)

Ingredients:
- 4 chicken drumsticks
- 1/4 cup white vinegar
- 1/3 cup soy sauce
- 1/4 cup sugar
- 1 onion, chopped.
- 5 cloves garlic, crushed
- 2 bay leaves
- 1/2 teaspoon kosher salt
- 1 teaspoon ground black pepper
- 2 tablespoons olive oil

Directions:
1. Select SAUTÉ on high heat. Wait 1 minute and add the oil to the bottom of the pot
2. Season the legs with salt and 1/2 teaspoon pepper.
3. Add the chicken drumsticks to the Instant Pot and brown for 4 minutes on each side.
4. Add the vinegar, soy sauce, sugar, onion, garlic, bay leaves and 1/2 teaspoon pepper.
5. Close and lock the lid. Select MANUAL and cook at HIGH pressure for 10 minutes
6. When the timer goes off, use a Quick Release.
7. Carefully Open the lid, Select the SAUTÉ setting on high heat and simmer for 10 minutes to reduce the sauce.
8. Press the CANCEL button to stop the cooking program.
9. Remove the bay leaves, Serve

Spicy Chicken Wings

(Prep + Cook Time: 20 minutes | **Serves:** 4)

Ingredients:
- 3-pound chicken wings
- 1/4 cup light brown sugar
- 2 tablespoons olive oil
- 1/2 teaspoon garlic powder
- 1/2 teaspoon cayenne pepper
- 1 ½ cups chicken broth or water
- 1/2 teaspoon black pepper
- 1/2 teaspoon paprika
- 1/2 teaspoon salt

Directions:
1. Rinse and dry the chicken wings with a paper towel. Put in the large bowl
2. In a medium bowl, combine the olive oil, sugar, garlic powder, cayenne pepper, black pepper, paprika, and salt. Mix well
3. Rub all sides of the chicken with the spice mix.
4. Pour the chicken broth into the Instant Pot and add the wings
5. Close and lock the lid. Select the MANUAL setting and set the cooking time for 10 minutes at HIGH pressure.
6. Once pressure cooking is complete, use a Quick Release
7. Carefully unlock the lid, if you want a crisp skin, slide under the broiler for 5-6 minutes then Serve.

BBQ Chicken Drumsticks

(Prep + Cook Time: 35 minutes | **Serves:** 5)

Ingredients:

- 6 chicken drumsticks
- 1/2 cup + 2 tablespoon water
- 1/2 cup sugar-free barbecue sauce
- 1 onion, chopped.
- 1 tablespoon olive oil
- 1 teaspoon garlic, minced
- 1 ½ tablespoon arrowroot

Directions:

1. Select the SAUTÉ setting on the Instant Pot and heat the oil
2. Add the onion and sauté for about 3 minutes, until softened
3. Add the garlic and cook for another 30 seconds.
4. Add 1/2 cup of water and barbecue sauce, stir well.
5. Add the chicken drumsticks to the pot. Close and lock the lid
6. Press the CANCEL button to reset the cooking program. Select MANUAL and cook at HIGH pressure for 10 minutes.
7. When the timer goes off, use a Quick Release. Carefully Open the lid
8. In a cup, whisk together the remaining water and arrowroot until combined. Add to the pot.
9. Select the SAUTÉ setting and cook on high heat for 5 minutes or until the sauce has thickened. Serve the drumsticks with the sauce

Turkey Meatballs

(Prep + Cook Time: 25 minutes | **Serves:** 2)

Ingredients:

- 1 pound' ground turkey
- 1 can (14 oz.) tomato puree
- 1/3 cup chicken broth or water
- 1/2 cup breadcrumbs
- 2 tablespoons green onion, chopped.
- 1/2 teaspoon kosher salt
- 1/4 teaspoon ground black pepper
- 1 ½ tablespoon buttermilk
- 1/2 tablespoon canola oil
- 1/2 tablespoon sesame seeds

For the sauce:

- 4 tablespoon soy sauce
- 1 clove garlic, minced
- 1 teaspoon ginger, grated
- 1 ½ tablespoon brown sugar
- 2 tablespoon canola oil
- 2 tablespoon rice vinegar
- 1/4 teaspoon ground black pepper
- 1/2 tablespoon cornstarch

Directions:

1. In a medium bowl, combine ground turkey, breadcrumbs, green onions, salt, pepper, and buttermilk. Mix well
2. Form 1 ½-inch meatballs and place in a bowl
3. In another bowl, combine all of the ingredients from the sauce list. Mix well.
4. Set your instant pot on SAUTÉ mode, add 1/2 tablespoon of canola oil and heat it up
5. Add the meatballs and brown for 2 minutes on each side.
6. Add the sauce, tomato puree and broth. Close and lock the lid.
7. Select the MANUAL setting and set the cooking time for 10 minutes at HIGH pressure
8. When the timer beeps, use a Quick Release.
9. Carefully unlock the lid, Transfer the meatballs with gravy to a serving bowl. Sprinkle with sesame seeds, Serve

Italian Chicken Dish

(Prep + Cook Time: 25 minutes | **Serves:** 5)

Ingredients:

- 8 boneless, skinless chicken thighs
- 2 cups cherry tomatoes
- 1/2 cup pitted green olives
- 1/2 cup thinly-sliced fresh basil
- 1/4 cup chopped fresh Italian parsley
- 2 medium-sized, chopped carrots
- 1 cup stemmed and quartered cremini mushrooms
- 1 chopped onion
- 3 cloves garlic, smashed
- 1 tablespoon tomato paste
- 1 tablespoon olive oil
- 1 teaspoon kosher salt
- 1/2 teaspoon ground black pepper

Directions:

1. Season the chicken thighs with ½ teaspoon salt and pepper
2. Select SAUTÉ on high heat. Wait 1 minute and add the oil to the bottom of the pot
3. Add the carrots, mushrooms, onions, and ½ teaspoon salt and sauté for about 5 minutes until soft.
4. Add the garlic and tomato paste and cook for another 30 seconds.
5. Add the cherry tomatoes, chicken thighs, and olives, stir well
6. Press the Cancel button to reset the cooking program, then select the MANUAL setting and set the cooking time for 10 minutes at HIGH pressure
7. When the timer goes off, use a Quick Release.
8. Carefully unlock the lid, Top with fresh basil and parsley, Serve

Thai Chicken Dish

(Prep + Cook Time: 25 minutes | **Serves:** 3)

Ingredients:

- 2-pound chicken thighs, boneless and skinless
- 1/2 cup fish sauce
- 1/4 cup extra virgin olive oil
- 1 cup lime juice
- 2 tablespoon coconut nectar
- 1 teaspoon mint, chopped.
- 2 teaspoon cilantro, finely chopped.
- 1 teaspoon ginger, grated

Directions:

1. In a medium bowl, whisk together lime juice, fish sauce, olive oil, coconut nectar, ginger, mint and cilantro until combined.
2. Add the chicken thighs to the instant pot. Pour the marinade on top
3. Close and lock the lid. Select Manual and cook at HIGH pressure for 10 minutes.
4. When the timer beeps, use a Quick Release.
5. Carefully unlock the lid, Serve

IP Shredded Chicken Breast

(Prep + Cook Time: 30 minutes | **Serves:** 4)

Ingredients:

- 1 ½ - 2-pound boneless chicken breasts
- 1/2 cup chicken broth
- 1/2 teaspoon ground black pepper
- 1/2 teaspoon garlic salt

Directions:

1. Season all sides of the chicken with the black pepper and salt
2. Add the chicken breasts to the Instant Pot and pour the chicken broth.
3. Close and lock the lid. Select MANUAL and cook at HIGH pressure for 8 minutes
4. Once cooking is complete, use a Natural Release for 10 minutes, then release any remaining pressure manually.
5. Remove the chicken from the pot and shred it with 2 forks, Serve

Lime Chili Chicken

(Prep + Cook Time: 35 minutes | **Serves:** 3)

Ingredients:
- 2-pound chicken breasts, bones removed
- 6 cloves garlic, minced
- 1/2 teaspoon liquid smoke
- 3/4 cup chicken broth or water
- Juice of 2 medium limes
- 1 ½ teaspoon chili powder
- 1 teaspoon cumin
- 1 teaspoon onion powder
- 1 teaspoon kosher salt
- 1 teaspoon ground black pepper

Directions:
1. Dump all of the ingredients into the Instant Pot and give it a little stir to mix everything evenly
2. Close and lock the lid. Select MANUAL and cook at HIGH pressure for 10 minutes.
3. When the timer goes off, let the pressure Release Naturally for 10 minutes, then release any remaining steam manually
4. Carefully Open the lid, Remove the chicken and shred it. Serve with the remaining juice from the Instant Pot.

Hunter Chicken

(Prep + Cook Time: 45 minutes | **Serves:** 5)

Ingredients:
- 8 chicken drumsticks, bone in
- 28 ounces' canned tomatoes and juice, crushed
- 1/2 cup black olives, pitted and sliced
- 1 yellow onion, chopped.
- 1 cup chicken stock
- 1 teaspoon garlic powder
- 1 teaspoon oregano, dried
- 1 bay leaf
- 1 teaspoon kosher salt

Directions:
1. Preheat the Instant Pot by selecting SAUTÉ.
2. Add the onion and cook for 6 to 7 minutes, until the onion is translucent
3. Add the stock, garlic powder, tomatoes, oregano, bay leaf and salt, stir well.
4. Put the chicken in the pot and stir. Close and lock the lid. Press the CANCEL button to reset the cooking program. Select the MANUAL setting and set the cooking time for 15 minutes at HIGH pressure.
5. Once timer goes off, allow to Naturally Release for 10 minutes, then release any remaining pressure manually
6. Uncover the pot, Remove the bay leaf. Divide the dish among plates, top with olives and serve.

Sesame Chicken

(Prep + Cook Time: 35 minutes | **Serves:** 5)

Ingredients:
- 6 boneless chicken thigh fillets
- 4 peeled and crushed cloves garlic
- 1 chunk peeled, grated fresh ginger
- 1/2 cup chicken stock
- 1 tablespoon rice vinegar
- 1 ½ tablespoon sesame seeds
- 5 tablespoons sweet chili sauce
- 5 tablespoon hoisin sauce
- 1 tablespoon soy sauce

Directions:
1. In a medium bowl, whisk together the chili sauce, hoisin sauce, ginger, garlic, vinegar, sesame seeds, soy sauce, and chicken stock until combined
2. Add the chicken thigh fillets to the Instant Pot and pour over the sauce mixture. Close and lock the lid. Select MANUAL and cook at HIGH pressure for 15 minutes
3. Once cooking is complete, let the pressure Release Naturally for 10 minutes. Release any remaining steam manually.
4. Open the lid, Serve with cooked rice, mashed potato or any other garnish

Buffalo Wings

(Prep + Cook Time: 25 minutes | **Serves:** 6)

Ingredients:

- 4-pound chicken wings, sectioned, frozen or fresh
- 1 - 2 tablespoon sugar, light brown
- 1/2 cup cayenne pepper hot sauce
- 1 tablespoon Worcestershire sauce
- 1/2 cup butter
- 1 ½ cups water
- 1/2 teaspoon kosher salt

Directions:

For the sauce:

1. In a microwavable container, mix the hot sauce with the Worcestershire sauce, butter, salt, and brown sugar; microwave for 20 seconds or until the butter is melted.

For the wings:

1. Pour the water into the Instant Pot and insert a steam rack
2. Place chicken wings on the steam rack and secure the lid
3. Select MANUAL and cook at HIGH pressure for 10 minutes.
4. When the timer beeps, use a Quick Release
5. Carefully unlock the lid. Preheat the oven to broil.
6. Carefully transfer the chicken wings to a baking sheet.
7. Brush the tops of the chicken wings with the sauce.
8. Place under the broiler for 4 to 5 minutes until browned
9. Brush the other side with the remaining sauce and broil for another 4-5 minutes then Serve.

Notes: If you want a milder sauce, use more butter. If you want a hotter sauce, use more hot sauce

Chicken Cacciatore

(Prep + Cook Time: 45 minutes | **Serves:** 4)

Ingredients:

- 4 chicken thighs, with the bone, skin removed
- 1/2 (14 oz.) can crushed tomatoes
- 2 tablespoons olive oil
- 1/2 cup diced green bell pepper
- 1/4 cup diced red bell pepper
- 1/2 cup diced onion
- 2 tablespoon chopped parsley or basil
- 1/2 teaspoon dried oregano
- 1 bay leaf
- 1 teaspoon kosher salt
- 1 teaspoon ground black pepper

Directions:

1. Select SAUTÉ on high heat. Wait 1 minute and add 1 tablespoon of oil to the bottom of the pot
2. Season the meat with salt and pepper
3. Brown the meat for a few minutes on each side. Remove the chicken from the pot and set aside
4. Pour another 1 tablespoon of oil into the pot; add bell peppers and onion and sauté for about 5 minutes or until soft and golden
5. Put the chicken thighs in the Instant pot. Pour over the tomatoes.
6. Add the oregano and bay leaf, stir well. Close and lock the lid
7. Press the CANCEL button to stop the SAUTE function. Select the MANUAL setting and set the cooking time for 25 minutes at HIGH pressure
8. Once cooking is complete, select CANCEL and let Naturally Release for 5 minutes, then do a Quick Release
9. Carefully unlock the lid and Serve.

Ginger Chicken Dish

(Prep + Cook Time: 35 minutes **| Serves:** 5)

Ingredients:
- 1 chicken cut into pieces
- 1 large onion, finely diced
- 1-inch ginger, finely grated
- 1/4 cup soy sauce
- 1/4 cup dry sherry
- 2 tablespoons olive oil
- 1/4 cup water
- Salt and ground black pepper to taste.

Directions:
1. Preheat the Instant Pot by selecting SAUTÉ. Add the oil.
2. Put the chicken in the Instant Pot and sauté until the chicken has turned light brown.
3. Add the soy sauce, onion, ginger, sherry, and water. Mix just until combined
4. Close and lock the lid. Press CANCEL and then select MANUAL and cook at HIGH pressure for 10 minutes.
5. Once cooking is complete, select Cancel and let Naturally Release for 5 minutes. Release any remaining steam manually
6. Carefully Open the lid, Season with salt and pepper to taste, Serve.

Turkey with Bean Chili.

(Prep + Cook Time: 50 minutes **| Serves:** 4)

Ingredients:
- 1 pound' ground turkey
- 1/2 cup red bell pepper, diced
- 1 cup cannellini beans, soaked for 8 hours
- 2 ½ cups chicken stock
- 2 cups onion, diced
- 1/2 cup Anaheim pepper, diced
- 3 tablespoon cilantro leaves, chopped.
- 1 teaspoon oregano
- 2 tablespoon chili powder
- 1 tablespoon olive oil
- 1 tablespoon salt
- 1/2 teaspoon black pepper

Directions:
1. Preheat the Instant Pot by selecting SAUTÉ. Add the oil.
2. Add the onion, Anaheim pepper, and bell pepper and sauté until the vegetables are translucent
3. Add the ground turkey, beans, chicken stock, oregano, chili powder, salt, and black pepper. Stir well. Close and lock the lid
4. Press the CANCEL button to reset the cooking program, then select the BEAN/CHILI setting and set the cooking time for 30 minutes.
5. When the timer beeps, let the pressure Release Naturally for 10 minutes, then release any remaining steam manually
6. Open the pot, Top with cilantro leaves and serve.

Tomato Chicken Drumsticks

(Prep + Cook Time: 40 minutes **| Serves:** 5)

Ingredients:
- 6 chicken drumsticks (24 oz), skin removed, on the bone
- 1 ½ cups tomato sauce
- 1 jalapeno, seeded, cut in halves
- 1/4 cup cilantro, chopped.
- 1 tablespoon apple cider vinegar
- 1 teaspoon oregano, dried
- 1 teaspoon olive oil
- 1/2 teaspoon salt
- 1/2 teaspoon ground black pepper

Directions:
1. In a medium bowl, combine the apple cider vinegar, oregano, salt and pepper
2. Add the chicken to the bowl and coat it well with the marinade. If desired, leave the chicken sit in the marinade for a couple of hours.
3. Set your instant pot on SAUTÉ mode, add the oil and heat it up

4. Lower the chicken into the pot and sear for 5-8 minutes on each side, until nicely browned.
5. Add the tomato sauce, a half of the jalapeno and cilantro. Close and lock the lid.
6. Press the CANCEL button to reset the cooking program, then select the MANUAL setting and set the cooking time for 20 minutes at HIGH pressure
7. Once pressure cooking is complete, use a Quick Release.
8. Unlock and carefully Open the lid, Serve with the remaining cilantro and jalapeno

Special Chicken Piccata

(Prep + Cook Time: 30 minutes | **Serves:** 4)

Ingredients:
- 4 chicken breasts skinless, boneless, 1 ½ to 1 ¾-pound
- 1 cup chicken broth
- 1/4 cup fresh lemon juice
- 1 tablespoon olive oil
- 2 tablespoon butter
- 2 tablespoon brined capers, drained
- 2 tablespoon flat-leaf fresh parsley, chopped.
- Cooked rice or pasta
- 1/4 teaspoon black pepper
- 1/2 teaspoon salt

Directions:
1. Select SAUTÉ on normal heat. Wait 2 minutes and add the oil to the bottom of the Instant Pot
2. Season the chicken with salt and pepper; add to the pot and brown the meat for 3 minutes on each side.
3. Add the broth. Close and lock the lid
4. Press the Cancel button to reset the cooking program, then select the MANUAL setting and set the cooking time for 5 minutes at HIGH pressure.
5. Once pressure cooking is complete, use a Quick Release
6. Unlock and carefully Open the lid, Remove the chicken from the pot to a serving bowl.
7. Select the SAUTÉ setting and simmer for 5 minutes to reduce the sauce.
8. Add fresh lemon juice
9. Add the butter. Once the butter is melted, add parsley and capers, stir
10. Press the CANCEL button to stop the cooking program.
11. Pour the sauce over chicken breasts. Serve with rice or pasta.

Shredded Chicken with Marinara

(Prep + Cook Time: 40 minutes | **Serves:** 5)

Ingredients:
- 4-pound chicken breasts
- 2 cups marinara sauce
- 1/2 cup chicken broth
- 1/2 teaspoon black pepper
- 1 teaspoon salt

Directions:
1. Add the chicken breasts, broth, pepper, and salt to the Instant Pot, stir well
2. Close and lock the lid. Select MANUAL and cook at HIGH pressure for 20 minutes
3. Once pressure cooking is complete, use a Quick Release.
4. Unlock and carefully Open the lid, Shred the chicken in the pot.
5. Select the SAUTÉ setting. Add the marinara sauce and simmer for 5 minutes
6. Serve with cooked rice, potato, peas or green salad.

Chicken Curry Recipe 2

(Prep + Cook Time: 40 minutes | **Serves:** 4)

Ingredients:

- 2-pound chicken breast or thighs
- 1 cup onion, chopped or 1/4 cup dry minced onion
- 16 ounces' canned coconut milk
- 16 ounces' canned tomato sauce
- 6 ounces' can tomato paste
- 2 cloves garlic, minced
- 2 tablespoon curry powder
- 3 tablespoon honey
- 1 teaspoon salt

Directions:

1. Combine all of the ingredients, except for the chicken, in the Instant Pot and stir to combine.
2. Add the chicken. Close and lock the lid
3. Select the MANUAL setting and set the cooking time for 15 minutes at HIGH pressure.
4. Once cooking is complete, let the pressure Release Naturally for 15 minutes. Release any remaining steam manually
5. Open the lid and gently stir. Serve with cooked rice, potato or peas.

Sweet Chicken Wings

(Prep + Cook Time: 35 minutes | **Serves:** 4)

Ingredients:

- 2-pound chicken wings
- 1 small lime, juiced
- 3 tablespoon honey
- 2 tablespoon soy sauce
- 1/2 cup water
- 1/2 teaspoon sea salt

Directions:

1. In a bowl, combine the soy sauce, lime juice, honey and salt
2. Rinse and dry the chicken wings with a paper towel.
3. Add the chicken wings and honey mixture to a Ziploc bag and shake a couple of times. Then refrigerate for 60 minutes.
4. Pour the water into the Instant Pot and add the chicken wings with marinade
5. Close and lock the lid. Select the MANUAL setting and set the cooking time for 15 minutes at HIGH pressure.
6. Once timer goes off, allow to Naturally Release for 10 minutes. Release any remaining steam manually.
7. Uncover the pot, Select SAUTÉ and continue to cook until the sauce thickens, Serve
8. If desired, season with some more herbs or spices.

Awesome Chicken Dinner

(Prep + Cook Time: 45 minutes | **Serves:** 4)

Ingredients:

- 2-pound boneless chicken thighs
- 1/4 cup honey
- 1/4 cup soy sauce
- 3 tablespoon organic ketchup
- 2 teaspoon garlic powder
- 1/4 cup coconut oil
- 1/2 teaspoon black pepper
- 1 ½ teaspoon sea salt

Directions:

1. Combine the soy sauce, ketchup, coconut oil, honey, garlic powder, pepper, and salt in the Instant Pot
2. Toss the chicken thighs in the mixture. Close and lock the lid.
3. Select the MANUAL setting and set the cooking time for 18 minutes at HIGH pressure
4. When the timer beeps, use a Quick Release.
5. Carefully unlock the lid. Select the SAUTÉ setting and simmer for 5 minutes or until the sauce begins to thicken.
6. Serve with vegetables

Creamy Cheesy Chicken

(Prep + Cook Time: 35 minutes | **Serves:** 6)

Ingredients:

- 1 pound' chicken breasts, boneless and skinless
- 8 ounces' cream cheese
- 1 can (10 oz.) rotel tomato, undrained
- 1 can (15 oz.) corn, undrained
- 1 can (15 oz.) black beans, drained and rinsed
- 1/4 cup parsley
- 1 package (1 oz.) dry ranch seasoning
- 1 ½ teaspoon chili powder
- 1 ½ teaspoon cumin

Directions:

1. Combine all of the ingredients, except cheese, in the Instant Pot
2. Close and lock the lid. Select MANUAL and cook at HIGH pressure for 20 minutes
3. When the timer goes off, let the pressure Release Naturally for 10 minutes, then release any remaining steam manually. Open the lid
4. Transfer the chicken to a plate and shred the meat.
5. Add the cheese to the pot and stir well. Close the lid a let sit for 5 minutes, until cheese is melted.
6. Open the lid and return the chicken to the pot. Stir to combine. Top with parsley and serve

Notes: Serve with tortilla chips or rice.

Salsa Chicken Delight

(Prep + Cook Time: 40 minutes | **Serves:** 3)

Ingredients:

- 2 pound' chicken breasts, skinless and boneless
- 2 cups chunky salsa, or your preference
- 2 teaspoon cumin
- A pinch of oregano
- 1 teaspoon kosher salt
- 1 teaspoon ground black pepper

Directions:

1. Add the chicken breasts to the Instant Pot and season with salt and pepper
2. Add the oregano, cumin and salsa, stir well.
3. Close and lock the lid. Select the POULTRY setting and set the cooking time for 25 minutes
4. When the timer beeps, use a Quick Release.
5. Carefully unlock the lid. Remove the chicken and shred it
6. You can use the shredded chicken in the casseroles or add to corn tortillas with some avocado, cilantro and a squeeze of lime juice for a quick meal.

Mustard Chicken with Potatoes

(Prep + Cook Time: 40 minutes | **Serves:** 7)

Ingredients:

- 2-pound chicken thighs
- 3-pound red potatoes, peeled and quartered
- 2 tablespoons olive oil
- 3/4 cup chicken broth
- 1/4 cup lemon juice
- 2 tablespoon Italian seasoning
- 3 tablespoon Dijon mustard
- 1 teaspoon salt
- 1 teaspoon ground black pepper

Directions:

1. Select the SAUTÉ setting on the Instant Pot and heat the oil
2. Add the chicken thighs to the pot and sauté for 2 - 3 minutes, until starting to brown.
3. Add the potatoes, Italian seasoning, and Dijon mustard. Cook, stir occasionally, for 2 minutes
4. Pour the broth and lemon juice into the pot, stir.
5. Season with salt and pepper. Close and lock the lid.

6. Press the CANCEL button to reset the cooking program. Select the POULTRY setting and set the cooking time for 15 minutes.
7. When the timer beeps, let the pressure Release Naturally for 10 minutes, then release any remaining steam manually
8. Carefully unlock the lid and Serve.

Chicken Curry Recipe

(Prep + Cook Time: 35 minutes | **Serves:** 4)

Ingredients:

- 1 pound' chicken breast, chopped.
- 5 ounces' canned coconut cream
- 6 potatoes, cut into halves
- 1 yellow onion, thinly sliced
- 1 bag (1 oz.) chicken curry base
- 1 tablespoon extra-virgin olive oil
- 1/2 bunch coriander, chopped.

Directions:

1. Select the SAUTÉ setting on the Instant Pot and heat the oil
2. Add the chicken and sauté for 2 minutes, until the chicken starts to brown
3. Add onion, stir and cook for 1 more minute.
4. In a medium bowl, combine the chicken curry base and coconut cream, stir well.
5. Pour into the pot, add potatoes and stir. Close and lock the lid
6. Press the CANCEL button to reset the cooking program, then select the MANUAL setting and set the cooking time for 15 minutes at HIGH pressure.
7. When the timer goes off, use a Quick Release
8. Carefully Open the lid, Top with coriander and serve.

Special Coca Cola Chicken

(Prep + Cook Time: 45 minutes | **Serves:** 4)

Ingredients:

- 4 chicken drumsticks
- 1 large finely onion, chopped.
- 1 small chopped chili
- 1 tablespoon balsamic vinegar
- 2 tablespoons olive oil
- 500 ml Coca Cola
- Salt and ground black pepper to taste

Directions:

1. Select SAUTÉ on high heat. Wait 1 minute and add the oil to the bottom of the pot
2. Season the chicken drumsticks with salt and pepper to taste.
3. Add the drumsticks to the Instant Pot and sear for 4 minutes on each side, until nicely browned.
4. Remove the chicken from the pot. Add the onions and sauté for about 3-5 minutes, until softened
5. Then add the chili, balsamic vinegar and Coca-Cola, stir.
6. Return the drumsticks to the pot. Close and lock the lid.
7. Press the CANCEL button to reset the cooking program. Select the MANUAL setting and set the cooking time for 10 minutes at HIGH pressure
8. Once cooking is complete, let the pressure Release Naturally for 10 minutes. Release any remaining steam manually.
9. Open the lid and Serve

Turkey Chili Delight

(Prep + Cook Time: 45 minutes | Serves: 4)

Ingredients:

- 1 pound' ground turkey (85% lean)
- 1 can tomato juice (5.5 oz.)
- 2 cups cooked chickpeas or white beans
- 2 - 3 cloves garlic, peeled
- 1 onion, diced
- 1/8 teaspoon cayenne
- 1 ½ teaspoon cumin
- 2 ½ tablespoon chili powder
- 1/2 cup water
- 1 ½ cups vegetable stock
- 1 yellow bell pepper, diced
- 2 cans tomatoes with chilies (10-ounce cans)

Directions:

1. Add the ground turkey and water to the Instant Pot.
2. Close and lock the lid. Select MANUAL and cook at HIGH pressure for 5 minutes
3. Turn off the heat and allow 5-10 minutes rest time and then do a Quick Release. Carefully Open the lid,
4. Break up the ground turkey with a wooden spoon or spatula.
5. Add the stock, chickpeas, garlic, onion, bell pepper, tomatoes, tomato juice, cayenne, cumin and chili powder, stir well to combine
6. Close and lock the lid. Select MANUAL and cook at HIGH pressure for 5 minutes.
7. Once pressure cooking is complete, allow 10-15 minutes rest time and then do a Quick Release.
8. Carefully Open the lid and Serve

Herbed Turkey Breast

(Prep + Cook Time: 50 minutes | Serves: 6)

Ingredients:

- 3-pound turkey breast
- 2 cups chicken broth
- 1 red onion, quartered
- 1 sprig fresh thyme
- 2 sprigs fresh rosemary
- 3 stalks celery, roughly chopped.
- 1 teaspoon dried oregano
- 1 teaspoon dried basil
- 1 teaspoon salt
- 1/2 teaspoon ground black pepper

Directions:

1. Prepare the Instant Pot by adding the broth to the pot and placing the steam rack in it
2. Add the rosemary and thyme to the pot
3. Season the turkey with salt, pepper, dried oregano, and dried basil.
4. Place the meat on the steam rack, breast side up. Add the onion and celery
5. Close and lock the lid. Select MANUAL and cook at HIGH pressure for 35 minutes.
6. When the timer beeps, select CANCEL and let Naturally Release for 10 minutes.
7. Open the lid, Transfer the turkey to a serving bowl and slice it. Serve with the gravy

Creamy Chicken and Bacon

(Prep + Cook Time: 35 minutes | Serves: 3)

Ingredients:

- 2-pound chicken breasts, skinless and boneless
- 1-ounce ranch seasoning
- 4-ounce cream cheese
- 2 slices bacon, chopped.
- 1 cup chicken stock
- Green onions, chopped for serving

Directions:

1. Select the SAUTÉ setting on the Instant Pot and add the bacon
2. Sauté the bacon for 4-5 minutes.
3. Add the chicken, stock, and ranch seasoning. Stir well.
4. Close and lock the lid. Select MANUAL and cook at HIGH pressure for 12 minutes

5. When the timer goes off, let the pressure Release Naturally for 5 minutes, then release any remaining steam manually
6. Carefully unlock the lid. Transfer the chicken to a plate and shred the meat.
7. Remove 2/3 cup of cooking liquid from the pot. Add the cheese, press the SAUTÉ button and continue to cook for 3 minutes
8. Return chicken to pot, stir. Select CANCEL to stop the cooking program. Add green onions, stir and serve.

Apricot Chicken

(Prep + Cook Time: 30 minutes | **Serves:** 5)

Ingredients:

- 2 ½-pound chicken thighs, skinless
- 1 pound' canned tomatoes, diced
- 1 tablespoon fresh ginger, grated
- 1/2 teaspoon cinnamon, ground
- Fresh parsley, chopped (optional)
- 1 tablespoon vegetable oil
- 1 teaspoon kosher salt
- 1 teaspoon ground black pepper
- 3 cloves garlic, minced
- 1 large onion, chopped.
- 1/8 teaspoon allspice powder
- 1/2 cup chicken broth
- 8-ounce canned apricots

Directions:

1. Set your instant pot on SAUTÉ mode, add the oil and heat it up
2. Season the chicken thighs with salt and pepper.
3. Add the chicken, garlic, and onion to the Instant pot.
4. Sprinkle with the allspice powder and cook for 5 minutes or until nicely browned
5. Pour the broth. Add the apricots, tomatoes, fresh ginger, and cinnamon to the pot. Stir well. Close and lock the lid.
6. Press the CANCEL button to reset the cooking program. Select the MANUAL setting and set the cooking time for 12 minutes at HIGH pressure
7. When the timer beeps, use a Quick Release
8. Carefully unlock the lid. Transfer the dish to a serving bowl, top with parsley and serve.

Delicious Chicken Puttanesca

(Prep + Cook Time: 45 minutes | **Serves:** 5)

Ingredients:

- 6 chicken thighs, skin on
- 6-ounce pitted black olives
- 14-ounce canned chopped tomatoes
- 2 cloves garlic, crushed
- 1 cup water
- 2 tablespoons olive oil
- 1/2 teaspoon red chili flakes or to taste
- 1 tablespoon capers, rinsed and drained
- 1 tablespoon fresh basil, chopped.
- 1 teaspoon kosher salt
- 1 teaspoon ground black pepper

Directions:

1. Select the SAUTÉ setting on the Instant Pot and heat the oil
2. Add the chicken thighs skin side down and Brown the meat for 4-6 minutes.
3. Transfer the meat to a bowl
4. Add the water, tomatoes, garlic, chili flakes, black olives, capers, fresh basil, salt and pepper to the Instant Pot. Stir well and bring to a simmer.
5. Return the chicken to the pot. Close and lock the lid.
6. Press the CANCEL button to reset the cooking program, then select the MAIN setting and set the cooking time for 16 minutes at HIGH pressure
7. Once timer goes off, allow to Naturally Release for 10 minutes, then release any remaining pressure manually.
8. Uncover the pot and Serve

Thanksgiving Turkey Dish

(Prep + Cook Time: 1 hour 20 minutes | **Serves:** 7)

Ingredients:

- 8-pound turkey, fresh or defrosted
- 1 medium-sized onion, quartered
- 2 cloves garlic cut in half
- 1 medium-sized carrot
- 1 celery stalk, quartered
- 2 cups water
- 1 bay leaf, dried
- 2 teaspoon salt
- 2 teaspoon ground black pepper

Directions:

1. Rub all sides of the turkey with salt and pepper.
2. Slice the meat to create stuffing pockets. Stuff with onions and set aside
3. Add the onion, garlic, carrot and celery to the Instant Pot.
4. Add the turkey and pour the water into the pot. Add the bay leaf.
5. Close and lock the lid. Select MANUAL and cook at HIGH pressure for 40 minutes
6. Once cooking is complete, use a Natural Release for 10 minutes, then release any remaining pressure manually. Open the lid,
7. Preheat the oven to 450 F.
8. Transfer the turkey to the baking sheet which is covered by parchment paper.
9. Drizzle with liquid from the pot and brown in the oven for another 15 to 20 minutes then Serve

Chicken Congee

(Prep + Cook Time: 65 minutes | **Serves:** 5)

Ingredients:

- 6 chicken drumsticks
- 1/2 cup scallions, chopped.
- 2 tablespoon sesame oil, optional
- 1 cup Jasmine rice
- 1 tablespoon fresh ginger
- 7 cups water
- Salt to taste

Directions:

1. Rinse the rice well.
2. Add the chicken, rice, water and ginger to the Instant Pot. Stir well
3. Close and lock the lid. Select the MANUAL setting and set the cooking time for 25 minutes at HIGH pressure.
4. Once cooking is complete, select CANCEL and let Naturally Release for 10 minutes. Release any remaining steam manually
5. Open the lid, Take the chicken out from the pot, shred the meat and discard the bones.
6. Return the chicken meat to the pot.
7. Select SAUTÉ and cook, stirring occasionally, for about 10 minutes, or until thickened
8. Top with scallions and sesame oil. Serve.

Simple Chicken Dish

(Prep + Cook Time: 35 minutes | **Serves:** 8)

Ingredients:

- 5-pound chicken thighs
- 1/2 cup soy sauce
- 1/2 cup white vinegar
- 4 cloves garlic, minced
- 3 bay leaves
- 1 teaspoon black peppercorns
- 1/2 teaspoon salt
- 1/2 teaspoon ground black pepper

Directions:

1. Add the garlic, soy sauce, vinegar, peppercorns, bay leaves, salt and pepper to the Instant Pot and stir well.
2. Add the chicken thighs. Stir to coat the chicken

3. Close and lock the lid. Select the POULTRY setting and set the cooking time for 15 minutes.
4. Once timer goes off, allow to Naturally Release for 10 minutes
5. Unlock the lid, Remove the bay leaves, stir and serve.

Turkey Verde and brown Rice.

(Prep + Cook Time: 35 minutes | **Serves:** 7)

Ingredients:
- 1 ½-pound turkey tenderloins
- 1/2 cup brown rice, long grain
- 1 small onion, sliced
- 1/2 cup salsa verde
- 1 cup chicken broth
- 1 tablespoon olive oil
- 1/2 teaspoon salt

Directions:
1. Select the SAUTÉ setting on the Instant Pot and heat the oil.
2. Add the onion. Stir and sauté for 3-4 minutes until the onion is translucent
3. Add the rice, salsa verde, broth, and salt. Stir well.
4. Press the CANCEL button to reset the cooking program.
5. Close and lock the lid. Select the MANUAL setting and set the cooking time for 18 minutes at HIGH pressure.
6. Once cooking is complete, let the pressure Release Naturally for 10 minutes. Release any remaining steam manually.
7. Uncover the pot, Transfer the turkey to a plate and slice the meat. Serve with rice

Turkey Broccoli Stew

(Prep + Cook Time: 30 minutes | **Serves:** 4)

Ingredients:
- 1 pound' turkey breast, cubed
- 2 tablespoon ghee or butter
- 1/2 onion, diced
- 1/2 teaspoon garlic powder
- 1 teaspoon thyme
- 1 carrot, sliced
- 2 celery stalks, chopped.
- 1 cup broccoli florets
- 3 ½ cups chicken broth
- Salt and ground black pepper to taste

Directions:
1. Preheat the Instant Pot by selecting SAUTÉ.
2. Once hot, add the butter and melt it.
3. Add the onions and sauté for 3 minutes.
4. Add the garlic and thyme and cook for 1 minute.
5. Add the carrot and celery and sauté for 2 more minutes
6. Put the turkey meat in the pot and stir. Cook until the turkey has turned light brown.
7. Add the broccoli and broth, stir well. Close and lock the lid
8. Press the CANCEL button to reset the cooking program, then select the MANUAL setting and set the cooking time for 25 minutes at HIGH pressure.
9. Once cooking is complete, select CANCEL and let Naturally Release for 15 minutes.
10. Uncover the pot, Taste and season more if necessary, Serve

Salsa Verde Chicken

(Prep + Cook Time: 25 minutes | **Serves:** 6)

Ingredients:
- 2 ½-pound boneless chicken breasts
- 1 teaspoon cumin
- 2 cup (16 oz) salsa verde
- 1 teaspoon smoked paprika
- 1 teaspoon salt

Directions:
1. Add the chicken breasts, paprika, cumin, and salt to the Instant Pot
2. Pour the salsa verde on top.
3. Close and lock the lid. Select the MANUAL setting and set the cooking time for 20 minutes at HIGH pressure.
4. Once pressure cooking is complete, use a Quick Release
5. Unlock and carefully Open the lid, Shred the meat, Serve.

Mouthwatering Chicken Dish

(Prep + Cook Time: 40 minutes | **Serves:** 4)

Ingredients:
- 2-pound chicken breast, boneless
- 1 (1 oz) packet ranch seasoning
- 8-ounce cream cheese
- 4-ounce cheddar cheese, shredded
- 6-8 bacon slices, cooked
- 1 cup water
- 3 tablespoon cornstarch

Directions:
1. Add the chicken breasts and cream cheese to the Instant Pot
2. Season with the ranch seasoning. Add 1 cup of water.
3. Close and lock the lid. Select MANUAL and cook at HIGH pressure for 25 minutes.
4. When the timer goes off, use a Quick Release.
5. Unlock and carefully Open the lid, Transfer the chicken to a plate and shred the meat
6. Select SAUTÉ and add the cornstarch. Stir well.
7. Add shredded chicken, cheese and bacon to the pot, stir. Sauté for 3 minutes.
8. Press the CANCEL button to stop the cooking program.
9. Close the lid and let the dish sit for a few minutes before serving

Mouthwatering Mojo Chicken Tacos

(Prep + Cook Time: 45 minutes | **Serves:** 3)6

Ingredients:
- 4 skinless, boneless chicken breasts

For the Mojo:
- 1/4 cup olive oil
- 8 cloves garlic, minced
- 1/4 cup chopped fresh cilantro + more for garnishing
- 2/3 cup fresh lime juice
- 2/3 cup orange juice
- 1 tablespoon grated orange peel
- 1 tablespoon dried oregano
- 2 teaspoon ground cumin
- 2 teaspoon Kosher salt
- 1/4 teaspoon ground black pepper

To serve:
- 8 – 12 mission organic corn tortillas
- 1 avocado, sliced
- 1/2 cup red onion, finely diced

Directions:
1. Add the chicken breasts to the Instant Pot.
2. In a bowl, whisk together all mojo ingredients until combined
3. Close and lock the lid. Select the POULTRY setting and set the cooking time for 20 minutes.

4. Once cooking is complete, select CANCEL and let Naturally Release for 10 minutes
5. Uncover the pot, Transfer the chicken to a plate and shred it. Return the meat to the pot and stir.
6. Preheat the oven to broil. Transfer shredded chicken with the sauce to a baking sheet.
7. Place under the broiler for 5 to 8 minutes, or until the edges of the chicken are brown and crispy
8. Top with cilantro. Serve in tacos with chopped onion and sliced avocado.

Turkey Breast Roast

(Prep + Cook Time: 60 minutes | **Serves:** 4)

Ingredients:
- 1 (3 pound) turkey breast roast, boneless
- 1 ½ cups chicken broth
- 2 tablespoon + 2 tablespoon garlic infused oil
- 2 teaspoon salt

Directions:
1. Rub all sides of the turkey with 2 tablespoons of oil and season with salt
2. Preheat the Instant Pot by selecting SAUTÉ. Add the remaining oil.
3. Put the meat in the pot and brown on both sides. Press the CANCEL button to stop SAUTE function.
4. Transfer the turkey breast roast to a bowl
5. Add the broth to the pot and deglaze the pot by scraping the bottom to remove all of the brown bits.
6. Insert the steam rack. Place the turkey meat on top.
7. Close and lock the lid. Select the MANUAL setting and set the cooking time for 30 minutes at HIGH pressure.
8. Once cooking is complete, select CANCEL and use a Natural Release for 10 minutes. Release any remaining steam manually
9. Open the lid and Serve.

Chicken Nachos

(Prep + Cook Time: 45 minutes | **Serves:** 6)

Ingredients:
- 2-pound chicken thighs, boneless, skinless
- 2/3 cup mild red salsa
- 1 package (1 oz) taco seasoning mix
- 1/3 cup mild Herdez salsa verde
- 1 tablespoon olive oil

Directions:
1. Select the SAUTÉ setting on the Instant Pot and heat the oil.
2. Add the chicken thighs and brown the meat nicely for a few minutes on each side
3. In a medium bowl, combine the taco seasoning and salsa.
4. Pour the mixture in the pot and stir well. Close and lock the lid.
5. Press the CANCEL button to reset the cooking program, then select the MANUAL setting and set the cooking time for 15 minutes at HIGH pressure.
6. Once cooking is complete, use a Natural Release for 10 minutes, then release any remaining pressure manually
7. Uncover the pot, Shred the meat. Serve with tortilla chips.

Buffalo Chicken

(Prep + Cook Time: 25 minutes | **Serves:** 3)

Ingredients:
- 2-pound chicken breasts, skinless, boneless and cut into thin strips
- 1/2 cup buffalo sauce
- 1/2 cup celery, chopped.
- 1/2 cup chicken stock
- 1/4 cup bleu cheese, crumbled
- 1 small yellow onion, chopped.

Directions:
1. Add the chicken breasts, onion, celery, buffalo sauce and stock to the Instant Pot
2. Close and lock the lid. Select MANUAL and cook at HIGH pressure for 12 minutes
3. Once timer goes off, allow to Naturally Release for 5 minutes, then release any remaining pressure manually.
4. Carefully unlock the lid. Remove 2/3 cup of cooking liquid
5. Add crumbled blue cheese to the pot and stir well, Serve.

Pina Colada Chicken

(Prep + Cook Time: 40 minutes | **Serves:** 3)

Ingredients:
- 2-pound chicken thighs cut into 1-inch pieces
- 1/2 cup coconut cream, full fat
- 1/2 cup green onion, chopped.
- 1 teaspoon arrowroot starch
- 2 tablespoon soy sauce
- 1 cup pineapple chunks, fresh or frozen
- 1 teaspoon cinnamon
- 1/8 teaspoon salt
- 1 tablespoon water

Directions:
1. Combine all of the ingredients, except green onion, in the Instant Pot and stir to combine
2. Close and lock the lid. Select the POULTRY setting and set the cooking time for 15 minutes.
3. Once timer goes off, allow to Naturally Release for 10 minutes, then release any remaining pressure manually.
4. Carefully Open the lid, Transfer the chicken to a serving bowl
5. In a cup, combine the arrowroot starch and water. Mix well.
6. Add the mixture to the instant pot, press the SAUTÉ button and continue to cook, stir occasionally, until the sauce begins to thicken
7. Serve the chicken with green onion and sauce.

Whole Chicken

(Prep + Cook Time: 45 minutes | **Serves:** 8

Ingredients:
- 1 medium-sized, whole chicken (3 pound)
- 1 minced green onion
- 1 tablespoon paprika
- 2 teaspoon ground black pepper
- 1/2 teaspoon cayenne pepper
- 2 tablespoon sugar
- 2 teaspoon kosher salt
- 1 tablespoon onion powder
- 1 tablespoon garlic powder
- 1 cup water or chicken broth
- 1 tablespoon cooking wine
- 2 teaspoon soy sauce

Directions:
1. In a medium bowl, combine the sugar, salt, onion powder, garlic powder, paprika, black pepper, and cayenne pepper
2. Prepare the Instant Pot by adding the water to the pot and placing the steam rack in it.
3. Pour the wine and soy sauce into the pot
4. Rub all sides of the chicken with the spice mix
5. Place the chicken on the steam rack and secure the lid.
6. Select the MANUAL setting and set the cooking time for 18 minutes at HIGH pressure.
7. Once timer goes off, allow to Naturally Release for 15 minutes
8. Carefully unlock the lid, Top with minced green onion and serve

Turkey with Apricot Glaze

(Prep + Cook Time: 60 minutes | **Serves:** 12

Ingredients:
- 9-pound turkey
- 6-ounce apricot jam
- 2 cups chicken stock
- 1 onion, peeled and diced
- 1 diced carrot
- 1/2 teaspoon cumin
- 1/2 teaspoon turmeric
- 1/2 teaspoon coriander
- 1 teaspoon salt
- 1 teaspoon ground black pepper

Directions:
1. Rinse the turkey and dry with paper towels.
2. In a bowl, combine the jam, cumin, turmeric, coriander, salt and pepper. Mix well.
3. Rub all sides of the turkey with the paste
4. Pour the broth into the Instant Pot, Add the onion and carrot.
5. Add the turkey. Close and lock the lid.
6. Select the POULTRY setting and set the cooking time for 40 minutes
7. Once timer goes off, allow to Naturally Release for 10 minutes, then release any remaining pressure manually, then Serve.
8. If desired, broil in the oven for a few minutes for a browned top

Cajun Chicken and Rice

(Prep + Cook Time: 45 minutes | **Serves:** 5)

Ingredients:
- 1 pound' chicken breasts, sliced
- 1 ½ cups white rice, rinsed
- 1 bell pepper, chopped.
- 1 onion, diced

Cajun spices:
- 1/4 teaspoon cayenne pepper
- 1 tablespoon paprika
- 3 cloves garlic, minced
- 2 cups chicken broth
- 1 tablespoon olive oil
- 1 tablespoon tomato paste

- 2 teaspoon dried thyme

Directions:
1. Select the SAUTÉ setting on the Instant Pot and heat the oil
2. Add the onion and garlic and cook until fragrant.
3. Add the chicken breasts and Cajun spices, stir well. Sauté for another 3 minutes.
4. Pour the broth and tomato paste into the pot. Stir to dissolve the tomato paste
5. Add the rice and bell pepper, stir. Close and lock the lid.
6. Press the CANCEL button to reset the cooking program. Select the MANUAL setting and set the cooking time for 20 minutes at HIGH pressure
7. Once cooking is complete, let the pressure Release Naturally for 10 minutes. Release any remaining steam manually then Serve

Awesome Goose Dish

(Prep + Cook Time: 50 minutes | **Serves:** 4)

Ingredients:
- 1 goose breast, fat trimmed off and cut into pieces
- 1 goose leg, skinless
- 1 goose thigh, skinless
- 1 yellow onion, chopped.
- 12-ounce canned mushroom cream
- 1 tablespoon olive oil
- 2 teaspoon garlic, minced
- 1 ½ cups water
- 1/2 teaspoon ground black pepper
- 1/2 teaspoon salt

Directions:

1. To preheat the Instant Pot, select SAUTÉ.
2. In a bowl, combine the oil, pepper, salt, and garlic. Mix well
3. Rub all sides of the goose with the spice mix.
4. Add the goose parts to the pot. Cook until the goose has turned light brown, do it in two batches.
5. Press the CANCEL button to stop SAUTE function.
6. Add the water, onion and mushroom cream, stir. Close and lock the lid
7. Select the MANUAL setting and set the cooking time for 20 minutes at HIGH pressure.
8. Once timer goes off, allow to Naturally Release for 5 minutes, then release any remaining pressure manually.
9. Uncover the pot, and Serve

Turkey Sausage and Cabbage.

(**Prep + Cook Time:** 25 minutes | **Serves:** 2)

Ingredients:

- 1/2 pound' turkey sausage, sliced
- 2 cloves garlic, minced
- 1/2 cabbage head, shredded
- 1/4 cup water or chicken broth
- 1/2 yellow onion, chopped.
- 1 teaspoon mustard
- 1 teaspoon balsamic vinegar
- 1 teaspoon sugar
- 1 tablespoon olive oil
- 1/2 teaspoon kosher salt
- 1/4 teaspoon ground black pepper

Directions:

1. Select the SAUTÉ setting on the Instant Pot and heat the oil
2. Add the onion and garlic and cook for 2 minutes.
3. Add the turkey sausage and sauté for another 5 minutes
4. Add the cabbage, water, mustard, vinegar, sugar, salt and pepper, stir well
5. Close and lock the lid. Select the MANUAL setting and set the cooking time for 5 minutes at HIGH pressure.
6. Once cooking is complete, use a Natural Release for 5 minutes, then release any remaining pressure manually.
7. Open the lid and Serve

Awesome Turkey Salsa Verde

(**Prep + Cook Time:** 40 minutes | **Serves:** 5)

Ingredients:

- 2 ½-pound turkey breast, chopped into cubes (1 ½ -inch)
- 16-ounce salsa verde
- 1/4 teaspoon turmeric
- 1/4 teaspoon cumin
- 1/4 teaspoon smoked paprika
- 1/4 teaspoon garlic salt
- 1/4 teaspoon ground black pepper

Directions:

1. In the Instant Pot, combine the salsa, turmeric, cumin, paprika, salt, and pepper, stir well.
2. Put the turkey cubes in the pot and toss until turkey is covered in sauce
3. Close and lock the lid. Select MANUAL and cook at HIGH pressure for 20 minutes.
4. When the timer beeps, use a Quick Release.
5. Carefully unlock the lid and Serve

Italian Duck Dish

(Prep + Cook Time: 30 minutes | **Serves:** 4)

Ingredients:

- 2-pound duck breasts, halved
- 1/2 cup sun-dried tomatoes, chopped.
- 1 cup spinach, chopped.
- 1/2 cup parmesan cheese, grated
- 1/2 tablespoon Italian seasoning
- 2 tablespoon olive oil
- 1/2 teaspoon ground black pepper
- 1/4 teaspoon salt
- 2 cloves garlic, minced
- 1/2 cup chicken stock
- 3/4 cup heavy cream

Directions:

1. In a bowl, combine the oil, Italian seasoning, pepper, salt, and garlic. Stir well
2. Rub all sides of the duck breasts with the spice mix.
3. Preheat the Instant Pot by selecting SAUTÉ.
4. Add the duck to the pot. Cook on both sides until the breasts have turned golden brown.
5. Press the CANCEL button to reset the cooking program.
6. Add the chicken stock. Close and lock the lid.
7. Select the MANUAL setting and set the cooking time for 4 minutes at HIGH pressure
8. Once pressure cooking is complete, use a Quick Release. Unlock and carefully Open the lid,
9. Add the heavy cream, tomatoes, spinach, and cheese, stir.
10. Close and lock the lid. Select MANUAL and cook at HIGH pressure for 5 minutes
11. When the timer beeps, use a Quick Release.
12. Carefully unlock the lid, Serve.

Sriracha Chicken

(Prep + Cook Time: 20 minutes | **Serves:** 4)

Ingredients:

- 4 diced chicken breasts
- 1/4 cup sugar
- 5 tablespoon soy sauce
- 2 - 3 tablespoon honey
- 4 tablespoon cold water
- 1 tablespoon minced garlic
- 2 - 3 tablespoon sriracha
- 2 tablespoon cornstarch

Directions:

1. In the Instant Pot, whisk together soy sauce, honey, sugar, 2 tablespoons of water, garlic, and sriracha until combined
2. Toss the chicken breasts in the mixture. Close and lock the lid.
3. Select MANUAL and cook at HIGH pressure for 9 minutes.
4. Meanwhile, in a small bowl combine 2 tablespoons of water and cornstarch
5. Once timer goes off, use a Quick Release.
6. Carefully unlock the lid, Pour the cornstarch mixture into the pot.
7. Select the SAUTÉ setting, simmer and stir occasionally until the sauce begins to thicken

Orange Chicken Delight

(Prep + Cook Time: 30 minutes | **Serves:** 4)

Ingredients:

- 4 chicken breasts
- 3/4 cup orange juice
- 3/4 cup barbecue sauce
- 1/4 cup water
- 2 tablespoon soy sauce
- 1 tablespoon cornstarch + 2 tablespoon water
- 2 tablespoon green onions, chopped.

Directions:

1. Add the chicken breasts, 1/4 cup of water, orange juice, barbecue sauce, and soy sauce to the Instant Pot. Stir well.
2. Close and lock the lid. Select the POULTRY setting and set the cooking time for 15 minutes
3. Once pressure cooking is complete, use a Quick Release. Unlock and carefully
4. Open the lid, in a cup, combine the cornstarch and 2 tablespoon of water.
5. Select the SAUTÉ setting and add the cornstarch slurry to the pot.
6. Simmer for 5 minutes or until the sauce has thickened. Add green onions and serve

Turkey Casserole.

(**Prep + Cook Time:** 50 minutes | **Serves:** 6)

Ingredients:

- 2-pound boneless turkey breast, about 4 pieces
- 2 small cans of creamy mushroom soup
- 1 bag (14 oz) Pepperidge Farm herb stuffing mix
- 1 medium-sized onion, sliced
- 1 celery stalk, sliced
- 1 bag (10 oz) frozen mixed vegetables
- 1/2 teaspoon salt
- 1/2 teaspoon ground black pepper
- 1 cup chicken broth

Directions:

1. Add the onion, celery, and frozen mixed vegetables to the Instant Pot
2. Season the turkey breast with salt and pepper.
3. Add the breasts to the pot. Pour the broth into the pot. Close and lock the lid.
4. Select the POULTRY setting and set the cooking time for 25 minutes
5. When the timer goes off, use a Quick Release.
6. Carefully Open the lid, Pour the mushroom soup into the pot and add stuffing mix.
7. Select the SAUTÉ setting and cook for another 8 minutes, stirring occasionally.
8. Transfer cooked turkey to a serving bowl and drizzle with the sauce, Serve

Potatoes and Chicken

(**Prep + Cook Time:** 35 minutes | **Serves:** 4)

Ingredients:

- 2-pound chicken thighs, skinless and boneless
- 2-pound red potatoes, peeled and cut into quarters
- 2 tablespoon extra virgin olive oil
- 3/4 cup chicken stock
- 3 tablespoon dijon mustard
- 1/4 cup lemon juice
- 2 tablespoon Italian seasoning
- 1 teaspoon salt
- 1 teaspoon ground black pepper

Directions:

1. Select the SAUTÉ setting on the Instant Pot and heat the oil.
2. Season the chicken thighs with ½ teaspoon salt and ½ teaspoon pepper
3. Add the chicken to the Instant Pot and brown the meat for 3 minutes on each side.
4. In a medium bowl, combine the stock, mustard, lemon juice and Italian seasoning
5. Pour the mixture over the chicken.
6. Add the potatoes, ½ teaspoon salt and ½ teaspoon pepper. Stir.
7. Press the CANCEL button to reset the cooking program, then select the MAIN setting and set the cooking time for 15 minutes at HIGH pressure
8. Once cooking is complete, let the pressure Release Naturally for 5 minutes. Release any remaining steam manually.
9. Open the lid and Serve

Olive Lemon Chicken

(Prep + Cook Time: 30 minutes | **Serves:** 3)

Ingredients:

- 4 chicken breasts, skinless and boneless
- 1 cup chicken broth
- 1 can pitted green olives
- 1/2 cup butter
- 1/2 teaspoon cumin
- 1 teaspoon salt
- 1/2 teaspoon ground black pepper
- Juice of 1 lemon

Directions:

1. To preheat the Instant Pot, select SAUTÉ. Once hot, add the butter and melt it
2. Season the chicken breasts with cumin, salt, and pepper.
3. Put the breasts into the pot and sauté for 3-5 minutes on each side, until nicely browned.
4. Add the lemon juice, broth and olives, stir well. Close and lock the lid
5. Press the CANCEL button to reset the cooking program. Select the MANUAL setting and set the cooking time for 10 minutes at HIGH pressure.
6. Once cooking is complete, use a Natural Release for 5 minutes, then release any remaining pressure manually
7. Open the lid and Serve.

Teriyaki Chicken

(Prep + Cook Time: 30 minutes | **Serves:** 3)

Ingredients:

- 2-pound chicken breasts, skinless and boneless
- A handful green onions, chopped.
- 2/3 cup teriyaki sauce
- 1 tablespoon honey
- 1/2 cup chicken stock
- 1/2 teaspoon salt
- 1/2 teaspoon ground black pepper

Directions:

1. Preheat the Instant Pot by selecting SAUTÉ on high heat.
2. Add the teriyaki sauce and honey, stir and simmer for 1 minute
3. Add the chicken, stock, salt and pepper. Stir well. Close and lock the lid.
4. Select the MANUAL setting and set the cooking time for 12 minutes at HIGH pressure.
5. Once cooking is complete, select CANCEL and use a natural release for 5 minutes. Release any remaining steam manually
6. Transfer the chicken to a plate and shred the meat.
7. Remove ½ cup of cooking liquid and return shredded chicken to the pot. Add green onions and stir, Serve.

BBQ Chicken

(Prep + Cook Time: 30 minutes | **Serves:** 3)

Ingredients:

- 2-pound chicken (breasts or thighs)
- 3 large potatoes, unpeeled and quartered
- 1 cup BBQ sauce
- 1/2 cup water
- 1 tablespoon Italian seasoning
- 1 tablespoon minced garlic
- 1 large onion, sliced

Directions:

1. Add the chicken, water, potatoes, BBQ sauce, Italian seasoning, garlic and onion to the Instant Pot. Stir well.
2. Close and lock the lid. Select MANUAL and cook at HIGH pressure for 15 minutes
3. Once pressure cooking is complete, use a Quick Release.
4. Unlock and carefully Open the lid, Transfer the chicken to a plate and shred it. Return shredded chicken to the pot
5. Stir well until fully coated with the sauce, Serve.

IP Braised Turkey Wings

(Prep + Cook Time: 55 minutes **| Serves:** 4)

Ingredients:

- 4 turkey wings
- 1 bunch thyme, roughly chopped.
- 1 yellow onions, sliced
- 1 ½ cups cranberries
- 1 cup walnuts
- 2 tablespoon vegetable oil
- 2 tablespoon butter
- 1 teaspoon kosher salt
- 1/2 teaspoon ground black pepper
- 1 cup orange juice

Directions:

1. Select the SAUTÉ setting on the Instant Pot and heat the oil.
2. Add the butter and melt it
3. Season the turkey wings with salt and pepper and put in the pot.
4. Brown turkey on both sides. Remove the wings from the pot
5. Add the onion, cranberries, walnuts, and thyme to the pot, stir and sauté for 2 minutes.
6. Add orange juice and return turkey wings to the pot, stir. Close and lock the lid.
7. Select the MANUAL setting and set the cooking time for 20 minutes at HIGH pressure
8. Once pressure cooking is complete, use a Natural Release for 10 minutes. Then release any remaining pressure manually.
9. Open the lid, Transfer the turkey to a serving bowl.
10. Set your Instant Pot on SAUTÉ mode and simmer the cranberry mix for 5 minutes, until the sauce begins to thicken
11. Serve turkey wings with cranberry sauce.

Goose Brest

(Prep + Cook Time: 25 minutes **| Serves:** 2)

Ingredients:

- 1 pound' goose breast, skinless, boneless and cut into 1/6 inch slices
- 1 sweet onion, chopped.
- 1/4 cup sweet chili sauce
- 1/4 cup extra virgin olive oil
- 2 teaspoon garlic, chopped.
- 1/2 cup water
- Salt and black pepper to taste

Directions:

1. Select the SAUTÉ setting on the Instant Pot and heat the oil
2. Add the garlic and onion, sauté for about 2 minutes.
3. Add the goose breast slices, pepper and salt, stir and cook for 2 minutes on both sides
4. Pour the chili sauce and water, stir.
5. Press the CANCEL button to reset the cooking program, then select the MANUAL setting and set the cooking time for 5 minutes at HIGH pressure
6. Once cooking is complete, use a Quick Release.
7. Unlock and carefully open the lid, and Serve.

Duck with Potato

(Prep + Cook Time: 50 minutes **| Serves:** 5)

Ingredients:

- 1 whole duck (medium), chopped into chunks
- 2-inch ginger root, sliced
- 4 cloves garlic, minced
- 4 potatoes, chopped into cubes
- 2 green onions cut into 2 inches in length
- 4 tablespoon sugar
- 1 cup water
- 4 tablespoon soy sauce
- 2 tablespoon olive oil
- 4 tablespoon rice wine
- 1/2 teaspoon salt

Directions:

1. Select the SAUTÉ setting on the Instant Pot and heat the oil.
2. Add the duck and cook until the duck has turned light brown
3. Add all of the ingredients, except the potato, to the Pot.
4. Close and lock the lid. Select the MANUAL setting and set the cooking time for 20 minutes at HIGH pressure.
5. When the timer goes off, use a Quick Release. Carefully Open the lid,
6. Add the potato and stir.
7. Close and lock the lid. Select MANUAL and cook at HIGH pressure for 5 minutes
8. Once cooking is complete, use a Natural Release for 10 minutes, then release any remaining pressure manually.
9. Open the lid and Serve

Special Turkey Goulash

(**Prep + Cook Time:** 35 minutes | **Serves:** 4)

Ingredients:

- 2-pound ground turkey breast
- 1 red onion, sliced
- 1 can (15 oz) diced tomatoes
- 2 cloves garlic, chopped.
- 1 red bell pepper, chopped.
- 1 green bell pepper, chopped.
- 1 cup chicken stock
- 1 tablespoon butter
- Salt and ground black pepper to taste

Directions:

1. To preheat the Instant Pot, select SAUTÉ
2. Add the butter; stir until butter melts, about 2 minutes.
3. Add the ground turkey and sauté for 5 minutes, stirring occasionally.
4. Add the tomatoes with their juices, onion, garlic, bell peppers, and chicken stock. Stir well
5. Close and lock the lid. Select MANUAL and cook at HIGH pressure for 15 minutes.
6. Once timer goes off, use a Quick Release.
7. Unlock and carefully open the lid, Taste and season with salt and pepper if necessary. Serve

Delicious Duck and Veggies

(**Prep + Cook Time:** 55 minutes | **Serves:** 5)

Ingredients:

- 1 whole duck (medium), chopped into chunks
- 2 carrots cut into pieces
- 1 cucumber cut into pieces
- 1 inch ginger pieces, chopped.
- 1 ½ teaspoon salt
- 1/2 teaspoon black pepper
- 1 ½ tablespoon red wine
- 1 cup water

Directions:

1. Rub all sides of the duck pieces with salt and pepper.
2. Add the duck to the Instant Pot.
3. Add the carrot, cucumber, ginger, water, and wine to the pot
4. Close and lock the lid. Select the MANUAL setting and set the cooking time for 20 minutes at HIGH pressure.
5. Once cooking is complete, select CANCEL and let Naturally Release for 10 minutes. Release any remaining steam manually
6. Uncover the pot and Serve.

Pork Recipes

Pork Chops with Rice

(Prep + Cook Time: 30 minutes | **Serves:** 4)

Ingredients:

- 4 pork chops, thin cut (1/2-inch thick)
- 1 carrot, chopped.
- 1/2 cup mixed vegetables, frozen
- 1 tablespoon olive oil
- 1 cup onions, finely chopped.
- 1 teaspoon sea salt
- 1 teaspoon freshly ground black pepper
- 1 cup basmati rice, rinsed
- 1 cup water

Directions:

1. Pour the oil into the Instant Pot.
2. Add the onions at the bottom, then add the rice and sprinkle with salt and pepper
3. Place the pork on the rice, then pour in the water.
4. Add the carrots and mixed vegetables to the pot. Don't stir
5. Close and lock the lid. Select MANUAL and cook at HIGH pressure for 7 minutes.
6. Once cooking is complete, let the pressure Release Naturally for 10 minutes. Release any remaining steam manually
7. Uncover the pot, Serve.

Pork shoulder with Tortillas

(Prep + Cook Time: 35 minutes | **Serves:** 4-5)

Ingredients:

- 2 pounds' pork shoulder, trimmed of excess fat
- 1/2 cup orange juice
- 1 ½ cups tomatoes, diced
- Some lettuce and sliced cucumber pieces
- 6 tortillas
- 3 cloves garlic, minced
- 1/2 cup onion, sliced
- 1 teaspoon ground cinnamon
- 1 tablespoon roasted and ground cumin
- 1 teaspoon oregano
- 1 dried chipotle pepper
- 1 teaspoon kosher salt
- 1 teaspoon ground black pepper

Directions:

1. Cut the pork shoulder into 2-inch pieces
2. In the Instant Pot, combine the garlic, onion, cinnamon, cumin, oregano, chipotle pepper, salt and black pepper.
3. Add the meat pieces and rub them all over until are coated. Let marinate for 30 minutes
4. Pour in the orange juice and tomatoes. Close and lock the lid.
5. Select MANUAL and cook at HIGH pressure for 30 minutes.
6. Once timer goes off, allow to Naturally Release for 10 minutes, then release any remaining pressure manually
7. Uncover the pot, Shred the meat in the pot. Select SAUTÉ and simmer for 5 minutes, or until thickened, stirring occasionally
8. Fill the tortillas with this mixture, layering with lettuce leaves and cucumber slices, Serve warm.

Turnip Greens with Bacon.

(Prep + Cook Time: 40 minutes | **Serves:** 2 - 3)

Ingredients:

- 1-pound turnip greens, rinsed
- 5 slices bacon, cut into small pieces
- 1/2 tablespoon extra-virgin olive oil
- 1/4 teaspoon ground black pepper
- 3/4 cup smoked ham hocks or necks
- 1/2 cup onion, diced
- 2 cups chicken broth
- Salt to taste

Directions:

1. Set your instant pot on SAUTÉ mode, add the oil and heat it up
2. Add the bacon and smoked ham. Sauté until the bacon begins to brown and some of the fat has rendered.
3. Add the onion, stir and cook until softened.
4. Pour in the broth, season with salt and pepper and stir.
5. Add the turnip greens
6. Press the CANCEL button to stop the SAUTE function, then select the MANUAL setting and set the cooking time for 20 minutes at HIGH pressure.
7. When the timer beeps, use a Quick Release
8. Carefully unlock the lid, Serve warm.

Pork Chili Green Beans

(Prep + Cook Time: 30 minutes | **Serves:** 2 - 3)

Ingredients:

- 1/2-pound ground pork
- 1-pound green beans, cut into ½-inch pieces
- 1 ½ cups coconut milk
- 1 tablespoon fish or soy sauce
- 2 tablespoon olive oil
- 4 cloves garlic, minced
- 2 - 3 pieces red thai chili, chopped.
- 1 shallot, thinly sliced

Directions:

1. Select the SAUTÉ setting on the Instant Pot and heat the oil
2. Add the ground pork and cook for 5-8 minutes, until the meat has turned light brown.
3. Then add the garlic, chili and shallots. Sauté for 2 to 3 minutes more
4. Add the green beans, stir and cook until a bit tender.
5. Add the coconut milk and soy sauce, stir.
6. Bring to a boil and cook for 5 minutes
7. Press the CANCEL key to stop the SAUTÉ function, Serve.

Pork Chops with Apples.

(Prep + Cook Time: 25 minutes | **Serves:** 4)

Ingredients:

- 2 apples, sliced
- 4 tablespoon butter
- 4 pork chops, ½-1 inch thick
- 1 teaspoon nutmeg
- 1 teaspoon cinnamon
- 4 tablespoon brown sugar
- Salt and ground black pepper to taste

Directions:

1. In a bowl; mix the nutmeg, cinnamon and brown sugar.
2. Season the sliced apples with this mix and stir to coat.
3. Preheat the Instant Pot by selecting SAUTÉ. Once hot, add the butter and melt it
4. Add the apples to the pot and sauté, stirring occasionally, for 2 minutes.
5. Rub both sides of the pork chops with salt and pepper.
6. Put the pork on the apples

7. Press the CANCEL key to stop the SAUTÉ function.
8. Close and lock the lid. Select MANUAL and cook at HIGH pressure for 10 minutes.
9. Once timer goes off, use a Quick Release
10. Carefully unlock the lid, Serve.

Barbeque Baby Back Ribs

(Prep + Cook Time: 60 minutes **| Serves:** 4-5)

Ingredients:
- 1 rack baby back ribs (1 ½ - 2 pound)
- 1/2 teaspoon garlic powder
- 1/2 teaspoon onion powder
- 1 cup water
- 1/2 cup knob creek bourbon (optional)
- Barbecue sauce
- 1 teaspoon kosher salt
- 1/2 teaspoon ground black pepper

Directions:
1. Remove the membrane from the back of the ribs.
2. In a large bowl, combine salt, pepper, garlic powder and onion powder
3. Add the ribs and rub all sides with the spice mix.
4. Prepare the Instant Pot by adding the water and bourbon to the pot and placing the steam rack in it.
5. Place the ribs on the steam rack and secure the lid.
6. Select the MANUAL setting and set the cooking time for 20 minutes at HIGH pressure
7. When the timer beeps, use a Natural Release for 10 minutes, then release any remaining pressure manually.
8. Open the lid, Preheat the oven to broil.
9. Place the ribs onto a baking tray and brush on all sides with the BBQ sauce
10. Place under the broiler for 5-10 minutes and serve.

Easy Pork Chops

(Prep + Cook Time: 30 minutes **| Serves:** 4)

Ingredients:
- 4 boneless pork chops
- 4 tablespoon hot sauce
- 4 tablespoon butter
- 1 cup mozzarella cheese, grated
- 2 tablespoon olive oil
- 1 cup water
- 1/2 teaspoon kosher salt or to taste
- 1/2 teaspoon ground black pepper

Directions:
1. Select the SAUTÉ setting on the Instant Pot and heat the oil.
2. Season the pork chops with salt and pepper
3. Add the meat to the pot and brown for 3 minutes on both sides.
4. Pour in the water and hot sauce.
5. Place the butter on top of each pork chops
6. Press the CANCEL key to stop the SAUTÉ function.
7. Close and lock the lid. Select MANUAL and cook at HIGH pressure for 10 minutes.
8. When the timer goes off, use a Quick Release.
9. Carefully unlock the lid, Sprinkle the pork chops with mozzarella cheese
10. Close the lid and let sit for 5 minutes; or broil in the oven for a few minutes to melt the cheese, Serve.

Pork Sausage Gravy.

(Prep + Cook Time: 35 minutes **| Serves:** 4)

Ingredients:
- 1-pound pork sausage
- 2 cups whole milk
- 1/4 cup flour
- 1/2 tablespoon olive oil
- 4 cloves garlic, minced
- Salt and ground black pepper to taste

Directions:
1. To preheat the Instant Pot, select SAUTÉ. Once hot, add the oil to the pot.
2. Add the garlic and sauté until fragrant
3. Add the pork sausage, stir and break into chunks with a spatula. Cook until brown.
4. Pour in 1 ½ cups of milk, stir.
5. Press the CANCEL key to stop the SAUTÉ function.
6. Close and lock the lid. Select MANUAL and cook at HIGH pressure for 5 minutes
7. When the timer goes off, do a Quick Release. Allow a 5 minutes rest time and then carefully open the lid.
8. Add the flour and remaining milk to the pot, stir until smooth
9. Season with salt and pepper to taste.
10. Select SAUTÉ and cook, stirring occasionally, until thickened, Serve warm.

Pork Belly Recipe

(Prep + Cook Time: 1 hour 10 minutes | **Serves:** 2)

Ingredients:
- 1-pound pork belly
- 1 clove garlic, minced
- 1 cup white wine
- Rosemary sprig
- 1 tablespoon olive oil
- Salt and ground black pepper to taste

Directions:
1. Select the SAUTÉ setting on the Instant Pot and heat the oil
2. Add the pork belly and sauté for 2 minutes per side, until starting to brown.
3. Season the meat with salt and pepper, add the garlic.
4. Pour in the wine and add the rosemary sprig.
5. Bring to a boil and press the CANCEL key to stop the SAUTÉ function
6. Select the MANUAL setting and set the cooking time for 35 minutes at HIGH pressure.
7. Once cooking is complete, use a Natural Release for 10 minutes, then release any remaining pressure manually
8. Open the lid, Slice the meat and serve.

Pork Chili Verde.

(Prep + Cook Time: 50 minutes | **Serves:** 8

Ingredients:
- 4 pounds' sirloin pork roast, cut into cubes (2 inch)
- 2 cups chicken stock
- 1 teaspoon ground black pepper
- 1 bunch cilantro leaves, chopped.
- 1 teaspoon fish or soy sauce
- 1-pound tomatillos, quartered
- 2/3-pound Poblano peppers, chopped.
- 2 onions, chopped.
- 5 cloves garlic, minced
- 2 chili peppers
- 1 tablespoon dried oregano
- 1 teaspoon cumin
- 1 ½ teaspoon salt

Directions:
1. Combine all of the ingredients, except cilantro and soy sauce, in the Instant Pot.
2. Close and lock the lid. Select MANUAL and cook at HIGH pressure for 35 minutes
3. When the timer goes off, use a Quick Release. Carefully unlock the lid,
4. Remove the pork from the pot.
5. Add the cilantro and soy sauce to the pot and then blend the sauce with an immersion blender
6. Return the meat to the pot, stir to combine and serve.

Spicy Pork Loin Recipe

(Prep + Cook Time: 55 minutes | **Serves:** 4-5)

Ingredients:

- 2 ½ pounds' pork loin roast, cut into 2-inch pieces
- 5 cups sauerkraut, drained and rinsed
- 4 small apples, peeled, cored and chopped.
- 3 tablespoon butter
- 4 cloves garlic, crushed
- 1/2 teaspoon kosher salt
- 1/2 teaspoon black pepper, ground
- 1 cup chicken broth
- 1/2 cup water, optional

Directions:

1. Season the pork pieces with salt and pepper.
2. Set your instant pot on SAUTÉ mode. Add and melt the butter
3. Add the meat and garlic, cook for 5-6 minutes, until start to brown.
4. Add the broth and close and lock the lid
5. Press the CANCEL key to stop the SAUTÉ function.
6. Select MANUAL and cook at HIGH pressure for 45 minutes.
7. When the timer beeps, use a Quick Release.
8. Carefully unlock the lid, Press the SAUTÉ key and add the sauerkraut and apples. Sauté for 10-12 minutes, stirring occasionally
9. Add the water, if the dish is too dry and serve.

Spicy Pork Mexican Style

(Prep + Cook Time: 1 hour 20 minutes | **Serves:** 4-5)

Ingredients:

- 2 pounds' pork shoulder, cut into 1 ½-inch pieces
- 1 tablespoon apple cider vinegar
- 2 teaspoon Mexican chili powder
- 1/2 teaspoon canned chipotle chili
- 1/4 cup soy sauce
- 1 teaspoon dried oregano, ground
- 1-ounce raisins, soaked in 1/2 cup hot water
- 1 cup water
- 4 cloves garlic, minced
- 1 cup red onions, chopped.
- 1/2 teaspoon kosher salt
- 1/4 teaspoon ground black pepper

Directions:

1. In a food processor, combine garlic, onions, apple cider vinegar, Mexican chili, chipotle chili, soy sauce, oregano and raisins (with soaking water). Add 1/2 cup of water and pulse until smooth and creamy
2. Add the pork pieces to the Instant Pot and rub with salt and pepper.
3. Pour in the spice mixture and stir to combine. Let marinate for 30 minutes
4. Add 1/2 cup of water. Close and lock the lid.
5. Select the MANUAL setting and set the cooking time for 25 minutes at HIGH pressure.
6. Once cooking is complete, select CANCEL and use a Natural Release for 15 minutes
7. Uncover the pot, to thicken sauces, use the SAUTÉ function. Cook for 5 minutes, Serve

Pork and Cabbages.

(Prep + Cook Time: 60 minutes | **Serves:** 6-7)

Ingredients:

- 1 head cabbage, chopped.
- 4 pounds' pork roast, cut into chunks
- 3 tablespoon coconut oil
- 4 cloves garlic, minced
- 2 large onions, chopped.
- 1 teaspoon kosher salt
- 1 teaspoon ground black pepper
- 1 cup water

Directions:

1. Preheat the Instant Pot by selecting SAUTÉ. Add and heat the oil
2. Add the garlic and onions and sauté for 5-6 minutes until the onion is translucent.

3. Put the pork chunks in the pot and cook for 5 minutes on all sides
4. Season with salt and pepper and pour the water, stir well.
5. Press the CANCEL key to stop the SAUTÉ function.
6. Close and lock the lid. Select MANUAL and cook at HIGH pressure for 35 minutes
7. When the timer beeps, use a Quick Release.
8. Carefully unlock the lid, Select SAUTÉ and add the cabbage, stir and bring to a simmer.
9. Simmer the dish for 5 minutes, Serve

Instant pot Pulled Pork

(Prep + Cook Time: 1 hour 30 minutes | **Serves:** 8

Ingredients:

- 2 pounds' pork shoulder, trimmed of excess fat
- 1 onion, chopped.
- 1/2 cup chicken stock
- 1/2 cup cream
- 1/2 cup tomato paste
- 3 tablespoon olive oil
- 1 teaspoon cayenne pepper
- 1 teaspoon garlic powder
- 1 tablespoon lemon juice
- 1 teaspoon salt
- 1 teaspoon ground black pepper

Directions:

1. To preheat the Instant Pot, select SAUTÉ. Once hot, add the oil.
2. Add the pork shoulder and roast for 9 minutes on both sides
3. Add the onion and cook for another 1 - 2 minutes.
4. Press the CANCEL key to stop the SAUTÉ function.
5. Add the chicken stock, cream, tomato paste, lemon juice, salt, pepper, cayenne and garlic powder, Stir well.
6. Close and lock the lid. Select MANUAL and cook at HIGH pressure for 50 minutes
7. Once cooking is complete, let the pressure Release Naturally for 10 minutes. Release any remaining steam manually.
8. Uncover the pot, Transfer the pork to a plate and shred the meat
9. Return shredded pork to the pot. Select SAUTE and cook for 6 to 8 minutes more, Serve.

Braised Pork v2

(Prep + Cook Time: 1 hour 25 minutes | **Serves:** 6-7)

Ingredients:

- 4 pounds' pork butt, cut into 2-inch pieces
- 1/4 cup garlic powder
- 1/4 cup onion, chopped.
- 2 cups chicken or bone broth
- 2 cups red wine
- 4-ounce lemon juice
- 1 tablespoon paprika
- 2 tablespoon olive oil
- 1 teaspoon kosher salt
- 1 teaspoon ground black pepper

Directions:

1. Preheat the Instant Pot by selecting SAUTÉ. Add and heat the oil.
2. Add the pork pieces and season with salt, pepper and garlic powder
3. Cook for 2-4 minutes, until starting to brown. You may have to do it in two batches.
4. Transfer the meat to a plate. Add the onion to the pot and sauté for 2 minutes.
5. Add the broth and deglaze the pot by scraping the bottom to remove all of the brown bits
6. Return the pork to the pot. Add the wine, lemon juice and paprika, stir well.
7. Press the CANCEL button to reset the cooking program, then select the MANUAL setting and set the cooking time for 50 minutes at HIGH pressure
8. Once cooking is complete, select CANCEL and let Naturally Release for 10 minutes. Release any remaining steam manually
9. Uncover the pot, Serve with cooked rice or potato.

Peppercorn Pork Brisket.

(Prep + Cook Time: 1 hour 20 minutes | **Serves:** 4-5)

Ingredients:

- 3 pounds' pork brisket, trimmed of excess fat
- 1 ½ cups chicken broth
- 1 ½ cups red wine
- 6 cloves garlic, peeled and minced
- 1 tablespoon fresh rosemary leaves, chopped.
- 1 tablespoon butter
- 1 cup mushrooms, sliced
- 1 teaspoon kosher salt
- 2 tablespoon peppercorn, crushed
- 2 cloves garlic, minced
- 2 ½ tablespoon all-purpose flour
- 1 tablespoon garlic powder
- 1 tablespoon olive oil

Directions:

1. In a bowl; combine the salt, peppercorn and garlic.
2. Rub all sides of the pork brisket with the spice mix.
3. In another bowl, mix together the flour and garlic powder
4. Roll brisket in flour mixture all over until it's coated.
5. Select the SAUTÉ setting on the Instant Pot and heat the oil.
6. Add the brisket and cook for 6 minutes on each side, until browned
7. Pour the broth and wine and deglaze the pot by scraping the bottom to remove all of the brown bits.
8. Add the peeled garlic and rosemary. Close and lock the lid
9. Press the CANCEL key to stop the SAUTÉ function.
10. Select MANUAL and cook at HIGH pressure for 45 minutes.
11. Once timer goes off, allow to Naturally Release for 20 minutes, then release any remaining pressure manually
12. Uncover the pot, Transfer the brisket to a serving plate.
13. Remove the cooking liquid from the pot to a bowl.
14. Add the butter to the pot and select SAUTÉ. Once the butter has melted, add the mushrooms and sauté until softened.
15. Return the cooking liquid to the pot and sauté for 1 minute more. Press the CANCEL key
16. Slice the meat and serve with mushroom gravy.

Pork Chops and Tomato Sauce.

(Prep + Cook Time: 35 minutes | **Serves:** 4)

Ingredients:

- 4 pork chops, boneless
- 8 mushrooms, sliced
- 1 ½ cups tomato paste
- 1 tablespoon soy sauce
- 1/4 teaspoon sesame oil
- 1 yellow onion, sliced

Directions:

1. In a bowl; combine the soy sauce with sesame oil.
2. Add the pork chops and stir until fully coated. Set aside for 15 minutes
3. To preheat the Instant Pot, select SAUTÉ.
4. Put the meat in the pot and cook for 5 minutes per side, until browned.
5. Add the onion, stir and sauté for another 2 minutes.
6. Add the mushrooms and tomato paste, stir. Close and lock the lid
7. Press the CANCEL button to reset the cooking program, then select the MANUAL setting and set the cooking time for 8 minutes at HIGH pressure.
8. Once cooking is complete, use a Natural Release for 10 minutes, then release any remaining pressure manually
9. Open the lid, Serve.

Asian Style Pork Ribs

(Prep + Cook Time: 1 hour 15 minutes | **Serves:** 6

Ingredients:

- 4 pounds' pork spare ribs
- 3 cloves garlic, minced
- 2 green onions, chopped.
- 3 ginger slices
- 1/4 cup rice wine
- 1/2 cup water
- 1/2 cup soy sauce
- 1/4 cup pear juice
- 2 teaspoon sesame oil
- 1 teaspoon vegetable oil

Directions:

1. Preheat the Instant Pot by selecting SAUTÉ. Add and heat the oil.
2. Add the garlic, onions and ginger, stir and sauté for 1 minute
3. Put the ribs into the pot and pour the wine, water, soy sauce, pear juice and sesame oil. Stir well and cook for 3 to 4 minutes.
4. Close and lock the lid. Select MANUAL and cook at HIGH pressure for 40 minutes
5. When the timer goes off, let the pressure Release Naturally for 10 minutes, then release any remaining steam manually.
6. Unlock the lid, Transfer the ribs to a serving plate.
7. Strain sauce from the pot
8. Serve the ribs with this sauce.

Peppers and Sausages

(Prep + Cook Time: 40 minutes | **Serves:** 4-5)

Ingredients:

- 10 Italian sausages
- 4 green bell peppers, cut into thin strips
- 4 cloves garlic, minced
- 1 tablespoon basil, dried
- 2 tablespoon olive oil
- 1 tablespoon Italian seasoning
- 1 ½ cups tomato sauce
- 28-ounce canned tomatoes, diced
- 1 cup water

Directions:

1. Select the SAUTÉ setting on the Instant Pot and heat the oil
2. Add the sausages and brown for 3 to 4 minutes.
3. Add the tomato sauce, tomatoes, bell peppers, garlic, basil, water and Italian seasoning, stir
4. Close and lock the lid. Select the MANUAL setting and set the cooking time for 20 minutes at HIGH pressure.
5. Once cooking is complete, use a Natural Release for 5 minutes, then release any remaining pressure manually
6. Open the lid, Serve.

Pork Loin Stroganoff

(Prep + Cook Time: 50 minutes | **Serves:** 4-5)

Ingredients:

- 2-pound pork loin, cut into 1/2-inch strips
- 1 onion, chopped.
- 3 carrots, chopped.
- 2 stalks of celery, chopped.
- 2 cups chicken broth
- 1 tablespoon flour
- 1 tablespoon Dijon mustard
- 1/2 cup sour cream
- 1 package egg noodles, cooked
- 1 tablespoon olive oil
- 1/2 teaspoon kosher salt
- 1/2 teaspoon ground black pepper

Directions:
1. Select the SAUTÉ setting on the Instant Pot and heat the oil
2. Season the meat with salt and pepper and put into the pot
3. Cook until all the meat is browned. You may have to do it in two batches.
4. Remove the pork from the pot. Add the onion and sauté for 3 minutes.
5. Pour in 1 cup of broth and deglaze the pot by scraping the bottom to remove all of the brown bits.
6. Add the carrots and celery.
7. In a bowl; combine 1 cup of broth, flour and Dijon mustard.
8. Pour the mixture in the pot. Stir well and bring to a boil
9. Press the CANCEL key to stop the SAUTÉ function.
10. Return the meat to the pot. Close and lock the lid.
11. Select MANUAL and cook at HIGH pressure for 7 minutes.
12. Once cooking is complete, use a natural release for 10 minutes, then release any remaining pressure manually
13. Open the lid. Select SAUTÉ on low heat.
14. Add the sour cream and mix well. Simmer for 1 minute.
15. Press the CANCEL key to stop the SAUTÉ function.
16. Serve the meat with the sauce and cooked noodles.

Pork Loin Chops with Mushroom Gravy

(Prep + Cook Time: 60 minutes | **Serves:** 4)

Ingredients:
- 4 boneless pork loin chops (6-7-ounce each)
- 6-ounce baby bella mushrooms, sliced
- 1 tablespoon butter
- 1/2 cup heavy whipping cream
- ¼ – ½ teaspoon cornstarch
- 1 tablespoon chopped fresh parsley
- 1 teaspoon onion powder
- 1 teaspoon salt
- 1 teaspoon black pepper
- 1 teaspoon garlic powder
- 1 tablespoon paprika
- 1/4 teaspoon cayenne pepper
- 2 tablespoon coconut oil
- 1/2 medium onion, sliced

Directions:
1. Rinse the pork chops and pat dry with paper towel.
2. In a bowl; combine the onion powder, salt, black pepper, garlic powder, paprika and cayenne powder.
3. Season the pork chops with 1 tablespoon of the spice mix and rub all sides of the pork chops with the spice mix
4. To preheat the Instant Pot, select SAUTÉ. Add and heat the oil.
5. Put the pork in the pot and cook for about 3 minutes on each side, until browned
6. Transfer the meat to a plate and select CANCEL.
7. Add the onions and mushrooms to the pot. Place the pork chops on the top. Close and lock the lid.
8. Select the MANUAL setting and set the cooking time for 25 minutes at HIGH pressure
9. Once cooking is complete, select CANCEL and use a Natural Release for 10 minutes. Open the lid.
10. Transfer the pork to a serving plate.
11. Select SAUTÉ and add the heavy cream, butter and remaining spice mix to the pot, Stir well.
12. Add the cornstarch and mix well. Let the sauce simmer for 5 minutes until start to thicken
13. Press the CANCEL key to stop the SAUTÉ function.
14. Pour the gravy over the pork chops. Season with parsley and serve.

Milk Braised Pork

(Prep + Cook Time: 60 minutes **| Serves:** 4)

Ingredients:

- 2 pounds' pork loin roast
- 2 tablespoon butter
- 2 tablespoon olive oil
- 1 bay leaf
- 2 cups milk
- 1 teaspoon sea salt
- 1/2 teaspoon ground black pepper

Directions:

1. Preheat the Instant Pot by selecting SAUTÉ and melt the butter. Add the oil
2. Put the pork loin in the pot fatty-side down and sear on all sides, until browned.
3. Season with salt, pepper and bay leaf. Add the milk. Close and lock the lid
4. Press the CANCEL key to stop the SAUTÉ function.
5. Select MANUAL and cook at HIGH pressure for 30 minutes.
6. When the timer goes off, let the pressure Release Naturally for 15 minutes, then release any remaining steam manually.
7. Remove the meat to a serving bowl and cover to keep a warm
8. Select SAUTÉ and cook until the sauce has thickened. Slice the meat and serve with sauce.

Juicy Pork Shoulder Recipe

(Prep + Cook Time: 60 minutes **| Serves:** 6-7)

Ingredients:

- 3 pounds' pork shoulder, boneless and cut into 2-inch pieces
- 2 tablespoon fresh cilantro, finely chopped.
- 1/4 cup orange juice, freshly squeezed
- 1/4 cup lime juice, freshly squeezed
- 5 cloves garlic, crushed
- 1/2 teaspoon cumin, ground
- 1 teaspoon sea salt
- 1/2 teaspoon ground black pepper
- 1/2 cup heavy cream, optional

Directions:

1. In the Instant Pot, combine the garlic, cumin, cilantro, orange juice, lime juice, salt and pepper
2. Add the meat pieces and rub them all over until are coated. Close the lid and let marinate for 45 minutes
3. Lock the lid. Select MANUAL and cook at HIGH pressure for 40 minutes.
4. When the timer goes off, use a Quick Release.
5. Carefully unlock the lid, Press the SAUTE button and cook for 5 minutes more, stirring occasionally
6. Optional: If desired, add 1/2 cup of heavy cream for a creamier sauce, stir and cook for 1 minute more, Serve.

Pork Tenderloin

(Prep + Cook Time: 45 minutes **| Serves:** 4-5)

Ingredients:

- 2 pounds' pork loin
- 1 yellow onion, chopped.
- 2 apples, chopped.
- 2 cups apple cider
- 2 tablespoon brown sugar
- 1/2 teaspoon sea salt or to taste
- 1/2 teaspoon ground black pepper
- 1 tablespoon dry onion, minced
- 2 tablespoon extra-virgin olive oil

Directions:

1. Rub all sides of the pork loin with salt, pepper and dried onion
2. Preheat the Instant Pot by selecting SAUTÉ. Add and heat the oil.
3. Add the meat and cook for 4 minutes on each side, until browned
4. Remove the pork loin from the pot.

5. Add the onion and sauté for 2 minutes
6. Add the apples and apple cider and deglaze the pot by scraping the bottom to remove all of the brown bits.
7. Return the pork to the Instant Pot and sprinkle with sugar.
8. Press the CANCEL button to reset the cooking program, then select the MANUAL setting and set the cooking time for 20 minutes at HIGH pressure
9. Once cooking is complete, select CANCEL and use a Natural Release for 5 minutes.
10. Open the lid. Slice the pork loin and serve with the remaining sauce

Garlic and Honey Pork Chops

(Prep + Cook Time: 35 minutes | **Serves:** 4)

Ingredients:
- 2 pounds' pork chops, boneless
- 1/4 cups honey
- 2 tablespoon water
- 2 cloves garlic, ground
- 1/2 teaspoon cinnamon
- 1/2 teaspoon fresh ginger, peeled and minced
- 1/2 teaspoon sea salt or to taste
- 1/4 teaspoon ground black pepper
- 1 tablespoon olive oil
- 2 tablespoon Dijon mustard
- 1/2 tablespoon maple syrup

Directions:
1. Rub all sides of the pork chops with salt and pepper.
2. Preheat the Instant Pot by selecting SAUTÉ. Add and heat the oil
3. Put the meat into the pot and cook for 3 to 4 minutes per side, until browned.
4. Meanwhile, in a bowl, combine the Dijon mustard, maple syrup, honey, water, garlic and cinnamon.
5. Pour the mixture into the pot
6. Press the CANCEL button to reset the cooking program, then select the MANUAL setting and set the cooking time for 15 minutes at HIGH pressure.
7. When the timer beeps, use a Quick Release.
8. Carefully unlock the lid, Serve with mashed potatoes and macaroni and cheese as sides

Pork Shoulder and Beans.

(Prep + Cook Time: 1 hour 45 minutes | **Serves:** 6-7)

Ingredients:
- 3 pounds' pork shoulder, cut into 1 ½ - inch pieces
- 1 large yellow onion, sliced
- 6 cups water or chicken broth
- 1 ½ cups tomatoes, chopped.
- 2 teaspoon chili powder
- 2 teaspoon garlic, minced
- 1/2 cup light brown sugar
- 1 sprig fresh thyme
- 1 bay leaf
- 1 ½ tablespoon vegetable oil
- 2 cups dried white beans
- 2 tablespoon Creole mustard
- 1/2 teaspoon ground black pepper
- 1 teaspoon kosher salt

Spices:
- 2 ½ tablespoon paprika
- 1 tablespoon black pepper
- 1 tablespoon cayenne pepper
- 1 tablespoon onion powder
- 1 tablespoon dried thyme
- 1 tablespoon dried leaf oregano
- 2 tablespoon garlic powder
- 2 teaspoon salt

Directions:
1. In a small bowl, combine all spices.
2. Sprinkle the pork pieces with spice mix and rub them all over until coated
3. Set your instant pot on SAUTÉ mode, add the oil and heat it up

4. Add the pork and cook, stirring occasionally, for 4 to 5 minutes until the meat has turned light brown. You may have to do it in two batches.
5. Transfer the meat to a bowl.
6. Add the onion to the pot and sauté for 2 minutes.
7. Add the beans and pour in the water/broth, mix well. Deglaze the pot by scraping the bottom to remove all of the brown bits.
8. Close and lock the lid. Select MANUAL and cook at HIGH pressure for 20 minutes
9. When the timer beeps, use a Natural Release for 15 minutes. Uncover the pot.
10. Add the tomatoes, chili powder, garlic, light brown sugar, thyme, mustard, black pepper, bay leaf and return pork to the pot. Stir
11. Close and lock the lid. Select Manual and cook at HIGH pressure for 20 minutes.
12. When the timer beeps, use a Natural Release for 15 minutes
13. Uncover the pot, elect SAUTÉ, bring to a simmer and season with salt. Simmer for 10 minutes. Serve.

Teriyaki Pork Tenderloin

(**Prep + Cook Time:** 45 minutes | **Serves:** 4)

Ingredients:
- 2 pork tenderloins (1-pound each), cut into half
- 2 cups teriyaki sauce
- Sesame seeds, toasted
- 4 green onions, chopped.
- 2 tablespoon olive oil
- Salt and ground black pepper to taste

Directions:
1. Set your instant pot on SAUTÉ mode, add the oil and heat it up
2. Rub all sides of the tenderloins with salt and pepper.
3. Add the tenderloins and cook for few minutes until lightly brown on both sides. You may have to do it in two batches.
4. Pour the teriyaki sauce over the meat. Close and lock the lid
5. Press the CANCEL button to reset the cooking program, then select the MANUAL setting and set the cooking time for 20 minutes at HIGH pressure.
6. Once cooking is complete, select CANCEL and let Naturally Release for 10 minutes. Release any remaining steam manually
7. Uncover the pot, Slice the meat, top with toasted sesame seeds and green onions, serve.

Pork Strips with Cumin and Paprika

(**Prep + Cook Time:** 1 hour 30 minutes | **Serves:** 4)

Ingredients:
- 2 pounds' pork tenderloin, cut into 2-inch strips
- 2 cup vegetable stock
- 4 cups lettuce, chopped.
- 3 tablespoon garlic, chopped.
- 2 tablespoon dried oregano
- 1/2 tablespoon ground cumin
- 3 tablespoon sweet paprika
- 1/2 teaspoon kosher salt
- 1/2 teaspoon ground black pepper
- 2 tablespoon olive oil

Directions:
1. In a large bowl, combine the garlic, oregano, cumin, paprika, salt and pepper. Mix well
2. Rub the pork strips all over until coated. Let marinate for at least 30 minutes.
3. Set your instant pot on SAUTÉ mode, add the oil and heat it up.
4. Add the meat and cook for 10 minutes until browned.
5. Pour in the vegetable stock and stir well. Close and lock the lid
6. Press the CANCEL button to reset the cooking program, then select the MANUAL setting and set the cooking time for 30 minutes at HIGH pressure.

7. Once cooking is complete, use a Natural Release for 15 minutes, then release any remaining pressure manually.
8. Open the lid. Serve the cooked pork with the chopped lettuce

Pork Baby Back Ribs

(Prep + Cook Time: 55 minutes | **Serves:** 4)

Ingredients:

- 3-3 ½ pounds' pork baby back ribs, trimmed of excess fat, cut into 4-rib pieces
- 4 tablespoon maple syrup divided
- 1 8-ounce can tomato sauce
- 1/4 teaspoon ground ginger
- 1/4 teaspoon ground cinnamon
- 1 ¼ teaspoon ground coriander
- 1 ¼ teaspoon garlic powder, divided
- 3 teaspoon chili powder divided
- 1 teaspoon kosher salt
- 1/2 teaspoon black pepper

Directions:

1. In a bowl; combine the coriander, 1 teaspoon garlic powder, 2 teaspoon chili powder, salt and pepper. Mix well
2. Brush the ribs with 2 tablespoons of maple syrup.
3. Rub all sides of the pork ribs with the spice mix.
4. Put the ribs in the Instant Pot
5. In another bowl, whisk together tomato sauce, 2 tablespoons of maple syrup, ¼ teaspoon garlic powder, 1 teaspoon chili powder, ginger and cinnamon until combined.
6. Pour the mixture into the pot and stir to coat ribs with sauce
7. Close and lock the lid. Select the MANUAL setting and set the cooking time for 27 minutes at HIGH pressure.
8. When the timer goes off, let the pressure Release Naturally for 5 minutes, then release any remaining steam manually.
9. Open the lid, Transfer the ribs to a serving bowl and cover to keep warm
10. Select SAUTÉ and cook on HIGH heat until the sauce has thickened, Serve the ribs with the sauce.

Rosemary Pork Tenderloin

(Prep + Cook Time: 40 minutes | **Serves:** 4-5)

Ingredients:

- 3 pounds' pork tenderloin, cut in half
- 1/2 cup water or vegetable broth
- 1/2 cup balsamic vinegar
- 2 tablespoon avocado oil, optional
- 1/4 cup cherry preserves
- 4 cloves garlic, minced
- 1/4 cup fresh rosemary, chopped.
- 2 tablespoon olive oil
- 1/2 teaspoon kosher salt
- 1/2 teaspoon ground black pepper

Directions:

1. Preheat the Instant Pot by selecting SAUTÉ. Add and heat the olive oil
2. Season the pork with salt and pepper. Add to the pot and cook for 2 to 3 minutes on each side, until browned
3. In a bowl; combine the water, balsamic vinegar, avocado oil, cherry, garlic and rosemary, mix well.
4. Pour the mixture into the pot. Close and lock the lid.
5. Press the CANCEL key to stop the SAUTÉ function.
6. Select MANUAL and cook at HIGH pressure for 22 minutes
7. When the timer goes off, let the pressure Release Naturally for 15 minutes, then release any remaining steam manually.
8. Open the lid, Remove the pork from the Instant Pot. Slice the meat and serve

Pulled Pork Tacos.

(Prep + Cook Time: 1 hour 25 minutes | **Serves:** 8

Ingredients:

- 4 pounds' pork shoulder, trimmed of excess fat (cut into 4 chunks)
- 1 large yellow onion, peeled and sliced
- 1 ½ cups chicken or beef broth
- 1 teaspoon freshly ground pepper
- 1/2 teaspoon garlic powder
- 1/2 teaspoon chipotle chili powder
- 1/2 teaspoon cumin
- 1 ½ teaspoon sea salt
- Tortillas

Directions:

1. In a large bowl, combine the salt, pepper, garlic powder, chili powder and cumin
2. Rub all sides of the meat with the spice mix.
3. Put the onion in the instant pot and place the pork shoulder on the onion slices
4. Pour the broth. Close and lock the lid.
5. Select MANUAL and cook at HIGH pressure for 60 minutes.
6. Once timer goes off, allow to Naturally Release for 10 minutes, then release any remaining pressure manually
7. Open the lid, Remove the pork from the pot and shred the meat.
8. If you want the crispy edges, broil in the oven for a few minutes, Use the shredded meat to make tacos and serve

BBQ Pulled Pork

(Prep + Cook Time: 1 hour 25 minutes | **Serves:** 4-5)

Ingredients:

- 3 pounds' pork roast, cut into 4 chunks
- 2/3 cup chicken broth
- 1/2 cup BBQ sauce
- 1/2 teaspoon kosher salt
- 1/2 teaspoon ground black pepper

Directions:

1. Rub all sides of the pork roast with salt and pepper.
2. Put the meat in the Instant Pot
3. Pour in the broth and BBQ sauce, stir.
4. Close and lock the lid. Select MANUAL and cook at HIGH pressure for 60 minutes
5. Once cooking is complete, select Cancel and let Naturally Release for 10 minutes. Release any remaining steam manually.
6. Uncover the pot, Shred the meat with two forks.
7. Serve with the gravy

Coconut Ginger Pork Recipe

(Prep + Cook Time: 1 hour 25 minutes | **Serves:** 4-5)

Ingredients:

- 3 pounds' pork butt or shoulder roast, boneless, trimmed of excess fat
- 1 tablespoon avocado oil or olive oil
- 1 onion, peeled and cut into 8 chunks
- 4 cloves garlic, finely chopped.
- 2-inch piece ginger, peeled and thinly sliced
- 1 can (14 oz) coconut milk
- Lime wedges for garnish
- 1 teaspoon kosher salt
- 1 teaspoon black pepper
- 1 teaspoon ground cumin
- 1 teaspoon garam masala (or coriander)

Directions:

1. In a bowl; combine the salt, pepper, cumin and garam masala.
2. Rub all sides of the pork with the spice mix.
3. Select the SAUTÉ setting on the Instant Pot and heat the oil

4. Add the onion and garlic, sauté for 2 minutes.
5. Add the meat and ginger. Pour in the coconut milk.
6. Close and lock the lid. Press the CANCEL button to reset the cooking program, then select the MANUAL setting and set the cooking time for 55 minutes at HIGH pressure
7. Once timer goes off, allow to Naturally Release for 15 minutes, then release any remaining pressure manually
8. Slice the meat and serve with lime wedges.

Smoked Pork Shoulder.

(Prep + Cook Time: 1 hour 30 minutes | **Serves:** 4-5)

Ingredients:
- 3 pounds' pork shoulder, cut into half
- 1 cup water or bone broth
- 2 tablespoon liquid smoke
- Steamed green beans for serving
- 2 tablespoon vegetable oil
- 3 cloves garlic, chopped.
- Salt and ground black pepper to taste

Directions:
1. Select the SAUTÉ setting on the Instant Pot and heat the oil
2. Add the garlic and sauté for 1 minute.
3. Season the meat with salt and pepper to taste.
4. Add the pork shoulder to the pot and cook for 5 minutes on both sides, until browned
5. Pour in the water and liquid smoke and deglaze the pot by scraping the bottom to remove all of the brown bits. Close and lock the lid.
6. Press the CANCEL button to reset the cooking program, then select the MANUAL setting and set the cooking time for 70 minutes at HIGH pressure
7. Once cooking is complete, let the pressure Release Naturally for 10 minutes. Release any remaining steam manually.
8. Uncover the pot, Transfer the pork to a plate and shred the meat
9. Serve with the sauce and green beans.

Delicious Pork Shoulder Recipe

(Prep + Cook Time: 1 hour 35 minutes | **Serves:** 4-5)

Ingredients:

- 3 pounds' pork roast, shoulder, sirloin, trimmed of excess fat
- 1 teaspoon cumin
- 1 tablespoon oregano, ground
- 1 large onion, sliced
- 1/4 cup lime juice
- 2 cloves garlic, peeled and slivered
- 1/4 cup orange juice
- 1 tablespoon olive oil
- 2 cups water
- 1 teaspoon ground black pepper
- 1 tablespoon sea salt

Directions:

1. With a knife, cut tiny holes in the meat and insert slivers of garlic
2. In a large bowl (or use a large Ziploc bag), combine the cumin, oregano, onion, lime juice, orange juice, salt and pepper. Mix well.
3. Add the pork roast to the bowl and rub all sides with the spice mix. Cover the bowl tightly with aluminum foil. Let marinate for at least 60 minutes or up to 12 hours in the refrigerator
4. Set your instant pot on SAUTÉ mode, add the oil and heat it up.
5. Add the pork roast to the pot and brown for 4 minutes per side.
6. Remove the meat from the pot. Add the water and remaining marinade and deglaze the pot
7. Place the steam rack in the Instant Pot.
8. Place the pork on the steam rack and secure the lid.
9. Press the CANCEL button to reset the cooking program, then select the MANUAL setting and set the cooking time for 50 minutes at HIGH pressure
10. Once cooking is complete, let the pressure Release Naturally for 10 minutes. Release any remaining steam manually.
11. Uncover the pot. Slice the meat and serve

Beef & Lamb Recipes

Tomato Beef Meatballs

(Prep + Cook Time: 1 hour 10 minutes | **Serves:** 4)

Ingredients:

- 1 ¼ pounds' ground beef
- 1 teaspoon garlic powder
- 2 tablespoon olive oil
- 1 onion, diced
- 2 cloves garlic, minced
- 1 can chopped tomatoes
- 1 teaspoon onion powder
- 1 teaspoon dried oregano
- 1/2 teaspoon celery salt
- Ground black pepper to taste

Directions:

1. In a large bowl, combine the ground beef, garlic powder, onion powder, oregano, celery salt and pepper to taste. Mix well
2. Shape the mixture into 1 ½-inch meatballs and place on a plate.
3. Set your instant pot on SAUTÉ mode, add the oil and heat it up
4. Add the onion and garlic, sauté until fragrant.
5. Add the meatballs. Cook, stirring gently, on all sides, until the meatballs start to brown.
6. Add the tomatoes, stir. Close and lock the lid.
7. Select the MEAT/STEW setting and set the cooking time for 35 minutes
8. Once timer goes off, allow to Naturally Release for 10 minutes, then release any remaining pressure manually.
9. Open the lid, Serve with cooked rice or mashed potatoes.

Herbs and Meatloaf.

(Prep + Cook Time: 55 minutes | **Serves:** 4)

Ingredients:

- 2 pounds' ground beef
- 1 cup almond flour
- 1 teaspoon rosemary
- Sweet and spicy pepper sauce (for example, Tabasco)
- 1 teaspoon thyme
- 2 tablespoon olive oil
- 2 eggs, beaten
- 2 cups water
- 1 teaspoon garlic powder
- 1/2 teaspoon salt
- 1/2 teaspoon ground black pepper

Directions:

1. In a large bowl, combine the ground beef, eggs, garlic powder, almond flour, rosemary, thyme, salt and pepper. Mix well.
2. Take a cake pan and grease with olive oil. Transfer the meat mixture to the prepared pan, press mixture firmly into pan
3. Pour the water into the Instant Pot and insert a steam rack.
4. Place the pan on the steam rack
5. Close and lock the lid. Select the MANUAL setting and set the cooking time for 35 minutes at HIGH pressure.
6. Once cooking is complete, select CANCEL and let Naturally Release for 10 minutes. Release any remaining steam manually
7. Uncover the pot, Transfer the meatloaf to a serving plate. Drizzle the sweet and spice pepper sauce over the top
8. If desired, top with green onions or parsley.

Beef and Pasta Casserole.

(Prep + Cook Time: 45 minutes | **Serves:** 4)

Ingredients:

- 1-pound ground beef
- 16-ounce tomato puree
- 17-ounce pasta (of your choice)
- 1 ½ cups mozzarella cheese, shredded
- 1 teaspoon kosher salt
- 1/2 teaspoon ground black pepper

- 2 tablespoon butter
- 1 yellow onion, chopped.
- 1 carrot, chopped.
- 1 celery stalk, chopped.
- 1 tablespoon red wine
- Water as needed

Directions:

1. Add the butter to the Instant Pot and select SAUTÉ.
2. Once the butter has melted, add the onion, carrot and celery. Stir until well coated and sauté for 5 minutes
3. Raise the heat to high. Add the ground beef, 1/2 teaspoon of salt and ground pepper, Stir well.
4. Cook, stirring occasionally, for 8-10 minutes until nicely browned
5. Add red wine, stir well and cook for another 1 minute, or until the wine has evaporated.
6. Press the CANCEL key to stop the SAUTÉ function.
7. Add the tomato puree, pasta and 1/2 teaspoon of salt. Pour enough water into the pot to cover the pasta, Stir well.
8. Close and lock the lid. Select MANUAL and cook at HIGH pressure for 5-6 minutes
9. When the timer beeps, use a Quick Release
10. Carefully unlock the lid, and drain off most of the cooking liquid, reserving 1/2 cup.
11. Add the cheese to the pot, stir and close the lid. Let the dish sit for 10-15 minutes. Serve with the remained sauce

Awesome Beef Short Ribs

(Prep + Cook Time: 1 hour 10 minutes | **Serves:** 6-7)

Ingredients:

- 12 beef short ribs
- 2 tablespoon sriracha sauce
- 1/4 cup raw honey
- 1/2 cup soy sauce
- 1 cup tomato paste

- 2 tablespoon olive oil
- 4 cloves garlic, minced
- 1/4 cup ginger root, diced
- 2 tablespoon apple cider vinegar
- 1/2 teaspoon salt

Directions:

1. Select the SAUTÉ setting on the Instant Pot and heat the oil.
2. Season the ribs with salt. Add to the pot and cook for 5 minutes on each side, until browned. Brown the short ribs in batches
3. Transfer the browned ribs to a plate.
4. Add the soy sauce, tomato paste, apple cider, garlic, ginger, sriracha and honey to the pot
5. Stir the mixture well, at the same time, deglaze the pot by scraping the bottom to remove all of the brown bits.
6. Return the ribs to the pot.
7. Press the CANCEL key to stop the SAUTÉ function.
8. Close and lock the lid. Select MANUAL and cook at HIGH pressure for 35 minutes
9. Once timer goes off, allow to Naturally Release for 10-15 minutes, then release any remaining pressure manually
10. Open the lid. Serve with the gravy.

Delicious Lamb Stew

(**Prep + Cook Time:** 50 minutes | **Serves:** 4)

Ingredients:

- 1 ½ pounds' lamb stew meat, cut into 1 ½-inch cubes
- 3 cups sweet potatoes, chopped.
- 3 cups carrots, chopped.
- 2 cans (14 ounces each) tomatoes, diced
- 4 cups kale, finely chopped (stems removed)

- 5 dried unsweetened apricots, finely chopped.
- 3 ½ cups chicken or beef broth
- 2 tablespoon olive oil
- 3 tablespoon soy sauce
- 3 cloves garlic, chopped.
- 1 big white onion, chopped.

Spices:

- 1/2 teaspoon allspice
- 1/2 teaspoon ground ginger
- 1/2 teaspoon curry powder
- 1 teaspoon cinnamon

- 1/2 teaspoon ground turmeric
- 1 teaspoon ground cumin
- 1 teaspoon salt
- 1/2 teaspoon ground black pepper

Directions:

1. Set your instant pot on SAUTÉ mode, add the oil and heat it up
2. Add the lamb cubes to the pot and cook until all the meat is browned.
3. Add the remaining ingredients and spices to the Instant Pot
4. Close and lock the lid. Select MANUAL and cook at HIGH pressure for 30 minutes.
5. Once cooking is complete, select Cancel and let Naturally Release for 10 minutes. Release any remaining steam manually.
6. Uncover the pot, Serve warm

Beef Sandwiches.

(**Prep + Cook Time:** 1 hour 10 minutes | **Serves:** 8

Ingredients:

- 4 pounds' beef roast, cut into small chunks (2 - 3 inch)
- 2 tablespoon brown sugar
- 2 ½ teaspoon garlic powder
- 2 teaspoon mustard powder
- 2 teaspoon paprika
- 2 teaspoon onion flakes
- 3 cups beef stock

- 8 hoagie rolls
- 8 slices provolone cheese
- 2 tablespoon Worcestershire sauce
- 1 tablespoon balsamic vinegar
- 4 tablespoon butter, soft
- 1 teaspoon salt
- 1 teaspoon ground black pepper

Directions:

1. Add the beef roast to the Instant Pot.
2. Season the meat with salt, pepper, sugar, garlic powder, mustard powder, paprika and onion flakes. Mix well.
3. Pour in the stock, Worcestershire sauce and balsamic vinegar, Stir well
4. Close and lock the lid. Select the MANUAL setting and set the cooking time for 40 minutes at HIGH pressure.
5. Once cooking is complete, let the pressure Release Naturally for 10 minutes. Release any remaining steam manually. Uncover the pot
6. Remove the meat from the pot and shred it. Strain the sauce and keep 1 cup for serving.
7. Butter the hoagie rolls and add the provolone cheese.
8. Load up the rolls with some shredded roast and close the sandwich up. Serve each sandwich with the sauce in a ramekin

Italian Beef Roast

(Prep + Cook Time: 1 hour 25 minutes | **Serves:** 6-7)

Ingredients:

- 2 pounds' boneless beef chuck roast
- 1 package cremini mushrooms, sliced
- 1 can crushed tomatoes
- 1/2 cup dried red wine
- 2 teaspoon dried oregano
- 2 bay leaves
- 1 ½ tablespoon Italian seasonings
- 6 cloves garlic, minced
- 1 cup chicken broth
- 8-ounce bacon, diced
- 2 onions, chopped.
- 1 teaspoon tomato paste
- Salt and ground black pepper to taste
- Parsley, optional

Directions:

1. To preheat the Instant Pot, select SAUTÉ.
2. Add the bacon to the pot and cook until lightly crispy and turn to cook the other side.
3. Remove the bacon from the pot. Add the onion and garlic and sauté until fragrant
4. Add the beef, bacon, mushrooms, broth, tomato paste, tomatoes, red wine, oregano and bay leaves.
5. Sprinkle with Italian seasonings, salt and pepper to taste
6. Press the CANCEL key to stop the SAUTÉ function.
7. Select the MEAT/STEW setting and set the cooking time for 60 minutes at HIGH pressure.
8. Once timer goes off, allow to Naturally Release for 10 minutes, then release any remaining pressure manually
9. Open the lid, if desired, top with parsley and serve.

Beef Stew with Carrots and Turnips

(Prep + Cook Time: 1 hour 10 minutes | **Serves:** 2 - 3)

Ingredients:

- 1-pound beef stew meat, 1 inch pieces
- 1-pound turnips, 1 inch pieces
- 1-pound carrots, 1 inch pieces
- 1 cup bone broth
- 1/4 cup fresh parsley, chopped.
- 2 tablespoon olive oil
- 1 teaspoon kosher salt
- 1 medium red onion, chopped.
- 1 teaspoon dried thyme
- 2 tablespoon cassava flour
- 1 cup dry red wine
- 1/4 cup soy sauce

Directions:

1. Set your instant pot on SAUTÉ mode, add 1 tablespoon of oil and heat it up
2. Season the beef with 1/2 teaspoon of salt.
3. Add the meat to the pot and cook for 7 minutes on all sides, until browned.
4. Transfer the meat to a plate
5. Add the onion and 1 tablespoon of oil to the pot and sauté for about 5 minutes, until softened.
6. Add the thyme and cassava flour, stir and cook for 1 minute
7. Pour the wine and deglaze the pot by scraping the bottom to remove all of the brown bits.
8. Add the soy sauce, turnips, carrots, broth and 1/2 teaspoon of salt.
9. Return the meat to the pot.
10. Close and lock the lid. Select the MEAT/STEW program and leave it on the default
11. Once cooking is complete, use a Natural Release for 10 minutes, then release any remaining pressure manually.
12. Open the lid, Top with parsley and serve.

Beef Chili with Sweet Potatoes and Pumpkin

(Prep + Cook Time: 1 hour 10 minutes | **Serves:** 4-5)

Ingredients:

- 1-pound beef, cut into chunks
- 14 ounces can tomatoes, diced
- 2 cups sweet potatoes, peeled and diced
- 1/2 large onion, diced
- 8 ounces can tomato sauce
- 3 cloves garlic
- 1 teaspoon garlic powder
- 2 teaspoon taco seasoning
- 1 tablespoon olive oil
- 1 cup pumpkin, peeled and cubed
- 2 carrots, peeled and diced
- 1/2 teaspoon salt
- 1/2 teaspoon pepper or to taste

Directions:

1. Select the SAUTÉ setting on the Instant Pot and heat the oil
2. Brown the beef chunks for 4 minutes on both sides.
3. Add the pumpkin, carrots, tomatoes, sweet potatoes, onion, tomato sauce, cloves garlic, garlic powder, salt, pepper and taco seasoning, Stir well
4. Press the CANCEL key to stop the SAUTÉ function.
5. Close and lock the lid. Select the MEAT/STEW setting and leave it on the default.
6. Once cooking is complete, select CANCEL and let Naturally Release for 10 minutes. Release any remaining steam manually
7. Uncover the pot, Slightly mash the sweet potatoes with a fork, stir and let the dish sit for 15 minutes, Serve.

Beef Short Ribs.

(Prep + Cook Time: 1 hour 10 minutes | **Serves:** 6-7)

Ingredients:

- 4 pounds' beef short ribs
- 3 cloves garlic, minced
- 4 to 6 carrots, cut into bite sized pieces
- 1 tablespoon dried thyme
- 1 ½ cups beef broth
- 2 cups onions, diced
- 2 tablespoon olive oil
- 1 teaspoon kosher salt
- 1 teaspoon ground black pepper

Directions:

1. Rinse and pat the ribs dry with paper towels.
2. Season the ribs with salt and pepper
3. Set your instant pot on SAUTÉ mode, add the oil and heat it up
4. Add the ribs to the pot and cook for 5 minutes on each side, until browned. Brown the short ribs in batches.
5. Transfer the browned ribs to a plate.
6. Add the garlic to the pot and cook for 1 minute.
7. Put the carrot, onion and thyme to the pot. Sauté for another 5 minutes, until softened
8. Add the broth and deglaze the pot by scraping the bottom to remove all of the brown bits.
9. Put the beef ribs back into the pot.
10. Press the CANCEL button to reset the cooking program, then select the MANUAL setting and set the cooking time for 35 minutes at HIGH pressure
11. Once cooking is complete, select CANCEL and let Naturally Release for 15 minutes. Release any remaining steam manually
12. Uncover the pot, Serve with cooked rice, potato or veggies.

Beef and Cabbage.

(Prep + Cook Time: 1 hour 25 minutes | **Serves:** 4-5)

Ingredients:

- 2 ½ pounds' beef brisket
- 1 cabbage heat, cut into 6 wedges
- 4 carrots, chopped.
- 3 cloves garlic, chopped.
- 2 bay leaves
- 4 cups water
- 3 turnips, cut into quarters
- 6 potatoes, cut into quarters
- Horseradish sauce for serving
- 1 teaspoon salt
- 1/2 teaspoon ground black pepper

Directions:

1. Add the beef brisket to the Instant Pot and season with salt and pepper.
2. Add the garlic and bay leaves. Pour the water into the pot
3. Close and lock the lid. Select the MANUAL setting and set the cooking time for 60 minutes at HIGH pressure.
4. Once cooking is complete, use a Quick Release the pressure. Open the lid.
5. Add the cabbage, carrots, turnips and potatoes to the pot
6. Close and lock the lid. Select MANUAL and cook at HIGH pressure for 6 minutes.
7. Once cooking is complete, select Cancel and use a Natural Release for 10 minutes
8. Uncover the pot, Serve with horseradish sauce.

IP Round Roast and Veggies

(Prep + Cook Time: 40 minutes | **Serves:** 6

Ingredients:

- 2 ½ pounds' round roast (top or bottom)
- 1-pound potatoes, quartered or cubed
- 2 tablespoon minced garlic
- 1 tablespoon thyme
- 2 - 3 cups sliced mushrooms
- 1 large white onion, sliced or diced
- 2 tablespoon olive oil
- 2 cups vegetable or beef broth
- 1 teaspoon kosher salt
- 1/2 teaspoon ground black pepper

Directions:

1. Add the olive oil, broth, garlic, salt, pepper and thyme to the pot, Mix well
2. Add the roast, mushrooms and onion, stir.
3. Close and lock the lid. Select MANUAL and cook at HIGH pressure for 25 minutes.
4. When the timer goes off, use a quick release. Carefully unlock the lid
5. Add the potatoes, stir.
6. Close and lock the lid. Select MANUAL and cook at HIGH pressure for another 10 minutes.
7. When the timer beeps, use a Quick Release.
8. Carefully unlock the lid, Serve

Beef Roast

(Prep + Cook Time: 1 hour 10 minutes | **Serves:** 6-7)

Ingredients:

- 4 pounds' beef chuck roast, cut into cubes (2 inches)
- 5 minced cloves garlic
- 1 peeled and chopped Granny Smith apple
- 2 tablespoon olive oil
- 1 cup beef broth
- 1/2 cup soy sauce
- 1 thumb of grated ginger
- Juice of one big orange
- 1 teaspoon salt
- 1 teaspoon ground black pepper

Directions:

1. Set your instant pot on SAUTÉ mode, add the oil and heat it up
2. Season the roast with salt and pepper.
3. Add the roast to the pot and cook until the meat has turned light brown
4. Transfer the meat to a plate.
5. Press the CANCEL key to stop the SAUTÉ function.
6. Add the beef broth and deglaze the pot by scraping the bottom to remove all of the brown bits
7. Pour the soy sauce and stir. Return the roast to the pot.
8. Place the garlic, apple and ginger on top. Pour over the orange juice.
9. Close and lock the lid. Select MANUAL and cook at HIGH pressure for 45 minutes.
10. When the timer beeps, use a Quick Release
11. Carefully unlock the lid, Serve.

Beef Curry Recipe

(Prep + Cook Time: 60 minutes | **Serves:** 4)

Ingredients:

- 1 tablespoon olive oil
- 1 ½ cups jarred tikka masala or madras curry sauce
- 1 ½ pounds' of beef chuck steak (trimmed to ¼" fat), cut into 2-inch cubes
- 1 cup beef broth
- 1/2 cup coconut milk

Optional toppings:

- Chopped coriander or basil leaves
- Sliced green chilies
- 1/2 teaspoon ground black pepper
- 1/2 teaspoon salt

Directions:

1. Preheat the Instant Pot by selecting SAUTÉ. Add the oil.
2. Season the beef with salt and pepper
3. Add the beef to the pot and brown steak on both sides.
4. Remove the beef from the pot. Add the broth and deglaze the pot by scraping the bottom to remove all of the brown bits
5. Press the CANCEL key to stop the SAUTÉ function.
6. Return the meat to the pot. Add coconut milk and tikka masala, stir well.
7. Close and lock the lid. Select MANUAL and cook at HIGH pressure for 25 minutes
8. When the timer goes off, use a Quick Release.
9. Carefully unlock the lid, If desired, serve with any additional toppings

Beef Bourguignon.

(Prep + Cook Time: 60 minutes | **Serves:** 4)

Ingredients:

- 1-pound flank steak
- 2 tablespoon fresh parsley, finely chopped.
- 2 tablespoon fresh thyme, finely chopped.
- 1 tablespoon maple syrup
- 1 tablespoon olive oil
- 1 large red onion, sliced
- 3 cloves garlic, minced
- 1 ½ cups shiitake mushroom caps
- 4 medium-sized carrots, sliced
- 8-ounce bacon slices
- 1 cup beef broth
- 1 cup red wine
- 1 teaspoon sea salt

Directions:

1. Preheat the Instant Pot by selecting SAUTÉ. Add the oil.
2. Add the steak and cook for 3 to 4 minutes on each side, until browned
3. Transfer the beef to a plate.
4. Add the onion, garlic, mushroom caps, carrots and bacon. Stir and cook for 4 to 5 minutes, until the onion is translucent.

5. Pour the broth and wine, stir. Return the steak to the pot
6. Add the salt, parsley and thyme, stir. Pour the maple syrup.
7. Press the CANCEL key to stop the SAUTÉ function.
8. Close and lock the lid. Select MANUAL and cook at HIGH pressure for 30 minutes.
9. Once timer goes off, allow to Naturally Release for 10 minutes, then release any remaining pressure manually.
10. Open the lid, Serve

Juicy Beef Meatloaf

(Prep + Cook Time: 55 minutes | **Serves:** 4-5)

Ingredients:
- 2 pounds' ground beef
- 1/2 cup panko breadcrumbs
- 1 yellow onion, grated
- 2 eggs, beaten
- 1/4 cup ketchup
- 1/3 cup milk
- 2 cups water
- Salt and ground black pepper to taste

Directions:
1. In a large bowl, combine the milk with breadcrumbs. Stir well and set aside for 4 to 6 minutes.
2. Then add whisked eggs, onion, salt and pepper to taste. Mix well
3. Add the ground beef to the bowl and stir well.
4. Prepare the Instant Pot by adding the water to the pot and placing the steam rack in it.
5. Place the meatloaf onto a sheet of nonstick aluminum foil and shape a loaf
6. Spread the ketchup on the top.
7. Place the meatloaf "boat" on the steam rack. Close and lock the lid.
8. Select MANUAL and cook at HIGH pressure for 35 minutes
9. Once timer goes off, allow to Naturally Release for 10 minutes, then release any remaining pressure manually.
10. Open the lid, Slice and serve with cooked potatoes or rice

Beef Chili

(Prep + Cook Time: 55 minutes | **Serves:** 4-5)

Ingredients:
- 1-pound ground beef
- 1/2-pound kidney beans, rinsed
- 1 green bell pepper, diced
- 7 cups beef broth
- 1 can diced tomatoes
- 1/4 cup tomato paste
- 1 medium white onion, diced
- 3 cloves garlic, chopped.
- 1 teaspoon salt
- 1/2 teaspoon ground black pepper

Directions:
1. Combine all of the ingredients in the Instant Pot and stir to mix
2. Close and lock the lid. Select the BEAN/CHILI program and leave it on the default.
3. Once cooking is complete, use a Natural Release for 10 minutes, then release any remaining pressure manually
4. Open the lid, Serve.

Beef and Chili Beans

(Prep + Cook Time: 40 minutes | **Serves:** 4-5)

Ingredients:

- 1 ½ pounds' stew meat
- 1 can (15 oz) kidney beans
- 1 can (15 oz) chili beans
- 1 teaspoon kosher salt
- 1/2 teaspoon ground black pepper
- 1 tablespoon olive oil
- 1 onion, chopped.
- 2 cloves garlic, minced
- 2 cups beef broth
- 1 cup tomatoes, diced
- 1 tablespoon mustard
- 1 tablespoon taco seasoning

Directions:

1. Select the SAUTÉ setting on the Instant Pot and heat the oil.
2. Add the stew meat to the pot and cook for 7 minutes on all sides, until browned
3. Add the onion and sauté for 2 minutes more.
4. Add the garlic and sauté for another 1 minute
5. Pour the broth. Add the beans, taco seasoning, mustard, salt and pepper, stir.
6. Press the CANCEL button to reset the cooking program, then select the BEAN/CHILI setting and leave it on the default
7. Once cooking is complete, use a Natural Release for 10 minutes, then release any remaining pressure manually.
8. Open the lid, Serve

Lamb Ribs Recipe

(Prep + Cook Time: 40 minutes | **Serves:** 6-7)

Ingredients:

- 8 lamb ribs
- 13-ounce veggie stock
- 2 carrots, chopped.
- 4 rosemary sprigs
- 4 cloves garlic, chopped.
- 3 tablespoon all-purpose flour
- 2 tablespoon extra-virgin olive oil
- Salt and ground black pepper to taste

Directions:

1. Preheat the Instant Pot by selecting SAUTÉ. Add and heat the oil
2. Season the lamb ribs with salt and pepper and put into the pot.
3. Brown the ribs on both sides. Add the garlic and sauté for 1 minute more.
4. Add the flour and stir. Add the stock, carrots, rosemary and stir. Close and lock the lid
5. Press the CANCEL key to stop the SAUTÉ function.
6. Select MANUAL and cook at HIGH pressure for 22 minutes
7. Once timer goes off, allow to Naturally Release for 5 minutes, then release any remaining pressure manually.
8. Uncover the pot. Discard the rosemary sprigs and serve ribs with sauce

Tender Pot Roast

(Prep + Cook Time: 1 hour 10 minutes | **Serves:** 6

Ingredients:

- 3 pounds' beef chuck roast
- 1 cup beef broth
- 1 cup red wine
- 3 cloves garlic
- 1 onion
- 3 tablespoon steak sauce, optional
- 4 carrots, chopped into large chunks
- 4 potatoes, large-sized, quartered
- 2 stalks celery, chopped.
- 2 tablespoon olive oil
- 1 teaspoon salt
- 1 teaspoon ground black pepper

Directions:

1. Set your instant pot on SAUTÉ mode, add the oil and heat it up
2. Add the roast to the pot and cook until the meat has turned light brown
3. Transfer the beef to a plate.
4. Add the beef broth and deglaze the pot by scraping the bottom to remove all of the brown bits
5. Pour the wine. Add the carrots, potatoes and celery to the pot. Top with the garlic and onion. Season with 1/2 teaspoon salt.
6. Put the beef on the vegetables. Sprinkle with 1/2 teaspoon salt and 1 teaspoon pepper, then spread with the steak sauce
7. Press the CANCEL button to reset the cooking program, then select the Manual setting and set the cooking time for 45 minutes at HIGH pressure.
8. Once cooking is complete, use a Natural Release for 15 minutes, then release any remaining pressure manually
9. Open the lid, Transfer the roast to a plate and slice it. Serve with the gravy and vegetables

Broccoli Beef Dish

(Prep + Cook Time: 60 minutes | **Serves:** 4)

Ingredients:

- 1-pound stew beef meat
- 1 bag (10-12 oz) frozen broccoli
- 1/2 cup beef or bone broth
- 1/4 cup soy sauce
- 2 tablespoon fish sauce
- 1 onion, quartered
- 1 clove garlic, large-sized, pressed
- 1 teaspoon ground ginger
- 1/2 teaspoon salt

Directions:

1. Add the beef meat, onion, garlic, ginger and salt to the Instant Pot, stir
2. Pour the broth, soy sauce and fish sauce into the pot, stir well.
3. Close and lock the lid. Select MANUAL and cook at HIGH pressure for 35 minutes
4. Once pressure cooking is complete, use a Quick Release
5. Unlock and carefully open the lid. Add the broccoli, close the lid and let sit for 15 minutes, Serve.

Lamb Casserole

(Prep + Cook Time: 60 minutes | **Serves:** 2 - 3)

Ingredients:

- 1-pound lamb stew meat, cubed
- 1-pound baby potatoes
- 2 carrot, chopped
- 1 onion, chopped
- 1 celery stalk, chopped.
- 2 tablespoon ketchup
- 2 tablespoon red wine
- 2 cup chicken stock
- 1 teaspoon sweet paprika
- 1 teaspoon cumin, ground
- 1/4 teaspoon oregano, dried
- 1/4 teaspoon rosemary, dried
- 1 tablespoon olive oil
- 3 cloves garlic, minced
- 2 tomatoes, chopped.
- Salt and ground black pepper to taste

Directions:

1. Select the SAUTÉ setting on the Instant Pot and heat the oil
2. Add the lamb and cook until the meat has turned light brown.
3. Add the garlic and sauté for 1 minute more.
4. Add all of the remaining ingredients and spices
5. Press the CANCEL button to reset the cooking program, then press the MANUAL button and set the cooking time for 35 minutes at HIGH pressure.
6. Once cooking is complete, let the pressure Release Naturally for 10 minutes. Release any remaining steam manually. Uncover the pot, Serve

Cheesy Beef Steak

(Prep + Cook Time: 1 hour 15 minutes | **Serves:** 4-5)

Ingredients:
- 3 pounds' beef chuck roast, cut into chunks (2 - 3 inch)
- 1 tablespoon oil
- 2 onions, sliced
- 2 tablespoon steak seasoning
- 1 cup mozzarella cheese
- 2 green bell peppers, sliced
- 8-ounce mushrooms, sliced
- 1 cup beef stock
- 1 teaspoon salt
- 1/2 teaspoon ground black pepper

Directions:
1. Select the SAUTÉ setting on the Instant Pot and heat the oil
2. Add the onion and sauté for 3 to 4 minutes, until softened.
3. Add the beef chunks and brown the meat for a few minutes on each side
4. Add the steak seasoning, bell peppers, mushrooms and stock.
5. Sprinkle with salt and pepper, Stir well.
6. Press the CANCEL key to stop the SAUTÉ function.
7. Close and lock the lid. Select MANUAL and cook at HIGH pressure for 40 minutes
8. When the timer goes off, use a Quick Release.
9. Carefully unlock the lid, Place the mozzarella cheese on top. Close the lid and let the dish sit for 15 minutes. Serve

Garlic Lamb Shanks

(Prep + Cook Time: 1 hour 10 minutes | **Serves:** 4)

Ingredients:
- 2 ½ pounds' lamb shanks, trimmed of excess fat
- 2 tablespoon tomato paste
- 1/2 cup sweet red wine
- 1/2 teaspoon dried rosemary
- 12 whole cloves garlic, peeled
- 3/4 cup chicken broth
- 2 teaspoon balsamic vinegar
- 1 tablespoon butter
- 1/2 teaspoon ground black pepper
- 1/2 teaspoon salt

Directions:
1. Rub all sides of the lamb with salt and pepper
2. Select the SAUTÉ setting on the Instant Pot and heat the oil
3. Add the lamb shanks and sauté on each side, until browned
4. Add the garlic and sauté for another 2 minutes.
5. Pour in the broth, tomato paste, red wine and rosemary, Stir well. Close and lock the lid
6. Press the CANCEL button to stop the SAUTE function, then select the MANUAL setting and set the cooking time for 35 minutes at HIGH pressure.
7. Once cooking is complete, use a Natural Release for 15 minutes, then release any remaining pressure manually.
8. Open the lid, Transfer the lamb to a serving bowl
9. Add the butter and balsamic vinegar to the pot.
10. Select SAUTÉ and cook the sauce until thickened, stirring occasionally, Serve the lamb shanks with sauce.

Beef with Feta and Olives

(Prep + Cook Time: 60 minutes | **Serves:** 4-5)

Ingredients:

- 2 pounds' beef stew meat, cubed (2 inches)
- 1 cup feta cheese
- 1 tablespoon olive oil
- 4 cups spicy diced tomatoes with juice
- 1/2 cup green olives, drained
- 1/2 cup black olives, drained
- 1/2 teaspoon kosher salt

Directions:

1. Select the SAUTÉ setting on the Instant Pot and heat the oil.
2. Add the beef and sauté until the cubes has turned light brown
3. Add the tomatoes, green and black olives and salt, stir well. Close and lock the lid.
4. Press the CANCEL key to stop the SAUTÉ function.
5. Select MANUAL and cook at HIGH pressure for 45 minutes
6. When the timer beeps, use a Quick Release.
7. Carefully unlock the lid, Taste and season more if necessary.
8. Add the feta cheese and serve with cooked rice or potatoes.

Teriyaki Beef

(Prep + Cook Time: 60 minutes | **Serves:** 4)

Ingredients:

- 2 cloves garlic, finely chopped.
- 1 piece (2 pound) flank steak, sliced into ½-inch strips

For the teriyaki sauce:

- 2 tablespoon fish sauce, optional
- 1 ½ teaspoon ground or fresh ginger, optional
- 1 tablespoon raw honey
- 1/4 cup soy sauce
- 1/4 cup maple syrup

Directions:

1. In a medium bowl, combine the soy sauce, maple syrup, honey, fish sauce and ginger. Mix well.
2. Add the sauce, steak strips and garlic to the Instant Pot, stir
3. Close and lock the lid. Select MANUAL and cook at HIGH pressure for 40 minutes.
4. Once timer goes off, allow to Naturally Release for 10 minutes, then release any remaining pressure manually
5. Uncover the pot, Serve.

Mexican Shredded Beef.

(Prep + Cook Time: 1 hour 45 minutes | **Serves:** 4-5)

Ingredients:

- 2 pounds' beef shoulder roast
- 1 large onion, chopped.
- 3 tablespoon garlic, minced
- 3 cups beef broth
- 1 cup tomato salsa or tomatillo salsa
- 1 teaspoon sea salt
- 1 teaspoon ground black pepper
- 1 tablespoon vegetable oil

Directions:

1. Rinse the meat and pat dry with a paper towels.
2. In a large bowl, rub all sides of the beef with salt and pepper
3. Preheat the Instant Pot by selecting Sauté. Add the oil.
4. Add the onion and garlic, sauté for 2 to 3 minutes, until translucent
5. Put the meat into the pot and add the broth.
6. Press the CANCEL key to stop the SAUTÉ function.
7. Close and lock the lid. Select MANUAL and cook at HIGH pressure for 85 minutes
8. When the timer goes off, use a Quick Release.

9. Carefully unlock the lid, Transfer the meat to a plate and shred it.
10. Add the tomato salsa to the Instant Pot and mix with remaining liquid
11. Select SAUTÉ and cook the sauce until thickened.
12. Add shredded beef and stir well and serve.

Beef Brisket with Cinnamon and Coriander

(Prep + Cook Time: 1 hour 25 minutes | **Serves:** 4-5)

Ingredients:
- 3 pounds' beef brisket, flat cut
- 1 teaspoon ground cinnamon
- 1/2 tablespoon dried oregano
- 1 tablespoon ground cumin
- 1 ½ tablespoon dried rosemary
- 1 ½ cup beef stock
- 1/4 cup soy sauce
- 1 tablespoon dried coriander
- 1/4 teaspoon salt

Directions:
1. In a bowl; combine the soy sauce, salt, coriander, cinnamon, oregano, cumin and rosemary. Mix well.
2. Rub all sides of the brisket with the spice mix.
3. Let marinate for at least 45 minutes or up to 9 hours in the refrigerator
4. Add the beef brisket to the Instant Pot.
5. Add the beef stock. Close and lock the lid.
6. Select the MANUAL setting and set the cooking time for 60 minutes at HIGH pressure
7. Once cooking is complete, use a Natural Release for 10 minutes, then release any remaining pressure manually.
8. Open the lid, Transfer the meat to a plate and slice it and serve

Shredded Beef

(Prep + Cook Time: 1 hour 20 minutes | **Serves:** 4-5)

Ingredients:
- 3 ½ pounds' beef chuck roast
- 2 tablespoon olive oil
- 2 ½ cups beef broth
- 1 teaspoon sea salt

Directions:
1. Preheat the Instant Pot by selecting SAUTÉ. Add the oil.
2. Season the meat with salt
3. Add the beef roast to the pot and sauté for 8-10 minutes on both sides, until browned.
4. Close and lock the lid. Press the CANCEL button to reset the cooking program, then select the MANUAL setting and set the cooking time for 75 minutes at HIGH pressure
5. Once cooking is complete, select CANCEL and let Naturally Release for 10 minutes. Release any remaining steam manually.
6. Uncover the pot, Remove the beef roast from the pot and shred the meat with 2 forks.
7. Return to the Instant Pot and stir with remaining liquid
8. Serve with cooked rice, potato or pasta. Also you can use the meat in sandwiches, burrito bowls, tacos and more.

IP Marinated Steak

(Prep + Cook Time: 50 minutes | **Serves:** 4

Ingredients:
- 2 pounds' flank steak
- 1/2 cup + 1 tablespoon olive oil
- 2 tablespoon onion soup mix, dried
- 1 tablespoon Worcestershire sauce
- 1/2 cup beef broth or water
- 1/4 cup apple cider vinegar
- 1/4 teaspoon salt
- 1/4 teaspoon pepper

Directions:

1. Select the SAUTÉ setting on the Instant Pot and heat 1 tablespoon of oil.
2. Add the flank steak to the pot and season with salt and pepper
3. Sauté on each side until start to brown.
4. Add the broth, vinegar, soup mix, Worcestershire sauce and 1/2 cup of oil, Stir well.
5. Press the CANCEL button to reset the cooking program. Close and lock the lid.
6. Then select the MEAT/STEW setting and set the cooking time for 35 minutes
7. Once cooking is complete, use a natural release for 5 minutes, then release any remaining pressure manually. Open the lid and Serve hot.

Wine Braised Beef Brisket.

(Prep + Cook Time: 1 hour 25 minutes | **Serves:** 4-5)

Ingredients:

- 3 pounds' beef brisket, flat cut
- 3 tablespoon olive oil
- 1 large onion, sliced
- 1 carrot, chopped.
- 1 stalk celery, diced
- 1 tablespoon tomato paste
- 2 cloves garlic, minced
- 1 cup beef broth
- 1 cup red wine
- 2 sprigs fresh thyme
- 1 bay leaf
- 1 teaspoon kosher salt
- 1 teaspoon ground black pepper

Directions:

1. Select the SAUTÉ setting on the Instant Pot and heat the oil (2 tablespoons)
2. Rub all sides of the beef brisket with salt and pepper.
3. Put the beef in the pot and brown the meat for 4 to 5 minutes on each side.
4. Transfer the meat to a plate
5. Pour in 1 tablespoon of oil and add onion, carrot, celery and tomato paste. Sauté for 4 to 5 minutes.
6. Add the garlic and cook for another 30-45 seconds.
7. Pour in the broth and red wine and deglaze the pot by scraping the bottom to remove all of the brown bits.
8. Return the meat to the pot and add thyme and bay leaf.
9. Press the CANCEL key to stop the SAUTÉ function.
10. Close and lock the lid. Select MANUAL and cook at HIGH pressure for 60 minutes
11. Once timer goes off, allow to Naturally Release for 10 minutes. Then release any remaining pressure manually.
12. Uncover the pot, Transfer the brisket to a serving plate and slice the meat.
13. Press the SAUTE key and simmer until the sauce thickens. Serve the brisket with sauce

Tasty Thyme Lamb

(Prep + Cook Time: 1 hour 15 minutes | **Serves:** 4)

Ingredients:

- 2 pounds' lamb shoulder
- 1 cup fresh thyme, chopped.
- 1 tablespoon ground black pepper
- 1 tablespoon turmeric
- 1 teaspoon sugar
- 1/4 cup chicken stock
- 1 tablespoon olive oil
- 1/2 cup water
- 4 tablespoon butter
- 1 teaspoon paprika
- 1 teaspoon oregano
- 1/4 cup rice wine

Directions:

1. In a large bowl, combine the thyme, black pepper, paprika, oregano, rice wine, turmeric, sugar and chicken stock. Mix well.
2. Rub all sides of the lamb shoulder with the spice mix.
3. Select the SAUTÉ setting on the Instant Pot and heat the oil

4. Add the lamb and brown for 5 minutes on both sides.
5. Add the remaining spice mixture, water and butter to the pot, stir.
6. Once the butter is melted, press the CANCEL key to stop the SAUTÉ function.
7. Close and lock the lid. Select MANUAL and cook at HIGH pressure for 45 minutes
8. When the timer goes off, let the pressure Release Naturally for 10 minutes, then release any remaining steam manually
9. Open the lid, if desired, broil in the oven for 8-10 minutes for a browned top.

Lamb with Black Beans.

(Prep + Cook Time: 45 minutes | **Serves:** 4-5)

Ingredients:

- 1-pound ground lamb
- 1 can undrained diced tomatoes
- 1 ½ tablespoon tomato paste
- 1 can (1 cup) chopped and undrained green chillies
- 2 cans drained black beans
- 2 tablespoon vegetable oil
- 1/2 cup chopped onion
- 1/2 teaspoon salt
- 1 ½ tablespoon chili powder
- 1/2 teaspoon cayenne
- 2 teaspoon cumin
- 1 ½ cups chicken broth

Directions:

1. Preheat the Instant Pot by selecting SAUTÉ. Add and heat the oil
2. Add the lamb, onion and salt and sauté for 5 minutes, stirring occasionally.
3. Add the chili powder, cayenne, cumin, tomatoes, tomato paste, green chilies, black beans and broth, Stir well
4. Press the CANCEL button to stop the SAUTE function, then select the MANUAL setting and set the cooking time for 20 minutes at HIGH pressure.
5. Once cooking is complete, select CANCEL and use a Natural Release for 10 minutes
6. Open the lid, serve with sour cream, if desired.

Beef Stroganoff

(Prep + Cook Time: 40 minutes | **Serves:** 4-5)

Ingredients:

- 2 pounds' chuck roast, thin slices (½ inch)
- 1 onion, small-sized
- 1 ¼ cups beef broth
- 1/2 cup sour cream
- 16-ounce cooked egg noodles, optional
- 1 cup mushrooms, sliced
- 2 cloves garlic, minced
- 4 tablespoon butter
- 1 teaspoon kosher salt
- 1 teaspoon ground black pepper

Directions:

1. Preheat the Instant Pot by selecting SAUTÉ. Melt the butter
2. Add the onion and sauté for about 3 minutes.
3. Season the meat strips with salt and pepper. Add to the pot.
4. Cook, stirring occasionally, for 2 minutes until starting to brown
5. Add the mushrooms and cook for 2 more minutes.
6. Add the garlic and sauté for 1 minute.
7. Press the CANCEL button to stop SAUTE function.
8. Pour the broth and stir well. Close and lock the lid.
9. Select MANUAL and cook at HIGH pressure for 15 minutes
10. When the timer goes off, use a Quick Release.
11. Carefully unlock the lid, Add the sour cream and mix well. Close the lid and let sit for 5 minutes.
12. Serve with cooked egg noodles

Lamb Ragout Recipe

(Prep + Cook Time: 1 hour 20 minutes | **Serves:** 4-5)

Ingredients:
- 1 ½ pounds' lamb, bone-in
- A handful parsley, finely chopped.
- 6 cloves garlic, minced
- 1 small yellow onion, chopped.
- 2 carrots, sliced
- 1 teaspoon oregano, dried
- 1 teaspoon vegetable oil
- 4 tomatoes, chopped.
- 2 tablespoon tomato paste
- 1/2-pound mushrooms, sliced
- Water as needed
- Salt and ground black pepper to taste

Directions:
1. Select the SAUTÉ setting on the Instant Pot and heat the oil
2. Add the lamb and sear for 4 minutes on each side, until nicely browned.
3. Add the tomatoes, tomato paste, mushrooms, garlic, onion, carrots, oregano and water to cover everything.
4. Season with salt and pepper, stir well
5. Close and lock the lid. Select the MANUAL setting and set the cooking time for 60 minutes at HIGH pressure.
6. When the timer beeps, use a Quick Release.
7. Carefully unlock the lid, Transfer the lamb to a plate, then discard bones and shred the meat
8. Return the shredded lamb to the pot, add the parsley and stir. Serve warm.

Beef Ragu

(Prep + Cook Time: 60 minutes | **Serves:** 4)

Ingredients:
- 1 ½ pounds' beef steak, cut into strips
- 1 carrot, chopped.
- 1 stalk of celery, minced
- 1 cup beef broth
- 1 teaspoon ground paprika
- 1 star anise
- 1 bay leaf
- 1/2 long red chili, chopped.
- 2 tablespoon olive oil
- 1 onion, chopped.
- 3 cloves garlic, minced
- 1 can crushed tomatoes
- 1 teaspoon kosher salt
- 1/2 teaspoon ground black pepper

Directions:
1. Select the SAUTÉ setting on the Instant Pot and heat the oil
2. Add the onion and garlic and sauté until fragrant.
3. Add the beef and cook for 3 minutes until the meat has turned light brown.
4. Add the rest of the ingredients
5. Press the CANCEL button to reset the cooking program, then select the MEAT/STEW setting and leave it on the default.
6. Once cooking is complete, select CANCEL and let Naturally Release for 10 minutes. Release any remaining steam manually
7. Uncover the pot, Serve.

BBQ Beef Brisket

(Prep + Cook Time: 1 hour 25 minutes | **Serves:** 4)

Ingredients:
- 2 pounds' beef brisket, flat cut
- 2/3 cup BBQ sauce, plus additional for serving
- 2 tablespoon liquid smoke
- 1 tablespoon Worcestershire sauce
- 1/2 cup water
- 1/4 teaspoon garlic salt
- 1/4 teaspoon celery salt
- 1 teaspoon seasoned meat tenderizer

Directions:

1. In a large bowl, combine the garlic salt, celery salt and seasoned meat tenderizer. Mix well
2. In the same bowl, rub all sides of the beef brisket with the spice mix. Pour the Worcestershire sauce and liquid smoke over the brisket
3. Cover the bowl tightly with aluminum foil and let marinate for at least 45 minutes or up to 9 hours in the refrigerator.
4. Pour the water and BBQ sauce into the Instant Pot.
5. Add the brisket and remaining liquid from the bowl to the pot
6. Close and lock the lid. Select MANUAL and cook at HIGH pressure for 50 minutes.
7. When the timer beeps, let the pressure Release Naturally for 15 minutes. Release any remaining steam manually.
8. Uncover the pot, Transfer the brisket to a serving plate. Slice the meat and serve with additional BBQ sauce

Beef Casserole.

(Prep + Cook Time: 50 minutes **| Serves:** 2 - 3)

Ingredients:

- 1-pound stewing steak, cut into cubes
- 2 tablespoon sun-dried tomato paste
- 1-pound tomatoes, quarter cut
- 1 ½ cup red wine
- 6 tablespoon fresh oregano, chopped.
- 2 tablespoon olive oil
- 2-ounce black olives
- 2-ounce green olives
- 2 onions, quarter cut
- 2 red bell peppers, quarter cut
- 1 yellow bell pepper, cut into thick strips
- 5-ounce water

Directions:

1. Preheat the Instant Pot by selecting SAUTÉ. Add the oil.
2. Add the beef and cook, stirring occasionally, for 5 minutes, until browned
3. Put the onion, red and yellow bell peppers into the pot. Cook for another 3 to 4 minutes.
4. Add the tomato paste, tomatoes, red wine, water, black and green olives, Stir well.
5. Press the CANCEL key to stop the SAUTÉ function.
6. Close and lock the lid. Select MANUAL and cook at HIGH pressure for 20 minutes
7. When the timer goes off, use a Quick Release.
8. Carefully unlock the lid, Top with fresh oregano and serve.

Aromatic Lamb Curry

(Prep + Cook Time: 1 hour 30 minutes **| Serves:** 4-5)

Ingredients:

- 1 ½ pounds' lamb stew meat, cubed
- 14-ounce can tomatoes, diced
- 3 medium carrots, sliced
- 1 medium onion, diced
- 1 medium zucchini, diced
- Cilantro, chopped.
- 1/2 cup coconut milk
- 4 cloves garlic, minced
- Juice of 1/2 lime
- 1-inch piece fresh ginger, grated
- 1/4 teaspoon sea salt
- 1/4 teaspoon ground black pepper
- 1 ½ tablespoon yellow curry powder
- 1/2 teaspoon turmeric
- 1 tablespoon butter

Directions:

1. In the Instant Pot, combine the milk, garlic, lime juice, ginger, salt and pepper. Mix well
2. Add the lamb cubes to the pot and stir well until fully coated.
3. Let marinate for at least 45 minutes.
4. Add the curry powder, turmeric, butter, tomatoes, carrots and onion.
5. Close and lock the lid. Select MANUAL and cook at HIGH pressure for 22 minutes

6. When the timer beeps, let the pressure Release Naturally for 10 minutes, then release any remaining steam manually.
7. Open the lid, Add the zucchini. Select SAUTE and simmer the dish for 6 to 8 minutes until the zucchini is tender. Top with cilantro and serve

Beef and Noodles

(Prep + Cook Time: 1 hour 10 minutes | **Serves:** 4-5)

Ingredients:
- 1 chopped onion
- 2 minced cloves garlic
- 2 cups water
- 3 pounds' boneless beef chuck roast, cut into 2-inch cubes
- 8-ounce egg noodles
- 2 tablespoon olive oil
- 1 teaspoon salt
- 1/2 teaspoon ground black pepper

Directions:
1. Select the SAUTÉ setting on the Instant Pot and heat the oil
2. Add the beef to the pot and sauté until the meat start to brown.
3. Season with salt and pepper and add the onion and garlic
4. Press the CANCEL key to stop the SAUTÉ function.
5. Pour over 1 cup of water and lock the lid.
6. Select the MANUAL setting and set the cooking time for 38 minutes at HIGH pressure.
7. Once cooking is complete, let the pressure Release Naturally for 10 minutes. Release any remaining steam manually. Uncover the pot
8. Remove the meat from the pot
9. Select SAUTÉ, then add 1 cup of water and bring liquid to a boil.
10. Add the noodles and cook for 9-10 minutes or until tender. Return the meat to the pot, stir and serve

Mongolian Beef.

(Prep + Cook Time: 50 minutes | **Serves:** 4-5)

Ingredients:
- 2 pounds' steak, sliced (1 inch thick)
- 3 medium-sized white onions, finely chopped.
- 3 tablespoon dark soy sauce
- 3 tablespoon brown sugar
- 1 ¼ cups + 1/2 cup water
- 2 tablespoon corn flour
- 1/2 cup green onions, chopped.
- 1 tablespoon olive oil
- 1/2 teaspoon kosher salt
- 1/4 teaspoon ground black pepper
- 4 cloves garlic, minced
- 1 teaspoon minced ginger

Directions:
1. Season the meat with salt and pepper
2. Select the SAUTÉ setting on the Instant Pot and heat the oil.
3. lower the beef slices into the pot and sear for 5-6 minutes on each side, until browned.
4. Remove the meat from the pot
5. Add the garlic, ginger and chopped onions, stir. Sauté for 2 to 3 minutes.
6. Add the soy sauce, brown sugar and 1 ¼ cups of water to the pot, mix just until combined.
7. Return the browned beef to the pot, stir.
8. Press the CANCEL button to reset the cooking program, then select the MANUAL setting and set the cooking time for 15 minutes at HIGH pressure.
9. Once cooking is complete, use a Natural Release for 10 minutes, then release any remaining pressure manually
10. Open the lid, in a bowl; whisk 1/2 cup of water and corn flour, until combined.
11. Set the instant pot on SAUTÉ mode.
12. Pour the mixture into the pot, stirring continuously. Simmer until the sauce thickens
13. Transfer the dish to a serving bowl and sprinkle with green onions.

Beef Stew

(Prep + Cook Time: 1 hour 10 minutes | **Serves:** 4-5)

Ingredients:

- 3 pounds' beef shoulder, cut into chunks
- 5 cloves garlic, minced
- 1/2 cup feta cheese, crumbled
- 1 cup beef broth
- 1 teaspoon red wine vinegar
- 1/2 cup sun-dried tomatoes
- 1 onion, sliced
- 1 tablespoon oregano
- 1/2 teaspoon marjoram
- 1 tablespoon dried basil
- 1 teaspoon dill
- 1 teaspoon sea salt
- 1/2 teaspoon ground black pepper

Directions:

1. Dump all of the ingredients, except the feta cheese, into the Instant Pot and give it a good stir to mix everything evenly
2. Close and lock the lid. Select MANUAL and cook at HIGH pressure for 40 minutes.
3. When the timer beeps, let the pressure Release Naturally for 10 minutes, then release any remaining steam manually
4. Uncover the pot, Top with feta cheese and serve.

Grandma's Garlic Lamb

(Prep + Cook Time: 45 minutes | **Serves:** 4-5)

Ingredients:

- 2 pounds' lamb shanks
- 6 cloves garlic, peeled
- 1 tablespoon tomato paste
- 1/2 teaspoon thyme
- 1 tablespoon olive oil
- 1 tablespoon balsamic vinegar
- 1 tablespoon butter
- 1 cup chicken broth

Directions:

1. Select the SAUTÉ setting on the Instant Pot and heat the oil
2. Add the garlic and sauté for 2 to 3 minutes, or until starting to brown.
3. Pour in the broth and tomato paste, Stir well.
4. Add the thyme and stir
5. Add the lamb shanks and secure the lid
6. Press the CANCEL key to stop the SAUTÉ function.
7. Select MANUAL and cook at HIGH pressure for 25 minutes.
8. Once cooking is complete, select CANCEL and use a Natural Release for 5 minutes
9. Release any remaining steam manually.
10. Uncover the pot, Transfer the lamb to a serving bowl.
11. Add the vinegar and butter to the pot. Stir until butter melts, about 1 - 2 minutes, Serve the lamb with sauce

Shredded Pepper Steak.

(Prep + Cook Time: 1 hour 30 minutes | **Serves:** 6-7)

Ingredients:

- 3-4 pounds' beef (cheap steak or roast cuts will all work)
- 1 jar (16 oz) mild pepper rings (banana peppers or pepperoncini)
- 1 tablespoon garlic powder
- Red chili flakes to taste
- 1/2 cup salted beef broth

Directions:

1. Add beef to the Instant Pot and season with garlic powder and red chili
2. Pour the pepper rings and broth into the pot, stir.

3. Close and lock the lid. Select the MANUAL setting and set the cooking time for 70 minutes at HIGH pressure.
4. Once cooking is complete, use a Natural Release for 10 minutes, then release any remaining pressure manually.
5. Open the lid, Shred the meat in the pot (or transfer to a plate) and stir and serve

Notes: The jarred peppers can typically be found in the "Italian" foods section of your grocery store.

Beef Stew with Vegetables.

(Prep + Cook Time: 55 minutes | **Serves:** 4-5)

Ingredients:

- 2 pounds' beef stew meat (1 ½ inch chunks)
- 1 medium onion, quartered
- 4 cloves garlic, minced
- 2 tablespoon balsamic vinegar or red wine
- 6 tablespoon tomato paste
- 4 medium potatoes, peeled and chopped. (1 inch chunks)
- 1 large sweet potato, peeled and chopped. (1 inch chunks)
- 2 ribs celery, chopped.
- 3 medium carrots, cut into slices

- 2 teaspoon Worcestershire sauce
- 5 cups beef broth
- 1 bay leaf
- 2 tablespoon fresh parsley, chopped. (for garnish)
- 1/2 teaspoon onion powder
- 1/3 cup flour
- 3 teaspoon Italian seasoning, divided
- 2 tablespoon olive oil
- 1 teaspoon sea salt
- 1/2 teaspoon ground black pepper

Directions:

1. In a large bowl, combine the salt, pepper, onion powder, flour and 1 teaspoon Italian seasoning. Mix well.
2. Add the meat to the bowl, stir and rub all chunks with the spice mix.
3. Set your instant pot on SAUTÉ mode, add the oil and heat it up.
4. Add the meet and brown on all sides
5. Remove the beef from the pot and place on a plate.
6. Add the onion and garlic to the pot and sauté for 1 - 2 minutes.
7. Pour in the balsamic vinegar and tomato paste and deglaze the pot by scraping the bottom to remove all of the brown bits
8. Press the CANCEL key to stop the SAUTÉ function.
9. Return the meat to the pot. Add the potatoes, sweet potato, celery, carrots, 2 teaspoons Italian seasoning, Worcestershire sauce, beef broth and bay leaf, Stir well.
10. Select the MANUAL setting and set the cooking time for 25 minutes at HIGH pressure.
11. Once timer goes off, allow to Naturally Release for 10 minutes, then release any remaining pressure manually
12. Open the lid, Top with fresh parsley and serve.

Rosemary Lamb

(Prep + Cook Time: 50 minutes | **Serves:** 6-7)

Ingredients:
- 4 pounds' lamb, boneless and cut into 1 - 2 inch cubes
- 3 tablespoon flour
- 1 ½ cups veggie stock
- 2 tablespoon olive oil
- 4 cloves garlic, minced
- 1 cup carrots, sliced
- 4 rosemary sprigs
- Salt and ground black pepper to taste

Directions:
1. Season the lamb with salt and pepper to taste.
2. Preheat the Instant Pot by selecting SAUTÉ. Add and heat the oil
3. Add the garlic and sauté for 1 minute.
4. Add the lamb and cook until browned, stirring occasionally. You may have to do it in two batches.
5. Add the flour and stir. Pour over the stock.
6. Add the carrots and rosemary. Close and lock the lid.
7. Press the CANCEL key to stop the SAUTÉ function.
8. Select MANUAL and cook at HIGH pressure for 25 minutes
9. Once cooking is complete, use a Natural Release for 10 minutes, then release any remaining pressure manually.
10. Open the lid, Remove the rosemary stems. Serve the lamb with sauce

Special Rabbit Stew

(Prep + Cook Time: 55 minutes | **Serves:** 4-5)

Ingredients:
- 1 rabbit, cut into 9 chunks
- 1 carrot, peeled and minced
- 2 celery stalks, minced
- 2 tomatoes, diced
- 2 tablespoon tomato paste
- 1 bunch rosemary sprigs
- 1/2 cup black olives, pitted
- 1 cup dry red wine
- 1 medium onion, peeled and minced
- 2 cups chicken broth
- 7 tablespoon olive oil
- Salt and ground black pepper to taste

Directions:
1. Season the rabbit with salt and pepper
2. Preheat the Instant Pot by selecting SAUTÉ. Add 2 tablespoon of oil and heat it.
3. Add the meat and brown on all sides for 5 minutes.
4. Add the wine and cook for another 2 minutes.
5. Add 5 tablespoons of oil, onion, carrot and celery, Stir well
6. Add the tomatoes, tomato paste and rosemary. Cook for 5 minutes more.
7. Add the black olives and broth and stir. Close and lock the lid.
8. Press the CANCEL button to stop the SAUTE function, then select the MANUAL setting and set the cooking time for 15 minutes at HIGH pressure
9. Once timer goes off, let the pressure Release Naturally for 10 minutes, then release any remaining pressure manually.
10. Uncover the pot, Taste and season with salt and pepper if necessary. Remove the rosemary sprigs, Serve

Soups Recipes

Fish Fillets Soup Recipe

(Prep + Cook Time: 20 minutes | **Serves:** 4-5)

Ingredients:
- 1-pound white fish fillets, boneless, skinless and cubed
- 1 carrot, chopped.
- 4 cups chicken stock
- 2 cups heavy cream
- 1 cup bacon, chopped.

Directions:
1. In the Instant Pot, combine the fish, bacon, carrot and stock, Stir well
2. Close and lock the lid. Select MANUAL and cook at HIGH pressure for 5 minutes.
3. When the timer goes off, use a Quick Release. Carefully unlock the lid
4. Add the heavy cream and stir. Select SAUTÉ and simmer the soup for 3 minutes and Serve

Barley Chicken Soup Recipe

(Prep + Cook Time: 35 minutes | **Serves:** 6)

Ingredients:
- 2 cups chicken breasts, sliced
- 1/2 cup pearl barley, rinsed and drained
- 1 cup red potatoes, peeled and diced
- 1 cup onion, diced
- 3/4 cup celery
- 3 cups chicken stock
- 2 cups water
- 1 tablespoon oregano
- 2 cups carrots, diced
- 1 bay leaf
- Salt and ground black pepper to taste

Directions:
1. Put all of the ingredients into the Instant Pot. Mix well.
2. Close and lock the lid. Select MANUAL and cook at HIGH pressure for 20 minutes
3. Once cooking is complete, select CANCEL and let Naturally Release for 5 minutes. Release any remaining steam manually.
4. Uncover the pot, and Serve

Beef and Cabbage Soup Recipe

(Prep + Cook Time: 35 minutes | **Serves:** 4-5)

Ingredients:
- 1-pound ground beef
- 14-ounce can diced tomatoes, undrained
- 4 cups water
- 2 tablespoon coconut oil
- 1 onion, diced
- 1 clove garlic, minced
- Salt and ground black pepper to taste
- 1 head cabbage, chopped.

Directions:
1. Preheat the Instant Pot by selecting SAUTÉ. Add and heat the oil
2. Add the onion and garlic and sauté for 2 minutes.
3. Add the beef and cook, stirring, for 2 to 3 minutes until lightly brown.
4. Pour in the water and tomatoes. Season with salt and pepper, stir well
5. Press the CANCEL key to stop the SAUTÉ function.
6. Close and lock the lid. Select MANUAL and cook at HIGH pressure for 12 minutes.
7. When the timer goes off, use a Quick Release.
8. Carefully unlock the lid, Add the cabbage, select SAUTÉ and simmer for 5 minutes then Serve

Tofu and Miso Soup Recipe

(Prep + Cook Time: 20 minutes | **Serves:** 4)

Ingredients:

- 1 cup silken tofu, cubed
- 1 carrot, chopped.
- 2 celery stalks, chopped.
- 1 tablespoon tamari sauce
- 2 tablespoon miso paste
- 1/2 onion, diced
- 4 cups water
- Salt to taste

Directions:

1. Combine all of the ingredients, except for the miso and salt, in the Instant Pot and stir to mix
2. Close and lock the lid. Select the POULTRY setting and set the cooking time for 7 minutes
3. When the timer goes off, use a Quick Release.
4. Carefully unlock the lid, Whisk together the miso paste with some of the soup.
5. Pour the mixture in the soup and stir. Season with salt and serve

Multi Bean Soup Recipe

(Prep + Cook Time: 55 minutes | **Serves:** 8-10

Ingredients:

- 1 bag of 15-bean soup blend (Hurst Beans brand)
- 8 cups vegetable stock
- 1 can tomatoes, crushed
- 1 onion, chopped.
- 3 cloves garlic, minced
- 1 red bell pepper, chopped.
- 2 carrots, peeled and chopped.
- 2 stalks celery, chopped.
- 3 sprigs fresh thyme
- 1 tablespoon olive oil
- 1 bay leaf
- Salt and ground black pepper to taste

Directions:

1. Set your instant pot on SAUTÉ mode, add the oil and heat it up.
2. Add the onion and garlic and sauté for 1 to 2 minutes until fragrant
3. Add the bell pepper, carrot and celery and sauté for another 6 minutes.
4. Add the beans, tomatoes, thyme, bay leaf and stock. Stir to combine.
5. Season with salt and pepper. Close and lock the lid.
6. Press the CANCEL button to reset the cooking program, then press the MANUAL button and set the cooking time for 30 minutes at HIGH pressure
7. Once cooking is complete, select CANCEL and let Naturally Release for 10 minutes. Release any remaining steam manually.
8. Uncover the pot, Stir and Serve

Butternut Squash Curry Soup Recipe

(Prep + Cook Time: 50 minutes | **Serves:** 4)

Ingredients:

- 1 butternut squash, peeled and cut into 1-inch cubes
- 1 large onion, chopped.
- 1 tablespoon curry powder
- 1 teaspoon olive oil
- 2 cloves garlic, minced
- 3 cups water
- 1/2 cup coconut milk
- 1 ½ teaspoon salt

Directions:

1. Preheat the Instant Pot by selecting SAUTÉ. Add and heat the oil.
2. Add the onion and sauté for about 5 minutes, until softened
3. Add the garlic and cook for another 1 minute.
4. Press the CANCEL key to stop the SAUTÉ function.
5. Pour in the water and add the squash. Sprinkle with salt and curry powder and stir well.

6. Select the SOUP setting and set the cooking time for 30 minutes
7. When the timer beeps, use a quick release.
8. Carefully unlock the lid, with an immersion blender, blend the soup until smooth.
9. Pour in the coconut milk and mix well. Serve with dried cranberries and pumpkin seeds

Garden Harvest Soup Recipe

(Prep + Cook Time: 30 minutes | Serves: 6-7)

Ingredients:
- 10 cup packaged vegetables of your choice
- 1 teaspoon rosemary
- 6 cups bone broth
- 1 can crushed tomatoes
- 1 teaspoon parsley
- 1 teaspoon basil
- 1 teaspoon thyme
- Salt and ground black pepper to taste

Directions:
1. Combine all of the ingredients in the Instant Pot and stir to mix.
2. Close and lock the lid. Select MANUAL and cook at HIGH pressure for 10 minutes
3. Once cooking is complete, select CANCEL and let Naturally Release for 10 minutes. Release any remaining steam manually.
4. Uncover the pot, taste for seasoning and add more salt if needed and serve

Pomodoro Soup Recipe

(Prep + Cook Time: 30 minutes | Serves: 8

Ingredients:
- 3 pounds' tomatoes, peeled and quartered
- 3 ½ cups vegetable broth
- 1 onion, diced
- 1 cup coconut cream
- 3 tablespoon vegan butter

Directions:
1. Preheat the Instant Pot by selecting SAUTÉ. Once hot, add the butter and melt it
2. Add the onion and sauté for 5 minutes.
3. Add the tomatoes and sauté for another 2 to 3 minutes.
4. Pour in the broth, stir. Close and lock the lid.
5. Press the CANCEL button to reset the cooking program, then press the SOUP button and set the cooking time for 6 minutes
6. When the timer beeps, use a Quick Release.
7. Carefully unlock the lid, Add the coconut cream and stir.
8. Select SAUTÉ again and cook for 1 - 2 minutes.
9. With an immersion blender, blend the soup to your desired texture and serve

Chicken and Bean Soup

(Prep + Cook Time: 65 minutes | Serves: 6

Ingredients:
- 1-pound chicken fillet, cut into 1 ½ inch strips
- 1 jalapeno pepper, chopped.
- 1 red bell pepper, sliced
- 1 white onion, sliced
- 1 cup cannellini beans
- 1 cup fresh dill, chopped.
- 4 tablespoon salsa
- 7 cups water
- 1/3 cup cream
- 1 teaspoon soy sauce
- 2 teaspoon kosher salt
- 1 teaspoon ground black pepper

Directions:

1. Put the cannellini beans and chicken in the Instant Pot.
2. Pour in the water and stir. Close and lock the lid
3. Select MANUAL and cook at HIGH pressure for 30 minutes.
4. When the timer beeps, use a Quick Release. Carefully unlock the lid,
5. Add the jalapeno pepper, bell pepper, onion and dill. Stir to combine.
6. Close and lock the lid, select the SOUP setting and set the cooking time for 15 minutes
7. When the timer goes off, use a Quick Release.
8. Carefully unlock the lid, Add the salsa, cream, soy sauce, salt and black pepper. Stir well, close the lid and let the soup sit for 10 minutes and Serve

Veggie Cheese Soup Recipe

(Prep + Cook Time: 30 minutes | **Serves:** 4-5)

Ingredients:

- 1 package vegetables, frozen
- 1 jar cheese sauce
- Mozzarella cheese, shredded
- 1 can cream mushroom soup
- Salt and ground black pepper to taste

Directions:

1. Add the vegetables to the Instant Pot.
2. Pour in the mushroom soup and cheese sauce, stir well.
3. Sprinkle with salt and pepper, stir
4. Top with Mozzarella cheese. Close and lock the lid.
5. Select MANUAL and cook at HIGH pressure for 7 minutes
6. Once timer goes off, allow to Naturally Release for 10 minutes, then release any remaining pressure manually.
7. Uncover the pot and Serve

Green Split Pea Soup Recipe

(Prep + Cook Time: 50 minutes | **Serves:** 6

Ingredients:

- 1-pound green split peas
- 6 cups beef broth
- 1 tablespoon olive oil
- 1 clove garlic, minced
- 1 cup onion, chopped.
- 1 cup chopped celery
- 1 cup chopped carrots
- 1 cup leftover ham, chopped.
- Salt and ground black pepper to taste

Directions:

1. Preheat the Instant Pot by selecting SAUTÉ. Add and heat the oil
2. Add the garlic, onion, celery and carrot. Stir and sauté for 5-6 minutes
3. Add the leftover ham, peas and broth. Stir to combine.
4. Season with salt and pepper. Close and lock the lid.
5. Press the CANCEL button to stop the SAUTE function, then select the BEAN/CHILI and leave it on the default.
6. When the timer goes off, let the pressure Release Naturally for 10 minutes, then release any remaining steam manually.
7. Open the lid, Taste for seasoning and add more salt if needed and serve

Buffalo Chicken Soup Recipe

(Prep + Cook Time: 35 minutes | **Serves:** 4)

Ingredients:

- 2 chicken breasts, boneless, skinless, frozen or fresh
- 1/3 cup hot sauce
- 1 clove garlic, chopped.
- 1/4 cup onion, diced
- 1/2 cup celery, diced
- 2 cups cheddar cheese, shredded
- 1 cup heavy cream
- 2 tablespoon butter
- 1 tablespoon ranch dressing mix
- 3 cups chicken broth

Directions:

1. In the Instant Pot, combine the chicken breasts, garlic, onion, celery, butter, ranch dressing mix, broth and hot sauce.
2. Close and lock the lid. Select MANUAL and cook at HIGH pressure for 10 minutes
3. Once cooking is complete, let the pressure Release Naturally for 10 minutes. Release any remaining steam manually.
4. Uncover the pot, Transfer the chicken to a plate and shred the meat. Return to the pot.
5. Add the cheese and heavy cream, Stir well. Let sit for 5 minutes and serve

Low Carb Soup Recipe

(Prep + Cook Time: 35 minutes | **Serves:** 4-5)

Ingredients:

- 6 slices cooked turkey bacon, diced
- 1 large yellow onion, diced
- 1 tablespoon onion powder
- 1 head cauliflower, coarsely chopped.
- 1 green bell pepper, chopped.
- 2 cups shredded Cheddar cheese
- 1 tablespoon olive oil
- 2 cloves garlic, minced
- 32-ounce chicken stock
- 1 tablespoon Dijon mustard
- 4 dashes hot pepper sauce
- 1 cup half and half
- Salt and ground black pepper

Directions:

1. Select the SAUTÉ setting on the Instant Pot and heat the oil
2. Add the garlic and onion and sauté for 3 to 4 minutes.
3. Add the onion powder, cauliflower, bell pepper and stock. Season with salt and pepper, Stir well
4. Close and lock the lid. Press the CANCEL button to stop the SAUTE function, then select the SOUP setting and set the cooking time for 15 minutes.
5. When the timer beeps, use a Quick Release. Wait for 5 minutes
6. Carefully unlock the lid, Add the Dijon mustard, hot sauce, turkey bacon, cheddar cheese and half and half. Stir to combine
7. Select SAUTÉ and simmer the soup for 4 to 5 minutes and Serve

Toscana Soup Recipe

(Prep + Cook Time: 40 minutes | **Serves:** 4-5)

Ingredients:

- 1-pound Italian sausages, chopped.
- 3 large russet potatoes, unpeeled and sliced thickly
- 2 tablespoon olive oil
- 1 onion, diced
- 4 cloves garlic, minced
- 1/4 cup water
- 2 cups kale, chopped.
- 3/4 cup heavy cream
- 6 cups chicken broth
- Salt and ground black pepper to taste

Directions:

1. Set your instant pot on SAUTÉ mode, add the oil and heat it up.
2. Add the onion, garlic and Italian sausages. Stir and sauté for 4 to 5 minutes, until the sausages have turned light brown
3. Add the potatoes, water and chicken broth and stir.
4. Sprinkle with salt and pepper.
5. Press the CANCEL key to stop the SAUTÉ function.
6. Close and lock the lid. Select MANUAL and cook at HIGH pressure for 20 minutes
7. When the timer goes off, use a Quick Release.
8. Carefully unlock the lid, set your instant pot on SAUTÉ mode, add the kale and heavy cream.
9. Simmer for 3 to 4 minutes. Press the CANCEL key and let it sit for 5 minutes then Serve

Chicken Soup Recipe

(Prep + Cook Time: 45 minutes | **Serves:** 4)

Ingredients:

- 2 frozen, boneless chicken breasts
- 1/2 big onion, diced
- 2 cups chicken stock
- 2 cups water
- 4 medium-sized potatoes, cut into chunks
- 3 carrots, peeled and cut into chunks
- Salt and ground black pepper to taste

Directions:

1. In the Instant Pot, combine the chicken breasts, potatoes, carrots, onion, stock, water, salt and pepper to taste
2. Close and lock the lid. Select MANUAL and cook at HIGH pressure for 25 minutes.
3. Once timer goes off, allow to Naturally Release for 10 minutes and then release any remaining pressure manually.
4. Uncover the pot, and Serve

Lentil Soup Recipe

(Prep + Cook Time: 35 minutes | **Serves:** 6

Ingredients:

- 1-pound red bliss or yukon gold potatoes
- 1 bunch rainbow chard or spinach, chopped.
- 2 celery stalks, diced (optional)
- 1 medium onion, chopped.
- 3 cloves garlic, minced
- 2 carrots, sliced into ¼ inch pieces
- 1 cup red lentils, rinsed
- 1 cup green or brown lentils, rinsed
- 2 tablespoon olive oil
- 1 ½ teaspoon smoked paprika
- 1 ½ teaspoon cumin
- 8 cups water
- Salt and ground black pepper to taste

Directions:

1. Select the SAUTÉ setting on the Instant Pot and heat the oil.
2. Add the onion, garlic, carrot, potatoes, celery, paprika and cumin. Sauté for 5 minutes.
3. Add the lentils and water, stir well. Close and lock the lid
4. Press the CANCEL button to stop the SAUTE function, then select the MANUAL setting and set the cooking time for 3 minutes at HIGH pressure.
5. When the timer beeps, use a Natural Release for 10 minutes
6. Uncover the pot, Add the chard and sprinkle with salt and pepper, Stir well
7. Let the soup sit for 5 minutes and serve.

Turkish Soup Recipe

(Prep + Cook Time: 40 minutes | **Serves:** 2 - 3)

Ingredients:

- 1 onion, chopped.
- 1 potato, chopped.
- 1 carrot, chopped.
- 1/2 cup celery
- 1/2 teaspoon coriander
- 1/2 teaspoon paprika
- 3 teaspoon olive oil
- 3 cloves garlic, minced
- 1 cup red lentils
- 1 tablespoon rice
- 3 cups water
- Salt to taste

Directions:

1. Select the SAUTÉ setting on the Instant Pot and heat the oil
2. Add the garlic and onion and sauté for 2 to 3 minutes, until fragrant
3. Add the lentils and rice and stir to combine.
4. Add the potato, carrot, celery, coriander, paprika and water, stir well.
5. Close and lock the lid. Press the CANCEL button to reset the cooking program, then press the MANUAL button and set the cooking time for 10 minutes at HIGH pressure
6. When the timer beeps, use a Natural Release for 5 minutes
7. Carefully uncover the pot, Season with salt and stir. Let the mixture sit for 10 minutes and then puree in a blender and serve

Cabbage Turkey Soup Recipe

(Prep + Cook Time: 35 minutes | **Serves:** 4-5)

Ingredients:

- 1-pound ground turkey
- 4 cups chicken broth
- 2 cups water
- 1 head cabbage, chopped.
- 1 tablespoon olive oil
- 2 cloves garlic, minced
- 1 pack frozen onion, cubed
- 1 pack cauliflower florets
- 1 jar marinara sauce
- Salt and ground black pepper to taste

Directions:

1. Select the SAUTÉ setting on the Instant Pot and heat the oil
2. Add the ground turkey and garlic and sauté, stirring occasionally, for 5-6 minutes, until all the meat is browned
3. Transfer the browned turkey to a bowl.
4. Press the CANCEL key to stop the SAUTÉ function.
5. Add the onion, cauliflower, marinara sauce, broth and water to the pot, Stir well.
6. Place the cabbage on top, Close and lock the lid. Select MANUAL and cook at HIGH pressure for 6 minutes.
7. When the timer beeps, use a Natural Release for 10 minutes.
8. Uncover the pot, Return the meat to the pot and stir well, Season with salt and pepper and serve

Pork Shank Soup Recipe

(Prep + Cook Time: 1 hour 40 minutes | **Serves:** 4-5)

Ingredients:

- 1 ½ pounds' pork shank, cleaned and trimmed of excess fat
- 2 carrots, cut into chunks
- 1 small piece of chenpi (dried mandarin peel)
- 2 jujubes, dried (optional)
- 4 ½ cups water
- 1 thin slice of ginger
- 1 large green radish, cut into chunks
- Sea salt to taste

Directions:
1. Soak the chenpi in cold water for 20 minutes.
2. Combine all of the ingredients in the Instant Pot and stir to mix
3. Close and lock the lid. Select MANUAL and cook at HIGH pressure for 35 minutes.
4. Once cooking is complete, let the pressure Release Naturally for 20 minutes. Release any remaining steam manually. Uncover the pot
5. Select SAUTÉ, bring the soup to a boil and cook for another 20 minutes.
6. Taste for seasoning and add more salt if needed and serve

Corn Chowder Recipe

(**Prep + Cook Time:** 30 minutes | **Serves:** 4)

Ingredients:
- 3 potatoes, cubed
- 4 cups chicken broth
- 1 cup milk plus 1 tablespoon flour
- 3 tablespoon butter
- 1 onion, chopped.
- 4 cups corn kernels
- 1 green bell pepper, diced
- 1 tablespoon olive oil
- 1 red bell pepper, diced
- Salt and ground black pepper to taste

Directions:
1. Preheat the Instant Pot by selecting SAUTÉ. Add and heat the oil.
2. Add the onion and sauté for 2 to 3 minutes until fragrant.
3. Add the potatoes, corn kernels and bell peppers. Sprinkle with salt and pepper, Stir well
4. Add the chicken broth and stir. Close and lock the lid.
5. Press the CANCEL button to reset the cooking program, then press the MANUAL button and set the cooking time for 6 minutes at HIGH pressure.
6. When the timer beeps, use a Quick Release
7. Carefully unlock the lid, Whisk together the milk and flour.
8. Select Sauté and pour the mixture in the pot.
9. Add the butter simmer for 3 minutes, stirring occasionally, until the chowder has thickened

Cheddar, Potato and Broccoli Soup

(**Prep + Cook Time:** 40 minutes | **Serves:** 4-5)

Ingredients:
- 2 pounds' Yukon gold potatoes, peeled and cut into small chunks
- 4 cups vegetable broth
- 1 cup half and half
- 1 cup cheddar cheese, shredded
- Chives or green onion, chopped, for garnish
- 1 broccoli head, medium-sized, broken into large florets
- 2 tablespoon butter
- 2 cloves garlic, crushed
- Salt and ground black pepper to taste

Directions:
1. To preheat the Instant Pot, select SAUTÉ. Once hot, add the butter and melt it
2. Add the garlic and sauté for 2 to 3 minutes, until browned.
3. Add the potato, broccoli and broth. Season with salt and pepper, Stir well
4. Press the CANCEL key to stop the SAUTÉ function.
5. Close and lock the lid. Select MANUAL and cook at HIGH pressure for 5 minutes
6. When the timer goes off, let the pressure Release Naturally for 10 minutes, then release any remaining steam manually
7. Open the lid, Add the half and half and 1/2 cup cheese. Using an immersion blender, blend until smooth.
8. Taste for seasoning and add more salt if needed.
9. Top with the remaining cheese and green onion. Serve warm

Barley Beef Soup Recipe

(Prep + Cook Time: 1 hour 10 minutes **| Serves:** 6-7)

Ingredients:

- 2 pounds' beef chuck roast, cut into 1 ½ inch steaks
- 4 large carrots, chopped.
- 1 stalk of celery, chopped.
- 1 cup pearl barley, rinsed
- 2 tablespoon olive oil
- 1 bay leaf
- 2 onions, chopped.
- 4 cloves of garlic, sliced
- 8 cups chicken stock
- 1 tablespoon fish sauce
- Salt and ground black pepper to taste

Directions:

1. Select the SAUTÉ setting on the Instant Pot and heat the oil.
2. Sprinkle the beef with salt and pepper. Put in the pot and brown for about 5 minutes. Turn and brown the other side.
3. Remove the meat from the pot.
4. Add the onion, garlic, carrots and celery. Stir and sauté for 6 minutes
5. Return the beef to the pot. Add the pearl barley, bay leaf, chicken stock and fish sauce, Stir well.
6. Close and lock the lid. Press the CANCEL button to reset the cooking program, then press the MANUAL button and set the cooking time for 30 minutes at HIGH pressure
7. Once cooking is complete, let the pressure Release Naturally for 15 minutes. Release any remaining steam manually.
8. Uncover the pot, Remove cloves garlic, large vegetable chunks and bay leaf. Taste for seasoning and add more salt if needed

Beef and Rice Soup Recipe

(Prep + Cook Time: 30 minutes **| Serves:** 4-5)

Ingredients:

- 1-pound beef meat, ground
- 1 potato, cubed
- 2 carrots, thinly sliced
- 1/2 cup white rice
- 15-ounce canned garbanzo beans, rinsed
- 14-ounce canned tomatoes, crushed
- 12-ounce spicy V8 juice
- 1/2 cup frozen peas
- 1 tablespoon vegetable oil
- 1 celery rib, chopped.
- 1 yellow onion, chopped.
- 3 cloves garlic, minced
- 28-ounce canned beef stock
- Salt and black pepper to taste

Directions:

1. To preheat the Instant Pot, select SAUTÉ.
2. Add the ground beef and cook, stirring, for 5 minutes, until browned.
3. Transfer the meat to a bowl
4. Add the oil, celery and onion. Stir and sauté for 5 minutes.
5. Add the garlic and sauté for another 1 minute
6. Add the potato, carrots, rice, beans, tomatoes, spicy juice, stock, browned beef, salt and pepper. Mix well.
7. Press the CANCEL key to stop the SAUTÉ function.
8. Close and lock the lid. Select MANUAL and cook at HIGH pressure for 5 minutes
9. When the timer beeps, use a Quick Release.
10. Carefully unlock the lid, Add the peas to the pot and stir. Let it sit for 5 minutes and serve

Noodle Chicken Soup Recipe

(Prep + Cook Time: 30 minutes | **Serves:** 6

Ingredients:

- 8 cups chicken broth or vegetable broth
- 8-ounce spaghetti noodles break in half
- 1 medium onion, diced
- 3 celery stalks, diced
- 2 large carrots, diced
- 5 cloves garlic, minced
- 2 cups spinach, chopped.
- 3 tablespoon butter
- 1 teaspoon oregano
- 1 teaspoon basil, dried
- 1 teaspoon thyme, dried
- 2 cups skinless and boneless chicken breasts, cooked and cubed
- Salt and ground black pepper to taste

Directions:

1. To preheat the Instant Pot, select SAUTÉ. Once hot, add the butter and melt it
2. Add the onion, celery, carrot and a big pinch of salt. Stir and sauté for 5 minutes until they're soft.
3. Add the garlic, oregano, basil and thyme. Stir well and sauté for 1 minute more.
4. Add the chicken, broth and noodles. Close and lock the lid
5. Press the CANCEL button to reset the cooking program, then press the MANUAL button and set the cooking time for 4 minutes at HIGH pressure.
6. When the timer beeps, use a Quick Release
7. Carefully unlock the lid, Add the spinach and season with salt and pepper. Stir to mix and serve

Chicken Moringa Soup Recipe

(Prep + Cook Time: 45 minutes | **Serves:** 6-7)

Ingredients:

- 1 ½ pounds' chicken breasts
- 1 cup tomatoes, chopped.
- 1 thumb-size ginger
- 2 cups moringa leaves or kale leaves
- 5 cups water
- 1 onion, chopped
- 2 cloves garlic, minced
- Salt and ground black pepper to taste

Directions:

1. Combine all of the ingredients, except moringa leaves, in the Instant Pot and stir to mix
2. Close and lock the lid. Press the POULTRY button and set the cooking time for 15 minutes.
3. When the timer beeps, let the pressure Release Naturally for 15 minutes, then release any remaining steam manually
4. Open the lid, Add the moringa leaves and stir. Select SAUTÉ and simmer for 3 minutes.
5. Taste for seasoning and add more salt if needed and serve

Smoked Turkey Soup Recipe

(Prep + Cook Time: 1 hour 20 minutes | **Serves:** 8

Ingredients:

- 10-12-ounce smoked turkey drumstick
- 2 cups black beans, dried
- 1/2 tablespoon olive oil
- 1 medium-size onion, chopped.
- 6 cups water
- 1 celery stalk, chopped.
- 1 large carrot, chopped.
- 1/2 cup parsley, chopped.
- 3 cloves garlic, pressed
- 2 bay leaves
- 1 teaspoon salt
- 1/4 teaspoon ground black pepper

Directions:

1. Preheat the Instant Pot by selecting SAUTÉ. Add and heat the oil.
2. Put the onion, celery, carrots and parsley in the pot.
3. Sauté for 8-10 minutes, until the veggies are softened.
4. Add the garlic and sauté for 1 minute more

5. Pour in the water. Add the turkey, beans, salt, pepper and bay leaves, stir.
6. Bring to a boil, close and lock the lid
7. Press the CANCEL button to reset the cooking program, then press the MANUAL button and set the cooking time for 30 minutes at HIGH pressure
8. Once cooking is complete, select CANCEL and let Naturally Release for 10 minutes. Release any remaining steam manually
9. Uncover the pot, Remove the bay leaves. Transfer the turkey drumstick to a plate. Shred the meat.
10. With an immersion blender, blend the soup to your desired texture. Return the meat to the pot and stir then Serve

Egg Roll Soup Recipe

(Prep + Cook Time: 50 minutes | **Serves:** 4-5)

Ingredients:
- 1-pound ground beef
- 2/3 cup coconut aminos or soy sauce
- 4 cups chicken broth
- 1/2 head cabbage, chopped.
- 2 cups carrots, shredded
- 1 tablespoon olive oil
- 1 onion, cubed
- 1 teaspoon garlic powder
- 1 teaspoon onion powder
- 1 teaspoon ground ginger
- Salt and ground black pepper to taste

Directions:
1. Select the SAUTÉ setting on the Instant Pot and heat the oil
2. Add the onion and ground beef. Cook for 4 to 5 minutes, stirring occasionally, until all the meat is browned.
3. Add the cabbage, carrots, garlic powder, onion powder, ginger, coconut aminos and broth, Stir well.
4. Season with salt and pepper and stir. Close and lock the lid
5. Press the CANCEL button to stop the SAUTE function, then select the SOUP setting and set the cooking time for 25 minutes
6. Once timer goes off, use a Quick Release.
7. Carefully unlock the lid, Let the soup sit for 5-10 minutes and serve

Basil and Tomato Soup Recipe

(Prep + Cook Time: 20 minutes | **Serves:** 8

Ingredients:
- 2 cans whole Roma tomatoes
- 3/4 cup heavy cream
- 1/2 cup fresh basil leaves, chopped.
- 1 cup vegetable broth
- Salt and ground black pepper to taste

Directions:
1. Combine all of the ingredients, except for the heavy cream, in the Instant Pot and stir to mix
2. Close and lock the lid. Select MANUAL and cook at HIGH pressure for 8 minutes.
3. When the timer beeps, use a Quick Release.
4. Carefully unlock the lid, Select the SAUTÉ setting on the Instant Pot
5. Add the heavy cream and stir. Simmer for 2 minutes.
6. Press the CANCEL key to stop the SAUTÉ function and serve

Split Pea Soup Recipe

(Prep + Cook Time: 55 minutes | **Serves:** 6

Ingredients:

- 1-pound split peas
- 1/4 teaspoon thyme
- 6 cups vegetable broth
- 1 yellow onion, diced
- 2 cloves garlic, minced
- 3 stalks celery, sliced
- 3 carrots, sliced
- 1/2 tablespoon smoked paprika
- 1 bay leaf
- 2 tablespoon olive or coconut oil
- Salt and fresh ground pepper

Directions:

1. Select the SAUTÉ setting on the Instant Pot and heat the oil.
2. Add the onion, garlic, celery and carrot. Stir and sauté for 5-6 minutes.
3. Add the peas, smoked paprika, bay leaf, thyme and broth. Stir to combine
4. Season with salt and pepper. Close and lock the lid.
5. Press the CANCEL button to reset the cooking program, then press the MANUAL button and set the cooking time for 15 minutes at HIGH pressure.
6. Once cooking is complete, use a Natural Release for 10 minutes, then release any remaining pressure manually
7. Open the lid, Taste for seasoning and add more salt if needed and serve

Beef Borscht Soup Recipe

(Prep + Cook Time: 40 minutes | **Serves:** 4-5)

Ingredients:

- 2 pounds' ground beef
- 2 large carrots, diced
- 3 stalks of celery, diced
- 3 beets, peeled and diced
- 1 onion, diced
- 2 cloves garlic, diced
- 3 cups shredded cabbage
- 6 cups beef stock
- 1/2 tablespoon thyme
- 1 bay leaf
- Salt and ground black pepper to taste

Directions:

1. Preheat the Instant Pot by selecting SAUTÉ
2. Add the ground beef and cook, stirring, for 5 minutes, until browned.
3. Combine all the rest ingredients in the Instant Pot and stir to mix. Close and lock the lid
4. Press the CANCEL button to stop the SAUTE function, then select the MANUAL setting and set the cooking time for 15 minutes at HIGH pressure.
5. Once timer goes off, allow to Naturally Release for 10 minutes, then release any remaining pressure manually
6. Uncover the pot, Let the dish sit for 5-10 minutes and serve

Minestrone Soup Recipe

(Prep + Cook Time: 40 minutes | **Serves:** 4-5)

Ingredients:

- 15-ounce can (or about 2 cups cooked, drained) white or cannellini beans
- 3 cloves garlic, minced
- 2 celery stalks, diced
- 1/2 cup fresh spinach or kale (without the stalks), chopped.
- 1 cup elbow pasta
- 1 large carrot, diced
- 1 teaspoon dried basil
- 1 teaspoon dried oregano
- 2 tablespoon olive oil
- 1 large onion, diced
- 28-ounce can tomatoes, diced
- 4 cups bone broth or vegetable broth
- 1 bay leaf
- Salt and ground black pepper to taste

Directions:

1. Preheat the Instant Pot by selecting SAUTÉ. Add and heat the oil.
2. Add the onion, garlic, celery and carrot. Stir and sauté for 5-6 minutes, until softened.
3. Add the basil, oregano, salt and pepper, stir
4. Add the tomatoes, spinach, pasta, broth and bay leaf. Stir to combine.
5. Press the CANCEL key to stop the SAUTÉ function.
6. Close and lock the lid. Select MANUAL and cook at HIGH pressure for 6 minutes
7. When the timer beeps, let sit the mixture for 2 minutes, then use a Quick Release
8. Carefully unlock the lid, Add the kidney beans and stir and serve

Sweet Potato and Lentil Soup Recipe

(**Prep + Cook Time:** 40 minutes | **Serves:** 6

Ingredients:

- 3/4-pound sweet potato, peeled and cut into 1/2-inch dice
- 1 cup green lentils
- 2 teaspoons olive oil
- 1/2 yellow onion, chopped.
- 1 large celery stalk, diced
- 4 cloves garlic, minced
- 1 teaspoon paprika
- 1 teaspoon ground cumin
- 4-ounce spinach leaves
- 1/2 teaspoon red pepper flakes
- 1 can (14 oz.) petite diced tomatoes
- 1 cup water
- 3 ½ cups vegetable broth
- Salt and ground black pepper to taste

Directions:

1. Press the SAUTÉ button on the Instant Pot and heat the oil.
2. Add the onion and celery and sauté for 4 to 5 minutes, until softened
3. Add the garlic, paprika and red pepper flakes, stir well. Sauté for 1 minute.
4. Add the sweet potato, lentil, tomatoes, water and broth, Stir well.
5. Season with salt and pepper
6. Press the CANCEL key to stop the SAUTÉ function.
7. Close and lock the lid. Select MANUAL and cook at HIGH pressure for 12 minutes
8. Once timer goes off, wait for 10 minutes and then use a Quick Release.
9. Carefully unlock the lid, Add the spinach and stir and serve.

Broccoli Cheddar Soup Recipe

(**Prep + Cook Time:** 25 minutes | **Serves:** 4-5)

Ingredients:

- 6 cups broccoli, chopped.
- 1/2 onion, chopped.
- 2 carrots, chopped.
- 4 cups chicken broth
- 1 ½ cups cheddar cheese, grated
- 1/4 cup heavy cream
- 1 tablespoon olive oil
- 1 teaspoon garlic salt

Directions:

1. Preheat the Instant Pot by selecting SAUTÉ. Add and heat the oil
2. Add the onion and sauté for 3 to 4 minutes until translucent.
3. Add the carrots and broccoli and sauté for 2 minutes more
4. Pour in the broth. Press the CANCEL key to stop the SAUTÉ function
5. Close and lock the lid. Select MANUAL and cook at HIGH pressure for 5 minutes
6. When the timer beeps, use a Quick Release.
7. Carefully unlock the lid, Let the dish chill for a while.
8. With an immersion blender, blend the soup to your desired texture.
9. Season with salt and add the cheese and heavy cream. Stir well for 1 to 2 minutes until the cheese melts and serve.

Black Bean Soup Recipe

(Prep + Cook Time: 1 hour 10 minutes | **Serves:** 6

Ingredients:

- 1-pound dried black beans, soaked overnight
- 4 cups water
- 1/2 cup red wine
- 5 cloves garlic, minced
- 1 onion, chopped
- 1 red bell pepper, chopped.
- 2 teaspoon ground oregano
- 1 teaspoon ground cumin
- 2 tablespoon olive oil
- 1 bay leaf
- 2 tablespoon sherry vinegar
- Salt and ground black pepper to taste

Directions:

1. Preheat the Instant Pot by selecting SAUTÉ. Add and heat the oil.
2. Add the garlic and onion and sauté for 2 minutes, until fragrant.
3. Add the bell pepper, oregano, cumin and bay leaf. Stir and sauté for 1 minute more
4. Add the beans and pour the water, wine and vinegar, Stir well
5. Sprinkle with salt and pepper. Close and lock the lid.
6. Press the CANCEL button to stop the SAUTE function, then select the BEAN/CHILI setting and set the cooking time for 45 minutes
7. When the timer beeps, use a Quick Release
8. Carefully unlock the lid, and Serve

Navy Bean Bacon and Spinach Soup Recipe

(Prep + Cook Time: 50 minutes | **Serves:** 6

Ingredients:

- 3 cans (15-ounce each) navy beans, rinsed and drained
- 1 large celery stalk, chopped.
- 2 tablespoon tomato paste
- 1 sprig fresh rosemary
- 2 bay leaves
- 4 cups chicken broth
- 3 cups baby spinach
- 1 cup water
- 4 slices bacon, chopped.
- 1 onion, chopped
- 1 large carrot, chopped.
- Salt and ground black pepper to taste

Directions:

1. Combine the 1 can beans with 1 cup of water
2. With an immersion blender, blend the mixture
3. Set your instant pot on SAUTÉ mode, add the bacon and sauté until crisp
4. Transfer the bacon to a plate lined with paper towel
5. Add the onion, carrot and celery to the pot and sauté for 5 minutes, until softened.
6. Add the tomato paste and stir.
7. Add 2 cans beans, pureed beans, rosemary, bay leaves and broth. Close and lock the lid
8. Press the CANCEL key to stop the SAUTÉ function
9. Close and lock the lid. Select MANUAL and cook at HIGH pressure for 15 minutes.
10. Once cooking is complete, let the pressure Release Naturally for 10 minutes. Release any remaining steam manually
11. Uncover the pot, Remove the rosemary and bay leaves. Add the spinach, season with salt and pepper and stir well. Let the dish sit for 5 minutes and serve.

Ham and Bean Soup Recipe

(Prep + Cook Time: 1 hour 10 minutes | **Serves:** 6-7)

Ingredients:

- 1-pound white beans, rinsed
- 1 can diced tomatoes
- 1 clove garlic, minced
- 1 leftover ham bone with meat
- 1 onion diced
- 1 teaspoon chili powder
- 1 lemon, juiced
- 8 cups chicken broth

Directions:

1. Combine all of the ingredients in the Instant Pot and stir to mix.
2. Close and lock the lid. Select the BEAN/CHILI setting and set the cooking time for 50 minutes.
3. When the timer beeps, use a Quick Release
4. Let the soup sit for 10 minutes.
5. Carefully unlock the lid, and Serve.

Potato and Ham Soup Recipe

(Prep + Cook Time: 40 minutes | **Serves:** 4-5)

Ingredients:

- 2 pounds' Yukon Gold potatoes, cut into small chunks
- 1/2 cup cheddar cheese, grated
- 8 cloves garlic, minced
- 1 onion, diced
- 2 tablespoon fried bacon bits
- 4 cups chicken broth
- A dash of cayenne pepper
- 1 cup cooked ham, diced
- 2 tablespoon butter
- Salt and ground black pepper to taste

Directions:

1. To preheat the Instant Pot, select SAUTÉ
2. Once hot, add the butter and melt it
3. Add the garlic and onion, sauté for 1 - 2 minutes, or until fragrant.
4. Add the potatoes and sauté for 3 minutes more
5. Add the cayenne pepper, cooked ham and cheese. Pour in the broth and stir well
6. Season with salt and pepper. Close and lock the lid
7. Press the CANCEL button to reset the cooking program, then press the MANUAL button and set the cooking time for 25 minutes at HIGH pressure
8. Once timer goes off, use a Quick Release.
9. Carefully unlock the lid, top with bacon bits and serve.

Sweet Potato Soup

(Prep + Cook Time: 45 minutes | **Serves:** 4)

Ingredients:

- 4 large red sweet potatoes, peeled and diced
- 6 carrots, peeled and diced
- 1/2 teaspoon thyme
- 1/2 teaspoon ground sage
- 2 tablespoon butter
- 1 whole onion, chopped.
- 4 cloves garlic, chopped.
- 1-quart vegetarian broth
- Salt and ground black pepper to taste

Directions:

1. Preheat the Instant Pot by selecting SAUTÉ. Once hot, add the butter and melt it.
2. Add the onion, garlic and carrots and sauté for about 8 minutes, until the onion is translucent
3. Add the sweet potatoes, thyme, sage and broth. Season with salt and pepper, stir well. Close and lock the lid
4. Press the CANCEL button to stop the SAUTE function, then select the MANUAL setting and set the cooking time for 20 minutes at HIGH pressure

5. Once timer goes off, use a Quick Release
6. Carefully unlock the lid, with an immersion blender, blend the soup to your desired texture and serve

Cauliflower Soup Recipe

(Prep + Cook Time: 25 minutes | **Serves:** 4)

Ingredients:

- 3 cups chicken broth
- 1 large onion, chopped.
- 1 medium cauliflower, chopped.
- 1 tablespoon butter
- Salt and ground black pepper to taste

Directions:
1. Preheat the Instant Pot by selecting SAUTÉ. Once hot, add the butter and melt it
2. Add the onion and sauté for 4 to 5 minutes, until softened
3. Add the broth, cauliflower, salt and pepper, Stir well. Close and lock the lid
4. Press the CANCEL button to stop the SAUTE function, then select the MANUAL setting and set the cooking time for 5 minutes at HIGH pressure
5. Once timer goes off, use a Quick Release
6. Carefully unlock the lid, with an immersion blender, blend the soup to your desired texture and serve

Pumpkin Soup Recipe

(Prep + Cook Time: 35 minutes | **Serves:** 2 - 3)

Ingredients:

- 1 ½ cups chicken stock
- 1/2 apple, peeled, cored and grated
- 1/2 butternut pumpkin, chunks
- 1/2 red potato or radishes, diced
- 1 cup coconut milk
- 2 bay leaves
- 1/2 tablespoon butter
- 1/2 brown onion, chopped.
- Pinch curry powder
- Salt and ground black pepper to taste

Directions:
1. Select the SAUTÉ setting on the Instant Pot and melt the butter
2. Add the onion, pumpkin, potato and curry powder. Stir and sauté for 7-9 minutes until the onion is browned
3. Add the stock, apple, bay leaves, salt and black pepper, stir. Close and lock the lid
4. Press the CANCEL button to reset the cooking program, then press the MANUAL button and set the cooking time for 5 minutes at HIGH pressure
5. Once cooking is complete, select CANCEL and use a Natural Release for 10 minutes.
6. Open the lid. Remove the bay leaves. Add the milk and stir well
7. With an immersion blender, blend the soup until smooth
8. Taste for seasoning and add more salt if needed and serve.

Sweet Potato & Chickpea Soup Recipe

(Prep + Cook Time: 45 minutes | **Serves:** 4-5)

Ingredients:

- 30-ounce canned chickpeas
- 8-ounce orange juice
- 2 onions, sliced
- 1-pound sweet potatoes, diced
- 4 cups vegetable broth
- 1/2 tablespoon olive oil
- Salt and ground black pepper to taste

Directions:

1. Press the SAUTÉ button on the Instant Pot and heat the oil.
2. Add the onion and sauté for 4 to 5 minutes, until soft.
3. Add the potatoes, chickpeas, orange juice and broth, Stir well
4. Press the CANCEL key to stop the SAUTÉ function
5. Close and lock the lid. Select MANUAL and cook at HIGH pressure for 5 minutes.
6. Once cooking is complete, let the pressure Release Naturally for 10 minutes. Release any remaining steam manually
7. Uncover the pot, Season with salt and pepper to taste and serve.

Chicken and Wild Rice Soup Recipe

(Prep + Cook Time: 30 minutes | **Serves:** 4-5)

Ingredients:

- 2 chicken breasts, skinless and boneless and chopped.
- 4-ounce cream cheese, cubed
- 1 cup milk
- 1 cup half and half
- 2 tablespoon cornstarch mixed with 2 tablespoon 2 tablespoon butter
- 1 cup yellow onion, chopped.
- 1 cup celery, chopped.
- 1 cup carrots, chopped.
- 6-ounce wild rice
- water
- 1 tablespoon parsley, dried
- 28-ounce chicken stock
- A pinch of red pepper flakes
- Salt and ground black pepper to the taste

Directions:

1. Preheat the Instant Pot by selecting SAUTÉ. Once hot, add the butter and melt it.
2. Add the onion, celery and carrot. Stir and sauté for 5 minutes.
3. Add the rice, chicken breasts, parsley, stock, red pepper, salt and black pepper, Stir well.
4. Close and lock the lid. Press the CANCEL button to stop the SAUTE function, then select the MANUAL setting and set the cooking time for 5 minutes at HIGH pressure
5. When the timer beeps, use a Quick Release
6. Carefully unlock the lid, Add the cornstarch mixed with water and stir
7. Add the cheese, milk, half and half and stir well.
8. Select SAUTÉ and cook for 3 minutes then Serve.

Beet Soup Recipe

(Prep + Cook Time: 60 minutes | **Serves:** 4)

Ingredients:

- 3/4-pound beets, peeled and chopped.
- 1 onion, chopped.
- 1/4 cup fresh basil leaves, chopped.
- 4 cups chicken broth
- Salt and ground black pepper to taste

Directions:

1. Combine all of the ingredients in the Instant Pot and stir to mix.
2. Close and lock the lid. Select the SOUP setting and set the cooking time for 35 minutes
3. When the timer goes off, let the pressure Release Naturally for 10 minutes, then release any remaining steam manually
4. Open the lid, and with an immersion blender, blend the soup until smooth. Taste for seasoning and add more salt if needed.

French Onion Soup Recipe

(Prep + Cook Time: 40 minutes | **Serves:** 4-5)

Ingredients:

- 3 pounds' onions, chopped.
- 1-pound cheese, grated
- 3 cups chicken stock
- 8 slices bread, toasted
- 1 tablespoon chives for garnish
- 6 tablespoon butter
- 1 teaspoon apple cider vinegar
- 1 teaspoon fish sauce (or soy sauce)
- 1/2 cup dry sherry
- 2 sprigs thyme
- 1 bay leaf
- Salt and ground black pepper to taste

Directions:

1. To preheat the Instant Pot, select SAUTÉ
2. Once hot, add the butter and melt it.
3. Add the onion and sauté for 10 minutes until caramelized, stirring occasionally
4. Add the vinegar, fish sauce, dry sherry, thyme, bay leaf, cheese and stock.
5. Season with salt and pepper, Stir well.
6. Place the bread slices on top. Close and lock the lid
7. Press the CANCEL key to stop the SAUTÉ function
8. Close and lock the lid. Select MANUAL and cook at HIGH pressure for 10 minutes
9. Once cooking is complete, let the pressure Release Naturally for 10 minutes. Release any remaining steam manually.
10. Uncover the pot, Remove the sprigs thyme. Top with chives and serve

Fish & Seafood Recipes

Delicious Squid Recipe

(Prep + Cook Time: 35 minutes | **Serves:** 2 - 3)

Ingredients:

- 1-pound squid
- 1 teaspoon onion powder
- 1 tablespoon chives
- 1 tablespoon lemon juice
- 2 tablespoon starch
- 1 tablespoon garlic, minced
- 3 tablespoon fish sauce
- 2 tablespoon butter
- 1/4 teaspoon chili pepper, chopped.
- 1 teaspoon salt
- 1 teaspoon white pepper

Directions:

1. Slice the squid
2. In a large bowl, combine the onion powder, starch, garlic, chives, chili pepper, salt and white pepper. Mix well
3. Add the squid to the spice mix. Stir gently
4. Season the mixture with the lemon juice and fish sauce, stir. Set aside the mixture for 10 minutes
5. Preheat the Instant Pot by selecting SAUTÉ. Once hot, add the butter and melt it.
6. Add the squid mixture to the pot and secure the lid
7. Select the STEW setting and cook for 13 minutes.
8. Once cooking is complete, uncover the pot and serve.

Special Shrimp Scampi

(Prep + Cook Time: 15 minutes | **Serves:** 2 - 3)

Ingredients:

- 1-pound shrimp, peeled and deveined
- 2 tablespoon olive oil
- 1 clove garlic, minced
- 1/3 cup tomato paste
- 10-ounce canned tomatoes, chopped.
- 1/3 cup water
- 1/4 teaspoon oregano, dried
- 1 tablespoon parsley, finely chopped.
- 1/2 teaspoon kosher salt
- 1/2 teaspoon ground black pepper to taste
- 1 cup parmesan, grated

Directions:

1. Preheat the Instant Pot by selecting SAUTÉ. Add and heat the oil
2. Add the garlic and sauté for 1 minute.
3. Add the shrimp, tomato paste, tomatoes, water, oregano, parsley, salt and pepper, stir
4. Close and lock the lid. Select MANUAL and cook at HIGH pressure for 3 minutes.
5. When the timer goes off, use a Quick Release
6. Carefully unlock the lid, Sprinkle with parmesan and serve

Fish Fillets in Ginger Sauce

(Prep + Cook Time: 20 minutes | **Serves:** 4)

Ingredients:

- 4 pieces white fish fillets
- 1 orange for juice and zest
- 1 teaspoon orange zest
- 1 cup white wine or fish stock
- 2 tablespoon olive oil
- 4 spring onions, chopped.
- 2 teaspoon ginger, grated
- Salt and ground black pepper to taste

Directions:

1. Rub the fish fillets with the olive oil and season with salt and pepper
2. In the Instant Pot, combine the ginger, orange juice, orange zest and wine

3. Pour the water into the pot and insert a steamer basket
4. Place the fish fillets in the basket. Close and lock the lid
5. Select the MANUAL setting and set the cooking time for 7 minutes at HIGH pressure.
6. When the timer beeps, use a Quick Release.
7. Carefully unlock the lid, Pour the sauce over the fish fillets and serve.

Salmon, Potatoes and Broccoli

(Prep + Cook Time: 30 minutes | **Serves:** 2 - 3)

Ingredients:
- 2 salmon fillets
- 1-pound new potatoes
- Fresh herbs, optional
- 1 cup water
- 1 cups broccoli, chopped.
- 1/2 tablespoon butter
- Salt and ground black pepper to taste

Directions:
1. In a bowl; season the potatoes with salt, pepper and fresh herbs.
2. Prepare the Instant Pot by adding the water to the pot and placing the steam rack in it.
3. Place the potatoes on the steam rack, close and lock the lid
4. Select MANUAL and cook at HIGH pressure for 2 minutes
5. Meanwhile, in a bowl, season the broccoli and salmon with salt and pepper
6. When the timer goes off, use a quick release. Carefully unlock the lid,
7. Place the broccoli and salmon on the steam rack, along with the potatoes.
8. Close and lock the lid. Select MANUAL and cook at HIGH pressure for 2 minutes more.
9. When the timer beeps, use a Natural Release for 10 minutes.
10. Uncover the pot, Transfer the potatoes to a separate bowl and add the butter. Gently stir to coat the potatoes with the butter
11. Serve the cooked fish with potatoes and broccoli

Sockeye Salmon

(Prep + Cook Time: 15 minutes | **Serves:** 4)

Ingredients:
- 4 wild sockeye salmon fillets
- 1/4 cup lemon juice
- 2 tablespoon assorted chili pepper seasoning
- 1 cup water
- Salt and ground black pepper to taste

Directions:
1. Season the salmon fillets with chili pepper, salt, pepper and lemon juice
2. Pour the water into the Instant Pot and insert a steamer basket.
3. Place the fillets in the basket.
4. Close and lock the lid. Select MANUAL and cook at HIGH pressure for 5 minutes.
5. When the timer goes off, use a quick release
6. Carefully unlock the lid, Serve.

Shrimp Risotto Delight

(Prep + Cook Time: 40 minutes | **Serves:** 4-5)

Ingredients:
- 1-pound peeled and cleaned shrimp
- 3/4 cup parmesan cheese
- 1 ½ cups Arborio rice
- 2 tablespoon dry white wine
- 4 ½ cups chicken broth
- 1/4 cup fresh herbs
- 4 tablespoon butter
- 2 cloves garlic, minced
- 1 yellow onion, chopped.
- Salt and ground black pepper to taste

Directions:

1. Preheat the Instant Pot by selecting SAUTÉ
2. Once hot, add 2 tablespoons of butter and melt it
3. Add the garlic and onion and sauté for 4 minutes
4. Add the rice, stir and cook for 1minute more
5. Pour the wine. Stir and cook for about 3 minutes, or until much of the wine has evaporated.
6. Pour 3 cups of broth. Season with salt and pepper. Close and lock the lid.
7. Press the CANCEL key to stop the SAUTÉ function.
8. Select MANUAL and cook at HIGH pressure for 9 minutes
9. Once pressure cooking is complete, use a Quick Release. Unlock and carefully open the lid
10. Add the shrimp with the remaining broth.
11. Select SAUTE and cook for 4 to 5 minutes, or until the shrimp has become bright pink and solid
12. Add the cheese and 2 tablespoons of butter, stir well. Top with fresh herbs and serve.

Fish Curry Recipe

(Prep + Cook Time: 30 minutes | **Serves:** 4)

Ingredients:

- 1 ½ pounds' fish fillets, cut into 2-inch pieces
- 2 cups unsweetened coconut milk
- 1 cup tomatoes, chopped.
- 2 Serrano peppers, seeded and chopped.
- 1 tablespoon fresh lemon juice
- 2 tablespoon olive oil
- 4 cloves garlic, minced
- 2 medium onions, chopped.
- 2 teaspoon fresh ginger, grated finely
- 1/2 teaspoon ground turmeric
- 1 teaspoon red chili powder
- 2 teaspoon ground cumin
- 2 teaspoon ground coriander
- 2 tablespoon curry powder
- Salt to taste

Directions:

1. Select the SAUTÉ setting on the Instant Pot and heat the oil
2. Add the garlic, onion and ginger and sauté for 4 minutes
3. Add the turmeric, chili powder, cumin, coriander and curry. Stir and cook for 1 minute more.
4. Pour in the coconut milk and stir well.
5. Add the fish, tomatoes and Serrano pepper, stir. Season with salt
6. Press the CANCEL key to stop the SAUTÉ function
7. Close and lock the lid. Select MANUAL and cook at LOW pressure for 5 minutes.
8. Once cooking is complete, use a Natural Release for 10 minutes, then release any remaining pressure manually
9. Open the lid, Drizzle the dish with the lemon juice and serve

Salmon Fillets with Lemon Sauce

(Prep + Cook Time: 15 minutes | **Serves:** 2 - 3)

Ingredients:

- 1-pound salmon fillets
- 1 tablespoon feta cheese, crumbled
- 2 slices lemon
- 2 sprigs fresh rosemary
- 1 clove garlic, minced
- 1 tablespoon lemon juice
- 1/4 teaspoon dried oregano
- 1/4 cup olive oil
- 1 tablespoon red wine vinegar
- 1 cup water
- Salt and ground black pepper to taste

Directions:

1. In a bowl; combine the olive oil, vinegar, garlic, lemon juice, oregano, salt, pepper and cheese. Mix well
2. Pour the water into the Instant Pot and set a steam rack in the pot
3. Place the salmon on the steam rack
4. Pour the mixture over the salmon fillets. Top with the lemon slices and rosemary

5. Close and lock the lid. Select MANUAL and cook at HIGH pressure for 5 minutes.
6. Once pressure cooking is complete, use a Quick Release.
7. Unlock and carefully open the lid, Serve the salmon with the sauce.

Tasty Tuna Casserole.

(Prep + Cook Time: 15 minutes | **Serves:** 4)

Ingredients:
- 14-ounce canned tuna, drained
- 20-ounce egg noodles
- 1 cup peas, frozen
- 4-ounce cheddar cheese, grated
- 1/4 cup breadcrumbs, optional
- 28-ounce cream of mushroom soup
- 3 cups water
- Salt and ground black pepper to taste

Directions:
1. In the Instant Pot, combine the water and mushroom soup. Mix well.
2. Add the egg noodles, tuna, peas, salt and pepper, stir.
3. Close and lock the lid. Select MANUAL and cook at HIGH pressure for 4 minutes.
4. Once cooking is complete, use a Quick Release.
5. Unlock and carefully open the lid, Sprinkle with cheese and breadcrumbs, close the lid and let it sit for 5 minutes, Serve.

Salmon Fish Pho

(Prep + Cook Time: 40 minutes | **Serves:** 6

Ingredients:
- 4 salmon fillets
- 12-ounce squid
- 1/4 cup soy sauce
- 1/4 teaspoon thyme
- 1/2 cup fresh dill
- 1/2 tablespoon coriander
- 1 teaspoon chili flakes
- 1 clove garlic, sliced
- 5 cups water
- 1 tablespoon kosher salt
- 1 teaspoon ground black pepper

Directions:
1. Preheat the Instant Pot by selecting SAUTÉ.
2. In the Instant Pot, combine the water, soy sauce, thyme, fresh dill, coriander, salt, black pepper and chili flakes. Mix well
3. Close the lid and sauté the mixture for 15 minutes
4. Cut the fish and squid into ½-1 inch pieces
5. When the time is over, remove all the ingredients from the pot except the liquid.
6. Add the salmon, squid and garlic. Stir very gently.
7. Close and lock the lid. Select MANUAL and cook at HIGH pressure for 10 minutes.
8. When the timer goes off, use a Quick Release.
9. Carefully unlock the lid, Serve with cooked rice noodles.

Awesome Shrimps Recipe

(Prep + Cook Time: 15 minutes | **Serves:** 4-5)

Ingredients:
- 2 pounds' shrimp
- 1 tablespoon garlic, minced
- 1 tablespoon lemon juice
- 1/2 cup white wine
- 1/2 cup chicken stock
- 1 tablespoon parsley for garnish
- 2 tablespoon butter
- Salt and ground black pepper to taste

Directions:
1. Add the butter, garlic and lemon juice to the Instant Pot.
2. Pour in the stock and wine, stir well

3. Add the shrimp and season with salt and pepper, stir well again
4. Close and lock the lid. Select MANUAL and cook at HIGH pressure for 3 minutes.
5. When the timer goes off, use a Quick Release
6. Carefully unlock the lid, Top with parsley and serve

Tuna with Peas

(Prep + Cook Time: 25 minutes | **Serves:** 4)

Ingredients:
- 2 cans tuna, drained
- 2 carrots, peeled and chopped.
- 1 can cream of celery soup
- 1/2 cup water
- 3/4 cup milk
- 2 tablespoon butter
- 1 cup frozen peas
- 1/4 cup diced onions
- 2 eggs, beaten
- Salt and ground black pepper to taste

Directions:
1. In the Instant Pot, combine all of the ingredients and stir to mix.
2. Select the MANUAL setting and set the cooking time for 15 minutes at HIGH pressure
3. When the timer beeps, use a quick release
4. Carefully unlock the lid, Serve

Salmon with Mayonnaise

(Prep + Cook Time: 25 minutes | **Serves:** 4-5)

Ingredients:
- 2 pounds' salmon fillet
- 1 tablespoon lemon juice
- 4 cloves garlic, minced
- 1 teaspoon dry basil leaves
- 2 tablespoon olive oil
- Green onion, chopped.
- 1/2 cup mayonnaise
- Salt and ground pepper to taste

Directions:
1. In a bowl; combine the mayonnaise, lemon juice, garlic and basil
2. Season the salmon with salt and pepper
3. Set your instant pot on SAUTÉ mode, add the oil and heat it up
4. Add the fillets and brown on both sides for 10 minutes.
5. Add the mayonnaise mixture to the pot and coat the fillets
6. Cook for 5 minutes more. Flip the salmon from time to time.
7. Transfer to a serving plate and top with chopped green onion.

Easy Salmon Fillets

(Prep + Cook Time: 30 minutes | **Serves:** 2)

Ingredients:
- 2 salmon fillets
- Salt and ground black pepper to taste
- 1 cup water

Directions:
1. Prepare the Instant Pot by adding the water to the pot and placing the steam rack in it.
2. Season the salmon with salt and pepper
3. Place the salmon fillets on the steam rack and secure the lid
4. Press the STEAM button and set the cooking time for 10 minutes
5. When the timer beeps, use a Natural Release for 10 minutes
6. Uncover the pot, Serve with lemon wedges

Jumbo Shrimp Recipe

(Prep + Cook Time: 15 minutes | **Serves:** 2 - 3)

Ingredients:

- 1-pound frozen jumbo shrimp, peeled and deveined
- 1 can (28 oz.) crushed tomatoes
- 1 bay leaf
- 1 teaspoon thyme
- 2 teaspoon olive oil
- 2 cloves garlic, minced
- 1 medium onion, chopped.
- 2 stalks celery, diced
- 1 bell pepper, diced
- 1 tablespoon tomato paste
- 1 teaspoon kosher salt
- 1/2 teaspoon pepper
- 1/4 teaspoon cayenne pepper

Directions:

1. Select the SAUTÉ setting on the Instant Pot and heat the oil.
2. Add the garlic, onion, celery and bell pepper. Sauté the veggies for 3 to 4 minutes.
3. Add the tomato paste and cook for 1 minute more, stirring occasionally
4. Add the shrimp, tomatoes, bay leaf, thyme, salt, pepper and cayenne pepper, stir well. Close and lock the lid.
5. Press the CANCEL key to stop the SAUTÉ function.
6. Select MANUAL and cook at HIGH pressure for 2 minutes
7. When the timer beeps, use a Quick Release.
8. Carefully unlock the lid, Serve with cooked rice.

Mediterranean Style Squid

(Prep + Cook Time: 25 minutes | **Serves:** 2 - 3)

Ingredients:

- 2 pounds' squid, chopped.
- 2 tablespoon olive oil
- 3 cloves garlic, chopped
- 3 sprigs fresh rosemary
- 1/2 cup Italian parsley, chopped.
- 1 cup red wine
- 3 stalks of celery, chopped
- 1 can (28 oz) crushed tomatoes
- 1 red onion, sliced
- Salt and ground black pepper to taste

Directions:

1. In a bowl; combine the olive oil, squid, salt and pepper
2. Add the wine, tomatoes, onion, garlic, rosemary and celery to the pot
3. Set a steamer basket in the pot.
4. Place the squid in the steamer basket
5. Close and lock the lid. Select MANUAL and cook at HIGH pressure for 4 minutes
6. Once timer goes off, let the pressure Release Naturally for 10 minutes, then release any remaining steam manually
7. Open the lid, Top with fresh parsley and serve

Instant Boiled Octopus

(Prep + Cook Time: 30 minutes | **Serves:** 6

Ingredients:

- 2 ½ pounds' whole octopus, cleaned and sliced
- 3 tablespoon lemon juice, freshly squeezed
- 1 cup water
- Salt and ground black pepper to taste

Directions:

1. Pour the water and lemon juice to the Instant Pot
2. Add the octopus and season with salt and pepper.
3. Close and lock the lid. Select MANUAL and cook at HIGH pressure for 15 minutes
4. When the timer goes off, use a Quick Release

5. Carefully unlock the lid, if not tender enough, return to the pot and cook for 5 minutes more, then Serve.

Oysters in Shell

(Prep + Cook Time: 15 minutes | **Serves:** 6

Ingredients:
- 36 in-shell oysters
- 6 tablespoon butter, melted
- 1 cup water
- Salt and ground black pepper to taste

Directions:
1. Clean the oysters well
2. Add the water, oysters, salt and pepper to the Instant Pot
3. Close and lock the lid. Select the MANUAL setting and set the cooking time for 3 minutes at HIGH pressure.
4. When the timer beeps, use a Quick Release.
5. Carefully unlock the lid, Serve with melted butter.

Mediterranean Cod

(Prep + Cook Time: 25 minutes | **Serves:** 2 - 3)

Ingredients:
- 1 ½ pounds' fresh (or frozen) cod fillets
- 1 can diced tomatoes
- 1 lemon juice, freshly squeezed
- 3 tablespoon butter
- 1 onion, sliced
- Salt and ground black pepper to taste

Directions:
1. Preheat the Instant Pot by selecting SAUTÉ.
2. Once hot, add the butter and melt it
3. Add the onion, tomatoes, lemon juice, salt and pepper. Stir well and sauté for 9 minutes.
4. Add the fish fillets to the pot and coat it well with the sauce
5. Press the CANCEL button to stop the SAUTE function, then select the MANUAL setting and set the cooking time for 3 minutes (for frozen - 5 minutes) at HIGH pressure.
6. Once pressure cooking is complete, use a Quick Release
7. Unlock and carefully open the lid, Serve the fish with sauce.

IP Steamed Tilapia

(Prep + Cook Time: 20 minutes | **Serves:** 2 - 3)

Ingredients:
- 1-pound tilapia fillets
- 1/2 cup green commercial chutney
- 1 cup water

Directions:
1. Prepare the Instant Pot by adding the water to the pot and placing a steamer basket in it.
2. Cut a large parchment paper and place the fish in the middle
3. Divide the green chutney between all the fillets
4. Roll paper edges together tightly to form a packet. Place in the steamer basket.
5. Close and lock the lid. Select MANUAL and cook at HIGH pressure for 10 minutes
6. When the timer beeps, use a Quick Release
7. Uncover the pot, and Serve

Steamed Asparagus and Shrimp

(Prep + Cook Time: 10 minutes | **Serves:** 2)

Ingredients:

- 1-pound shrimp, frozen or fresh, peeled and deveined
- 1 teaspoon olive oil
- 6-ounce asparagus
- 1 cup water
- 1/2 tablespoon Cajun seasoning (or your choice of seasoning)

Directions:

1. Prepare the Instant Pot by adding the water to the pot and placing the steam rack in it
2. Put the asparagus on the steam rack.
3. Place the shrimp on the asparagus and drizzle with olive oil. Season with Cajun seasoning.
4. Select the STEAM setting and set the cooking time for 2 minutes at LOW pressure.
5. When the timer goes off, use a Quick Release
6. Carefully unlock the lid, Serve.

Tiger Prawns Paella

(Prep + Cook Time: 30 minutes | **Serves:** 2 - 3)

Ingredients:

- 1 cup tiger prawns, peeled and deveined
- 3/4 cup green peas, frozen
- 3/4 cup risotto rice or paella rice
- 1 cup sweet corn
- 1 tablespoon fresh parsley, finely chopped.
- 1 whole lemon, quartered
- A pinch of saffron threads
- 1 tablespoon olive oil
- 1 small red onion, roughly chopped.
- 1 red bell pepper, chopped.
- 2 chorizo sausage slices
- 2 cups vegetable stock (or chicken stock)
- 1 teaspoon salt

Directions:

1. Preheat the Instant Pot by selecting SAUTÉ. Add and heat the oil
2. Add the onion and chorizo slices. Stir and sauté for 3 minute.
3. Add the tiger prawns and cook for 2 to 3 minutes more, stirring occasionally
4. Add the rice and stock, Stir well.
5. Add the peas, sweet corn and parsley. Season with salt and saffron
6. Close and lock the lid. Select MANUAL and cook at HIGH pressure for 7 minutes.
7. Once pressure cooking is complete, use a Quick Release.
8. Unlock and carefully open the lid, Place the lemon on top. Close the lid and let sit for 10 minutes and serve

Poached Salmon.

(Prep + Cook Time: 20 minutes | **Serves:** 2 - 3)

Ingredients:

- 2 salmon fillets with skin
- 1/2 teaspoon fennel seeds
- 4 scallions, chopped.
- 2 cups chicken broth
- 1/2 cup dry white wine
- 1 teaspoon lemon zest
- 1/4 cup fresh dill
- 1 bay leaf
- Salt and ground black pepper to taste

Directions:

1. Place the steam rack in the Instant Pot.
2. Season the salmon fillets with salt and pepper
3. Place the fillets on the steam rack.
4. Pour in the broth and wine.
5. Sprinkle the fish with lemon zest, fresh dill, fennel seeds and scallions. Add the bay leaf

6. Select the MANUAL setting and set the cooking time for 5 minutes at HIGH pressure.
7. Once cooking is complete, use a Natural Release for 5 minutes, then release any remaining pressure manually
8. Open the lid, Serve the salmon fillets with sauce

Salmon with Broccoli

(Prep + Cook Time: 25 minutes **| Serves:** 2)

Ingredients:
- 8-ounce salmon fillet
- 8-ounce broccoli
- 1 cup water
- Salt and ground black pepper to taste

Directions:
1. Add the water to the Instant Pot and place a steam rack on top.
2. Cut the broccoli into florets
3. Season the salmon fillets and broccoli with salt and pepper to taste. Place them on the steam rack.
4. Close and lock the lid. Select STEAM and cook for 5 minutes
5. Once cooking is complete, use a Natural Release for 10 minutes, then release any remaining pressure manually
6. Open the lid, Serve

Cod in Orange Sauce

(Prep + Cook Time: 15 minutes **| Serves:** 4)

Ingredients:
- 4 cod fillets, boneless
- 1 cup white wine
- 4 spring onions, chopped.
- Juice from 1 orange
- A small ginger piece, grated
- Salt and ground black pepper to taste.

Directions:
1. Add the ginger, wine and orange juice to the Instant Pot, mix well
2. Place a steamer basket on top
3. Place the cod fillets in the basket. Season with salt and pepper.
4. Close and lock the lid. Select MANUAL and cook at HIGH pressure for 7 minutes
5. When the timer goes off, use a Quick Release
6. Carefully unlock the lid, Serve the fish with sauce and sprinkle with green onions

Salmon and Rice.

(Prep + Cook Time: 20 minutes **| Serves:** 2)

Ingredients:
- 2 wild salmon fillets, frozen
- 1 tablespoon butter
- 1/4 cup vegetable soup mix, dried
- A pinch of saffron
- 1/2 cup jasmine rice
- 1 cup chicken stock
- Salt and ground black pepper to taste

Directions:
1. In the Instant Pot, combine the rice, stock, butter, soup mix and saffron, Stir well
2. Place the steam rack in the pot
3. Sprinkle salmon with salt and pepper. Place the fish on the steam rack
4. Press the MANUAL button and set the cooking time for 5 minutes at HIGH pressure.
5. When the timer beeps, use a Natural Release for 10 minutes.
6. Uncover the pot, Serve.

Shrimp Curry Recipe

(Prep + Cook Time: 15 minutes | **Serves:** 2 - 3)

Ingredients:

- 1-pound shrimp, peeled and deveined
- 1 tablespoon garlic, minced
- 8-ounce unsweetened coconut milk
- 1 teaspoon curry powder
- 2 cups water
- Salt and ground black pepper to taste

Directions:

1. Add the water to the Instant Pot and insert a steam rack
2. In a large bowl, combine the shrimp, coconut milk, garlic and curry powder. Season with salt and pepper
3. Pour the mixture into the pan and place the dish on the steam rack, uncovered.
4. Close and lock the lid. Select the MANUAL setting and set the cooking time for 4 minutes at LOW pressure.
5. When the timer beeps, use a Quick Release
6. Carefully unlock the lid, Stir the curry and serve

Fish and Vegetables Asian Style

(Prep + Cook Time: 40 minutes | **Serves:** 2)

Ingredients:

- 2 fillets white fish
- 1/2-pound frozen vegetables of your choice
- 1 clove garlic, minced
- 2 teaspoon grated ginger
- 1/4 long red chili, sliced
- 1 tablespoon honey
- 2 tablespoon soy sauce
- 1 cup water
- Salt and ground black pepper to taste

Directions:

1. Add the water to the Instant Pot and place a steam rack on top
2. Put the vegetables in the pan
3. Place the pan on the steam rack
4. In a bowl; combine the garlic, ginger, red chili, honey, soy sauce, salt and pepper, Stir well.
5. Add the fillets to the bowl coat it well with the mixture.
6. Place the fish fillets on the vegetables. Close and lock the lid.
7. Press the STEAM button and set the cooking time for 15 minutes
8. Once cooking is complete, select Cancel and let Naturally Release for 10 minutes. Release any remaining steam manually
9. Uncover the pot, Serve

Delicious Dijon Salmon

(Prep + Cook Time: 15 minutes | **Serves:** 2)

Ingredients:

- 2 fish fillets or steaks, such as salmon, cod, or halibut (1-inch thick)
- 2 teaspoon Dijon mustard
- 1 cup water
- Salt and ground black pepper to taste

Directions:

1. Pour the water into the Instant Pot and insert a steam rack
2. Sprinkle the fish with salt and pepper
3. Place the fillets on the rack skin-side down and spread the Dijon mustard on top of each fillets or steaks
4. Close and lock the lid. Select MANUAL and cook at HIGH pressure for 5 minutes.
5. When the timer goes off, use a Quick Release
6. Carefully unlock the lid, Serve.

Cranberries Plov

(Prep + Cook Time: 30 minutes **| Serves:** 4)

Ingredients:

- 1 package (16 oz) frozen seafood blend
- 3 cups water
- 1 bell pepper, red or yellow, sliced
- 3 big carrots, shredded
- 1 ½ cups basmati rice, organic
- 2 - 3 tablespoon butter
- 1 onion, large-sized, chopped.
- 1/2 cup dried cranberries
- Salt and ground black pepper to taste
- 1 lemon, sliced (optional)

Directions:

1. To preheat the Instant Pot, select SAUTÉ
2. Once hot, add the butter and melt it
3. Add the onion, bell pepper and carrots. Sauté for 5-7 minutes, stirring occasionally
4. Add the seafood blend, rice and cranberries, stir well.
5. Season with salt and pepper to taste.
6. Pour in water. Close and lock the lid.
7. Select RICE and leave it on the default
8. When the timer beeps, use a Natural Release for 10 minutes
9. Uncover the pot, if you like, you can squeeze fresh lemon juice over the dish and Serve.

Mussels with Wine

(Prep + Cook Time: 15 minutes **| Serves:** 4)

Ingredients:

- 3 pounds' mussels, cleaned and debearded
- 6 tablespoon butter
- 1 ½ cups chicken stock
- 4 shallots, chopped.
- 1 cup white wine

Directions:

1. Add the butter to the Instant Pot and select SAUTÉ.
2. Once the butter has melted, add the shallots and sauté for 2 minutes.
3. Pour in the wine, stir and cook for another 1 minute.
4. Add the stock and mussels, stir well. Close and lock the lid
5. Press the CANCEL button to stop the SAUTE function, then select the MANUAL setting and set the cooking time for 3 minutes at HIGH pressure.
6. Once pressure cooking is complete, use a Quick Release.
7. Unlock and carefully open the lid, remove unopened mussels and serve.

Seafood Paella Delight

(Prep + Cook Time: 35 minutes **| Serves:** 6)

Ingredients:

- 2 cups chopped white fish and scallops
- 1 green bell pepper, diced
- 2 cups rice
- A few saffron threads
- 2 cups fish stock
- 2 cups mussels and shrimp
- 4 tablespoon olive oil
- 1 onion, diced
- 1 red bell pepper, diced
- Salt and ground black pepper to taste

Directions:

1. Set your instant pot on SAUTÉ mode, add the oil and heat it up
2. Add the onion and bell peppers and sauté for 4 minutes
3. Add the fish, rice and saffron, stir. Cook for 2 minutes more.
4. Pour in the fish stock and season with salt and pepper, stir
5. Place the shellfish on top
6. Press the CANCEL key to stop the SAUTÉ function

7. Close and lock the lid. Select MANUAL and cook at HIGH pressure for 6 minutes.
8. Once cooking is complete, select CANCEL and let Naturally Release for 10 minutes. Release any remaining steam manually.
9. Uncover the pot, Stir the dish and let sit for 5 minutes and serve.

Instant pot Steamed Fish

(Prep + Cook Time: 30 minutes | **Serves:** 4)

Ingredients:
- 4 white fish fillet
- 1-pound cherry tomatoes cut into halves
- 1 cup olives, pitted and chopped.
- 1 tablespoon olive oil
- 1 clove garlic, minced
- 1/2 teaspoon thyme, dried
- 1 cup water
- Salt and ground black pepper to taste

Directions:
1. Prepare the Instant Pot by adding the water to the pot and placing the steamer basket in it
2. Place the fish fillets in the basket
3. Place the tomatoes and olives on top. Add the olive oil, garlic, thyme, salt and pepper
4. Close and lock the lid. Select MANUAL and cook at LOW pressure for 10 minutes.
5. Once cooking is complete, select Cancel and use a Natural Release for 10 minutes
6. Open the lid, Serve the fish with tomatoes mix

Dill Lemon Cod

(Prep + Cook Time: 15 minutes | **Serves:** 2)

Ingredients:
- 2 cod fillets
- 2 sprigs fresh dill
- 4 slices lemon
- 1 cup water
- 1/4 teaspoon garlic powder
- 2 tablespoon butter
- Salt and ground black pepper to taste

Directions:
1. Prepare the Instant Pot by adding the water to the pot and placing the steam rack in it.
2. Place the cod fillets on the steam rack. Sprinkle with salt, pepper and garlic powder.
3. On each fillet, place in order: 1 sprig of dill, 2 lemon slices and 1 tablespoon of butter.
4. Close and lock the lid. Select MANUAL and cook at HIGH pressure for 5 minutes.
5. Once pressure cooking is complete, use a Quick Release
6. Unlock and carefully open the lid, Serve

Alaskan Cod

(Prep + Cook Time: 15 minutes | **Serves:** 2)

Ingredients:
- 1 large fillet wild Alaskan Cod
- 2 tablespoon butter
- 1 cup cherry tomatoes, chopped.
- Salt and ground black pepper to taste

Directions:
1. Pour the tomatoes in the Instant Pot
2. Place the fish on top
3. Season with salt and pepper
4. Close and lock the lid. Select MANUAL and cook at HIGH pressure for 8 minutes.
5. When the timer beeps, use a Quick Release
6. Carefully unlock the lid, Place the butter on the cod fillet. Close the lid and let the dish sit for 1 minute then Serve

Cheesy Haddock

(Prep + Cook Time: 20 minutes | **Serves:** 2)

Ingredients:
- 1-pound fresh or frozen haddock fillets
- 1 tablespoon butter
- 1 tablespoon flour
- 1/2 cup milk
- 1 cup parmesan cheese, grated
- 1 cup water
- 1/4 teaspoon salt
- Ground black pepper to taste

Directions:
1. To preheat the Instant Pot, select SAUTÉ. Add the butter and melt it
2. Add the flour, salt and pepper, stir well. Sauté for 1 minute
3. Gradually pour the milk, cook for 3-5 minutes, stirring occasionally, until the sauce is smooth and thick.
4. Add the cheese to the pot and stir.
5. Press the CANCEL key to stop the SAUTÉ function.
6. In a pan, combine the fish fillets with sauce. Cover tightly with foil.
7. Clean the inner pot with water.
8. Pour a cup of water into the pot and set a steam rack in it
9. Place the pan on the steam rack.
10. Select MANUAL and cook at HIGH pressure for 5 minutes
11. Once pressure cooking is complete, use a Quick Release. Unlock and carefully open the lid and Serve

Seafood Gumbo Recipe

(Prep + Cook Time: 25 minutes | **Serves:** 4)

Ingredients:
- 12-ounce sea bass filets cut into 2" chunks
- 1-pound medium to large raw shrimp, deveined
- 1 ½ tablespoon Cajun or creole seasoning
- 1 ½ tablespoon ghee or avocado oil
- 1 yellow onion, diced
- 2 celery ribs, diced
- 3/4 cups bone broth
- 14-ounce diced tomatoes
- 1/8 cup tomato paste
- 2 bay leaves
- 1 bell pepper, diced
- Salt and ground black pepper to taste

Directions:
1. Rub all sides of the fillets with salt, pepper and half of Cajun or creole seasoning
2. Preheat the Instant Pot by selecting SAUTÉ. Add and heat the oil or melt ghee.
3. Add the fish to the pot and cook for 2 minutes per side
4. Remove the fillets from the pot. Add the remaining Cajun or creole seasoning, onions and celery
5. Sauté for 2 minutes until fragrant
6. Add the broth, tomatoes, tomato paste, bay leaves, bell pepper, shrimp and cooked fish
7. Press the CANCEL button to reset the cooking program, then press the MANUAL button and set the cooking time for 5 minutes at HIGH pressure.
8. Once pressure cooking is complete, use a Quick Release.
9. Unlock and carefully open the lid and Serve.

Almond Tilapia Recipe

(Prep + Cook Time: 15 minutes | **Serves:** 4)

Ingredients:
- 4 tilapia fillets
- 1/4 teaspoon lemon pepper
- 2 tablespoon Dijon mustard
- 2/3 cup sliced almonds
- 1 cup water
- 1 teaspoon olive oil

Directions:
1. Add the water to the Instant Pot and place the steam rack on top
2. In a bowl; combine the oil, lemon pepper and Dijon mustard, mix well
3. Brush the fish fillets with the mixture.
4. Transfer the fillets to the almond to coat both sides.
5. Place on the steam rack. Close and lock the lid.
6. Select MANUAL and cook at HIGH pressure for 5 minutes.
7. When the timer goes off, use a Quick Release
8. Carefully unlock the lid, then Serve.

Tasty Scallops

(Prep + Cook Time: 15 minutes | **Serves:** 2)

Ingredients:
- 1-pound sea scallops, shells removed
- 1/2 cup soy sauce
- 1/2 teaspoon ground ginger
- 1/2 teaspoon garlic powder
- 1 cup water
- 1 tablespoon olive oil
- 3 tablespoon maple syrup
- 1/2 teaspoon salt

Directions:
1. Prepare the Instant Pot by adding the water to the pot and placing the steam rack in it
2. In a 6 to 7-inch baking pan, put the scallops, olive oil, maple syrup, soy sauce, ginger, garlic powder and salt
3. Place the pan on the steam rack.
4. Select the STEAM setting and set the cooking time for 6 minutes
5. When the timer beeps, use a Quick Release
6. Carefully unlock the lid

Delicious Lobster Tails

(Prep + Cook Time: 30 minutes | **Serves:** 4)

Ingredients:
- 4 lobster tails, cut in half
- 1/2 cup white wine
- 1/2 cup butter, melted
- 1 cup water

Directions:
1. Pour the water and wine into the Instant Pot and insert a steamer basket
2. Place the lobster tails in the basket.
3. Select the MANUAL setting and set the cooking time for 5 minutes at LOW pressure.
4. Once cooking is complete, use a Natural Release for 10 minutes and then release any remaining pressure manually.
5. Open the lid, Transfer the legs to a serving bowl
6. Add melted butter and serve.

Crab Legs Recipe

(Prep + Cook Time: 10 minutes | **Serves:** 4-5)

Ingredients:

- 4 pounds' king crab legs, broken in half
- 3 lemon wedges
- 1 cup water
- 1/4 cup butter

Directions:

1. Pour the water into the Instant Pot and insert a steamer basket.
2. Place the crab legs on the rack
3. Close and lock the lid. Select MANUAL and cook at HIGH pressure for 3 minutes
4. When the timer goes off, use a Quick Release
5. Carefully unlock the lid, Transfer the legs to a serving bowl; add melted butter and lemon wedges and serve.

Crab in Coconut Milk

(Prep + Cook Time: 15 minutes | **Serves:** 2 - 3)

Ingredients:

- 1-pound crabs, halved
- 3 cloves garlic, minced
- 1 can coconut milk
- 1 thumb-size ginger, sliced
- 1 lemongrass stalk
- 1 tablespoon olive oil
- 1 onion, chopped.
- Salt and ground black pepper to taste

Directions:

1. Preheat the Instant Pot by selecting SAUTÉ. Add and heat the oil.
2. Add the onion and sauté for 2 minutes.
3. Add the garlic and sauté for 1 minute more
4. Add the crabs, coconut milk, ginger, lemongrass stalk, salt and pepper
5. Press the CANCEL key to stop the SAUTÉ function.
6. Close and lock the lid. Select MANUAL and cook at HIGH pressure for 6 minutes.
7. When the timer goes off, use a Quick Release.
8. Carefully unlock the lid and Serve

Salmon with Pecan

(Prep + Cook Time: 25 minutes | **Serves:** 2 - 3)

Ingredients:

- 2 salmon fillets
- 1/4 cup flour
- 1 egg, beaten
- 1/4 cup pecans, finely chopped.
- 1 cup water
- 1/2 cup olive oil
- 1/2 teaspoon salt

Directions:

1. Preheat the Instant Pot by selecting SAUTÉ. Add and heat the oil.
2. Season the fillets with salt
3. Dip the fillets in the flour, then in whisked egg, then in pecans
4. Add to the pot and brown the fish on both sides
5. Press the CANCEL button to stop the SAUTE function
6. Remove the salmon from the pot and place the steam rack in it. Pour in the water.
7. Place the fillets on the steam rack. Close and lock the lid
8. Select the MANUAL setting and set the cooking time for 4 minutes at HIGH pressure.
9. When the timer beeps, use a Natural Release for 10 minutes.
10. Uncover the pot, Serve.

Snacks & Appetizers

Pumpkin and Cinnamon Muffins

(Prep + Cook Time: 30 minutes | **Serves:** 18)

Ingredients:
- 3/4 cup pumpkin puree
- 1/4 cup coconut flour
- 1/2 cup erythritol
- 1/2 teaspoon nutmeg, ground.
- 4 tablespoon ghee
- 2 tablespoon flaxseed meal
- 1/2 teaspoon baking powder
- 1/2 teaspoon baking soda
- 1 ½ cups water
- one egg
- 1 teaspoon cinnamon powder

Directions:
1. In a bowl, mix ghee with pumpkin puree, egg, flaxseed meal, coconut flour, erythritol, baking soda, baking powder, nutmeg and cinnamon, stir well and divide into a greased muffin pan
2. Add the water to your instant pot, add the steamer basket, add muffin pan inside, close the lid and cook on High for 20 minutes
3. Arrange muffins on a platter and serve as a snack

Squash and Beets Dip

(Prep + Cook Time: 30 minutes | **Serves:** 8)

Ingredients:
- 4 beets; peeled and chopped.
- 1 butternut squash; peeled and chopped.
- 1 yellow onion; chopped.
- 1 bunch basil; chopped.
- 2 bay leaves
- 8 carrots; chopped.
- 2 tablespoon olive oil
- 5 celery ribs
- 8 garlic cloves; minced.
- 1 cup veggie stock
- 1/4 cup lemon juice
- Salt and black pepper to the taste

Directions:
1. Set your instant pot on Sauté mode; add oil, heat it up, add celery, carrots and onions, stir and cook for 3 minutes
2. Add beets, squash, garlic, stock, lemon juice, basil, bay leaves, salt and pepper; then stir well. seal the instant pot lid and cook on High for 12 minutes.
3. Discard bay leaves, blend dip using an immersion blender, transfer to a bowl and serve as a snack

Cajun Shrimp Appetizer

(Prep + Cook Time: 7 minutes | **Serves:** 4)

Ingredients:
- 1-pound shrimp, peeled and deveined
- 1/2 tablespoon Cajun seasoning
- 1 cup water
- 1 teaspoon extra virgin olive oil
- 1 bunch asparagus, trimmed

Directions:
1. Pour the water in your instant pot, add steamer basket, add shrimp and asparagus inside, drizzle Cajun seasoning and oil over them, toss a bit, close the lid and cook on High for 3 minutes
2. Arrange on appetizer plates and serve as an appetizer.

Shrimp Recipe

(Prep + Cook Time: 18 minutes | **Serves:** 2)

Ingredients:
- 1/2-pound big shrimp, peeled and deveined
- 2 teaspoon Worcestershire sauce
- 1 teaspoon Creole seasoning
- 2 teaspoon olive oil
- Juice of 1 lemon
- Salt and black pepper to the taste

Directions:
1. In your instant pot, mix shrimp with Worcestershire sauce, oil, lemon juice, salt, pepper and seasoning; then stir well. seal the instant pot lid and cook on High for 4 minutes
2. Arrange shrimp on a lined baking sheet, introduce in preheated broiler and broil for 4 minutes more.
3. Arrange on a platter and serve

Easy Leeks Platter

(Prep + Cook Time: 20 minutes | **Serves:** 4)

Ingredients:
- 4 leeks, washed, roots and ends cut off
- 1 tablespoon ghee
- 1/3 cup water
- Salt and black pepper to the taste

Directions:
1. Put leeks in your instant pot, add water, ghee, salt and pepper; then stir well. seal the instant pot lid and cook on High for 5 minutes.
2. Set the pot on sauté mode; cook leeks for a couple more minutes, arrange them on a platter and serve as an appetizer

Cauliflower Dip Recipe

(Prep + Cook Time: 20 minutes | **Serves:** 6)

Ingredients:
- 6 cups cauliflower florets
- 1/2 cup coconut milk
- 7 cups veggie stock
- 2 tablespoon ghee
- 8 garlic cloves; minced.
- Salt and black pepper to the taste

Directions:
1. Set your instant pot on Sauté mode; add ghee, heat it up, add garlic, salt and pepper, stir and cook for 2 minutes
2. Add stock and cauliflower to the pot, heat up, seal the instant pot lid and cook on High for 7 minutes.
3. Transfer cauliflower and 1 cup stock to your blender, add milk and blend well for a few minutes
4. Transfer to a bowl and serve as a dip for veggies

Easy Mango Dip

(Prep + Cook Time: 23 minutes | **Serves:** 4)

Ingredients:
- 2 mangos; peeled and chopped.
- 1 shallot; chopped.
- 1 ¼ apple cider vinegar
- 1/2 teaspoon cinnamon powder
- 2 red hot chilies; chopped.
- 1 tablespoon coconut oil
- 1/4 teaspoon cardamom powder
- 2 tablespoon ginger; minced.
- 1/4 cup raisins
- 5 tablespoon stevia
- 1 apple, cored and chopped.

Directions:
1. Set your instant pot on Sauté mode; add oil, heat it up, add shallot and ginger, stir and cook for 3 minutes
2. Add cinnamon, hot peppers, cardamom, mangos, apple, raisins, stevia and cider; then stir well. seal the instant pot lid and cook on High for 7 minutes.
3. Set the pot on simmer mode, cook your dip for 6 minutes more, transfer to bowls and serve cold as a snack.

Tomato Dip Recipe

(Prep + Cook Time: 25 minutes | **Serves:** 20)

Ingredients:
- 2-pound tomatoes; peeled and chopped.
- 1 apple, cored and chopped.
- 1 yellow onion; chopped.
- 3-ounce dates chopped.
- 3 teaspoon whole spice
- 1/2-pint balsamic vinegar
- 4 tablespoon stevia
- Salt to the taste

Directions:
1. Put tomatoes, apple, onion, dates, salt, whole spice and half of the vinegar in your instant pot; then stir well. seal the instant pot lid and cook on High for 10 minutes
2. Set the pot on simmer mode, add the rest of the vinegar and stevia; then stir well. cook for a few minutes more until it thickens, transfer to bowls and serve as a snack.

Prosciutto and Asparagus Appetizer

(Prep + Cook Time: 10 minutes | **Serves:** 4)

Ingredients:
- 8 asparagus spears
- 8-ounce prosciutto slices
- 2 cups water
- A pinch of salt

Directions:
1. Wrap asparagus spears in prosciutto slices and place them on a cutting board
2. Add the water to your instant pot, add a pinch of salt, add steamer basket, place asparagus inside, seal the instant pot lid and cook on High for 4 minutes.
3. Arrange asparagus on a platter and serve as an appetizer

Spicy Salsa

(Prep + Cook Time: 13 minutes | **Serves:** 4)

Ingredients:
- 2 avocados, pitted; peeled and chopped.
- 1 red onion; chopped.
- 2 tablespoon lime juice
- 2 tablespoon cumin powder
- 1/2 tomato; chopped.
- 3 jalapeno pepper; chopped.
- Salt and black pepper to the taste

Directions:
1. In your instant pot, mix onion with avocados, peppers, salt, black pepper, cumin, lime juice and tomato; then stir well. seal the instant pot lid and cook on Low for 3 minutes.
2. Divide into bowls and serve

Zucchini Rolls Recipe

(Prep + Cook Time: 18 minutes | **Serves:** 24)

Ingredients:

- 3 zucchinis, thinly sliced
- 2 tablespoon olive oil
- 24 basil leaves
- 2 tablespoon mint; chopped.
- 1 ½ cups water
- 1 ⅓ cup ricotta cheese
- Salt and black pepper to the taste
- 1/4 cup basil; chopped.
- Tomato sauce for serving

Directions:

1. Set your instant pot on sauté mode; add zucchini slices, drizzle the oil over them, season with salt and pepper, cook for 2 minutes on each side and transfer to a plate
2. In a bowl, mix ricotta with chopped basil, mint, salt and pepper; then stir well. divide this into zucchini slices and roll them
3. Add the water to your instant pot, add steamer basket, add zucchini rolls inside, seal the instant pot lid and cook on High for 3 minutes.
4. Arrange on a platter and serve with tomato sauce on the side

Tasty Okra Bowls

(Prep + Cook Time: 25 minutes | **Serves:** 6)

Ingredients:

- 28-ounce canned tomatoes; chopped.
- 1-pound okra, trimmed
- 6 scallions; chopped.
- 3 green bell peppers; chopped.
- 2 tablespoon olive oil
- 1 teaspoon stevia
- Salt and black pepper to the taste

Directions:

1. Set your instant pot on Sauté mode; add oil, heat it up, add scallions and bell peppers, stir and cook for 5 minutes.
2. Add okra, salt, pepper, stevia and tomatoes; then stir well. close the lid, cook on High for 10 minutes, divide into small bowls and serve as an appetizer salad

Artichokes

(Prep + Cook Time: 25 minutes | **Serves:** 4)

Ingredients:

- 4 big artichokes, trimmed
- 2 cups water
- 2 teaspoon balsamic vinegar
- Salt and black pepper to the taste
- 2 tablespoon lemon juice
- 1/4 cup olive oil
- 2 garlic cloves; minced.
- 1 teaspoon oregano; dried

Directions:

1. Add the water to your instant pot, add the steamer basket, add artichokes inside, seal the instant pot lid and cook on High for 8 minutes
2. In a bowl, mix lemon juice with vinegar, oil, salt, pepper, garlic and oregano and stir very well.
3. Cut artichokes in halves, add them to lemon and vinegar mix, toss well, place them on preheated grill over medium high heat, cook for 3 minutes on each side, arrange them on a platter and serve as an appetizer

Tomatoes Appetizer

(Prep + Cook Time: 20 minutes | **Serves:** 4)

Ingredients:
- 4 tomatoes, tops cut off and pulp scooped
- 1/2 cup water
- 1 yellow onion; chopped.
- 1 tablespoon ghee
- 2 tablespoon celery; chopped.
- 1/2 cup mushrooms; chopped.
- 1 cup cottage cheese
- 1/4 teaspoon caraway seeds
- Salt and black pepper to the taste
- 1 tablespoon parsley; chopped.

Directions:
1. Set your instant pot on sauté mode; add ghee, heat it up, add onion and celery, stir and cook for 3 minutes.
2. Add tomato pulp, mushrooms, salt, pepper, cheese, parsley and caraway seeds; then stir well. cook for 3 minutes more and stuff tomatoes with this mix
3. Add the water to your instant pot, add the steamer basket, and stuffed tomatoes inside, seal the instant pot lid and cook on High for 4 minutes
4. Arrange tomatoes on a platter and serve as an appetizer

Instant Chili Dip

(Prep + Cook Time: 20 minutes | **Serves:** 8)

Ingredients:
- 5 ancho chilies; dried and chopped.
- 2 garlic cloves; minced.
- 1 ½ cups water
- 2 tablespoon balsamic vinegar
- 1/2 teaspoon cumin, ground.
- 1 ½ teaspoon stevia
- 1 tablespoon oregano; chopped.
- Salt and black pepper to the taste

Directions:
1. In your instant pot mix water chilies, garlic, salt, pepper, stevia, cumin and oregano; then stir well. seal the instant pot lid and cook on High for 8 minutes
2. Blend using an immersion blender, add vinegar; then stir well. set the pot on simmer mode and cook your chili dip until it thickens
3. Serve with veggie sticks on the side as a snack

French Endives

(Prep + Cook Time: 17 minutes | **Serves:** 4)

Ingredients:
- 4 endives, trimmed and halved
- 1 tablespoon ghee
- 1 tablespoon lemon juice
- Salt and black pepper to the taste

Directions:
1. Set your instant pot on Sauté mode; add ghee, heat it up, add endives, season with salt and pepper, drizzle lemon juice, close the lid and cook them on High for 7 minutes
2. Arrange endives on a platter, drizzle some of the cooking juice over them and serve as an appetizer.

Artichoke Dip Recipe

(Prep + Cook Time: 15 minutes | **Serves:** 6)

Ingredients:
- 14-ounce canned artichoke hearts
- 16-ounce parmesan cheese, grated
- 10-ounce spinach, torn
- 1 teaspoon onion powder
- 8-ounce cream cheese
- 8-ounce mozzarella cheese, shredded.
- 1/2 cup chicken stock
- 1/2 cup coconut cream
- 1/2 cup mayonnaise
- 3 garlic cloves; minced.

Directions:

1. In your instant pot, mix artichokes with stock, garlic, spinach, cream cheese, coconut cream, onion powder and mayo; then stir well. seal the instant pot lid and cook on High for 5 minutes
2. Add mozzarella and parmesan, stir well, transfer to a bowl and serve as a snack.

Turkey Meatballs

(Prep + Cook Time: 16 minutes | **Serves:** 16 p)

Ingredients:

- 1-pound turkey meat, ground.
- one egg
- 1/2 teaspoon garlic powder
- 1/2 cup mozzarella cheese, shredded.
- 2 tablespoon olive oil
- 1/4 cup tomato paste
- 2 tablespoon basil; chopped.
- 1/4 cup coconut flour
- 2 tablespoon sun-dried tomatoes; chopped.
- Salt and black pepper to the taste

Directions:

1. In a bowl, mix turkey with salt, pepper, egg, flour, garlic powder, sun-dried tomatoes, mozzarella and basil, stir well and shape 12 meatballs out of this mix
2. Set your instant pot on sauté mode; add oil, heat it up, add meatballs, stir and brown for 2 minutes on each side.
3. Add tomato paste over them, toss a bit, seal the instant pot lid and cook on High for 8 minutes.
4. Arrange meatballs on a platter and serve them right away

Shrimp Appetizer

(Prep + Cook Time: 15 minutes | **Serves:** 4)

Ingredients:

- 1-pound shrimp, peeled and deveined
- 3/4 cup pineapple juice
- 2 tablespoon coconut aminos
- 3 tablespoon vinegar
- 1 cup chicken stock
- 3 tablespoon stevia

Directions:

1. Put shrimp, pineapple juice, stock, aminos and stevia in your instant pot, stir a bit, seal the instant pot lid and cook on High for 4 minutes
2. Arrange shrimp on a platter, drizzle cooking juices all over and serve as an appetizer

Eggplant Spread

(Prep + Cook Time: 20 minutes | **Serves:** 6)

Ingredients:

- 2-pound eggplant, peeled and cut into medium chunks
- 3 olives, pitted and sliced
- 1/4 cup olive oil
- 4 garlic cloves; minced.
- 1/2 cup water
- 1/4 cup lemon juice
- 1 bunch thyme; chopped.
- 1 tablespoon sesame seed paste
- Salt and black pepper to the taste

Directions:

1. Set your instant pot on sauté mode; add oil, heat it up, add eggplant pieces, stir and cook for 5 minutes.
2. Add garlic, water, salt and pepper; then stir well. close the lid, cook on High for 3 minutes, transfer to a blender, add sesame seed paste, lemon juice and thyme, stir and pulse really well
3. Transfer to bowls, sprinkle olive slices on top and serve as an appetizer.

Italian Dip

(Prep + Cook Time: 30 minutes | **Serves:** 4)

Ingredients:
- 4-ounce cream cheese, soft
- 4 black olives, pitted and chopped.
- 2 cups water
- 1/2 cup mozzarella cheese
- 1/4 cup coconut cream
- 1/4 cup mayonnaise
- 1/4 cup parmesan cheese, grated
- 1/2 cup tomato sauce
- 1 tablespoon green bell pepper; chopped.
- 6 pepperoni slices; chopped.
- 1/2 teaspoon Italian seasoning
- Salt and black pepper to the taste

Directions:
1. In a bowl, mix cream cheese with mozzarella, coconut cream, mayo, salt and pepper, stir and divide this into 4 ramekins.
2. Layer tomato sauce, parmesan cheese, bell pepper, pepperoni, Italian seasoning and black olives on top
3. Add the water to your instant pot, add the steamer basket, add ramekins inside, seal the instant pot lid and cook on High for 20 minutes.
4. Serve this dip warm with veggie sticks on the side.

Zucchini Dip Recipe

(Prep + Cook Time: 20 minutes | **Serves:** 4)

Ingredients:
- 2-pound zucchini; chopped.
- 1 yellow onion; chopped.
- 1 tablespoon olive oil
- 2 garlic cloves; minced.
- 1/2 cup water
- 1 bunch basil; chopped.
- Salt and white pepper to the taste

Directions:
1. Set your instant pot on Sauté mode; add oil, heat it up, add onion, stir and sauté for 3 minutes
2. Add zucchini, salt, pepper and water; then stir well. seal the instant pot lid and cook on High for 3 minutes
3. Add garlic and basil, blend everything using an immersion blender, set the pot on simmer mode and cook your dip for a few more minutes until it thickens.
4. Transfer to a bowl and serve as a tasty snack

Zucchini Hummus Recipe

(Prep + Cook Time: 16 minutes | **Serves:** 4)

Ingredients:
- 4 cups zucchini; chopped.
- 3 tablespoon veggie stock
- 1/4 cup olive oil
- 1/2 cup lemon juice
- 1 tablespoon cumin, ground.
- 3/4 cup sesame seeds paste
- 4 garlic cloves; minced.
- Salt and black pepper to the taste

Directions:
1. Set your instant pot on sauté mode; add half of the oil, heat it up, add zucchini and garlic, stir and cook for 2 minutes
2. Add stock, salt and pepper, close the lid and cook on High for 4 minutes more
3. Transfer zucchini to your blender, add the rest of the oil, sesame seeds paste, lemon juice and cumin, pulse well, transfer to bowls and serve as a snack

Italian Mussels Appetizer

(Prep + Cook Time: 20 minutes | **Serves:** 4)

Ingredients:
- 28-ounce canned tomatoes; chopped.
- 2 jalapeno peppers; chopped.
- 1/2 cup white onion; chopped.
- 1/2 cup basil; chopped.
- 1/4 cup balsamic vinegar
- 1/4 cup veggie stock
- 1/4 cup olive oil
- 2-pound mussels, scrubbed
- 2 tablespoon red pepper flakes, crushed.
- 2 garlic cloves; minced.
- Salt to the taste

Directions:
1. Set your instant pot on Sauté mode; add oil heat it up, add tomatoes, onion, jalapenos, stock, vinegar, garlic and pepper flakes, stir and cook for 5 minutes.
2. Add mussels; then stir well. close the lid, cook on Low for 4 minutes, add salt and basil; then stir well. divide everything into small bowls and serve as an appetizer

Surprising Oysters

(Prep + Cook Time: 16 minutes | **Serves:** 3)

Ingredients:
- 6 big oysters, shucked
- 2 tablespoon melted ghee
- 1 ½ cups water
- 1 lemon cut into wedges
- 1 tablespoon parsley
- 3 garlic cloves; minced.
- A pinch of sweet paprika

Directions:
1. Divide ghee, parsley, paprika and garlic in each oyster.
2. Add the water to your instant pot, add steamer basket, add oysters, close the lid and cook on High for 6 minutes
3. Arrange oysters on a platter and serve with lemon wedges on the side

Crab and Cheese Dip

(Prep + Cook Time: 30 minutes | **Serves:** 8)

Ingredients:
- 8 bacon strips, sliced
- 8-ounce cream cheese
- 12-ounce crab meat
- 4 garlic cloves; minced.
- 4 green onions; minced.
- 1 cup parmesan cheese, grated
- 2 poblano pepper; chopped.
- 2 tablespoon lemon juice
- 1/2 cup mayonnaise
- 1/2 cup coconut cream
- Salt and black pepper to the taste

Directions:
1. Set your instant pot on sauté mode; add bacon, cook until it's crispy, transfer to paper towels, drain grease and leave aside
2. In a bowl, mix coconut cream with cream cheese, mayo, half of the parmesan, poblano peppers, garlic, lemon juice, green onions, salt, pepper, crab meat and bacon and stir really well.
3. Clean your instant pot, add crab mix, spread the rest of the parmesan on top, seal the instant pot lid and cook on High for 14 minutes
4. Divide into bowls and serve as a snack.

Sausage and Cheese Dip

(Prep + Cook Time: 15 minutes | **Serves:** 4)

Ingredients:
- 2 cups Mexican cheese, cut into chunks
- 1 cup Italian sausage; cooked and chopped.
- 5-ounce canned tomatoes and green chilies; chopped.
- 4 tablespoon water

Directions:
1. In your instant pot, mix sausage with cheese, tomatoes and chilies and water; then stir well. close the lid, cook on High for 5 minutes.
2. blend a bit using an immersion blender, transfer to a bowl and serve as a dip

Asian Squid Appetizer

(Prep + Cook Time: 25 minutes | **Serves:** 4)

Ingredients:
- 4 squid, tentacles from 1 squid separated and chopped.
- 1 tablespoon mirin
- 2 tablespoon stevia
- 4 tablespoon coconut aminos
- 1 cup cauliflower rice
- 14-ounce fish stock

Directions:
1. In a bowl, mix chopped tentacles with cauliflower rice, stir well and stuff each squid with the mix.
2. Place squid in your instant pot, add stock, aminos, mirin and stevia; then stir well. seal the instant pot lid and cook on High for 15 minutes
3. Arrange stuffed squid on a platter and serve as an appetizer.

Mussels Bowls

(Prep + Cook Time: 12 minutes | **Serves:** 4)

Ingredients:
- 2-pound mussels, scrubbed
- 12-ounce veggie stock
- 1 tablespoon olive oil
- 8-ounce spicy sausage; chopped.
- 1 tablespoon sweet paprika
- 1 yellow onion; chopped.

Directions:
1. Set your instant pot on Sauté mode; add oil, heat it up, add onion and sausages, stir and cook for 5 minutes.
2. Add stock, paprika and mussels; then stir well. close the lid, cook on Low for 2 minutes, divide into bowls and serve as an appetizer

Salmon Patties

(Prep + Cook Time: 17 minutes | **Serves:** 4)

Ingredients:
- 1-pound salmon meat; minced.
- 1 teaspoon olive oil
- one egg, whisked
- 4 tablespoon coconut flour
- 2 tablespoon lemon zest, grated
- Salt and black pepper to the taste
- Arugula leaves for serving

Directions:
1. Put salmon in your food processor, blend it, transfer to a bowl, add salt, pepper, lemon zest, coconut and egg, stir well and shape small patties out of this mix.
2. Set your instant pot on sauté mode; add oil, heat it up, add patties and cook them for 3 minutes on each side.
3. Arrange arugula on a platter, add salmon patties on top and serve as an appetizer

Delicious Shrimp Appetizer

(Prep + Cook Time: 30 minutes | **Serves:** 16)

Ingredients:

- 10-ounce shrimp, cooked, peeled and deveined
- 11 prosciutto slices
- 1/3 cup blackberries, ground.
- 1/3 cup veggie stock.
- 2 tablespoon olive oil
- 1 tablespoon mint; chopped.
- 2 tablespoon erythritol

Directions:

1. Wrap each shrimp in prosciutto slices and drizzle oil over them.
2. In your instant pot, mix blackberries with mint, stock and erythritol; then stir well. set on simmer mode and cook for 2 minutes
3. Add steamer basket, and wrapped shrimp, close the lid and cook on High for 2 minutes
4. Arrange wrapped shrimp on a platter, drizzle mint sauce all over and serve

Mushroom Dip

(Prep + Cook Time: 45 minutes | **Serves:** 6)

Ingredients:

- 10-ounce shiitake mushrooms; chopped.
- 10-ounce Portobello mushrooms; chopped.
- 10-ounce cremini mushrooms; chopped.
- 1 tablespoon thyme; chopped.
- 1/2 cup coconut cream
- 1 yellow onion; chopped.
- 1/4 cup olive oil
- 1 tablespoon coconut flour
- 1-ounce parmesan cheese, grated
- 1 tablespoon parsley; chopped.
- 3 garlic cloves; minced.
- 1 ¼ cup chicken stock
- Salt and black pepper to the taste

Directions:

1. Set your instant pot on Sauté mode; add oil, heat it up, add onion, salt, pepper, flour, garlic and thyme, stir well and cook for 5 minutes
2. Add stock, shiitake, cremini and Portobello mushrooms; then stir well. seal the instant pot lid and cook on High for 25 minutes.
3. Add cream, cheese and parsley; then stir well. set the pot on Simmer mode, cook dip for 5 minutes more, transfer to bowls and serve as a dip.

Instant Cod Puddings

(Prep + Cook Time: 30 minutes | **Serves:** 4)

Ingredients:

- 1-pound cod fillets, skinless, boneless cut into medium pieces
- 2 tablespoon parsley; chopped.
- 4-ounce coconut flour
- 2 teaspoon lemon juice
- 2 eggs, whisked
- 2-ounce ghee, melted
- 1/2-pint coconut milk, hot
- 1/2-pint shrimp sauce
- 1/2-pint water
- Salt and black pepper to the taste

Directions:

1. In a bowl, mix fish with flour, lemon juice, shrimp sauce, parsley, eggs, salt and pepper and stir.
2. Add milk and melted ghee, stir well and leave aside for a couple of minutes.
3. Divide this mix greased ramekins
4. Add the water to your instant pot, add the steamer basket, add puddings inside, seal the instant pot lid and cook on High for 15 minutes
5. Serve the warm

Zucchini Appetizer Salad Recipe

(Prep + Cook Time: 16 minutes | **Serves:** 4)

Ingredients:
- 1 zucchini, roughly sliced
- 1/4 cup tomato sauce
- 1 cup mozzarella, shredded.
- A pinch of cumin, ground.
- A drizzle of olive oil
- Salt and black pepper to the taste

Directions:
1. In your instant pot, mix zucchini with oil, tomato sauce, salt, pepper and cumin, toss a bit, seal the instant pot lid and cook on High for 6 minutes
2. Divide between appetizer plates and serve right away.

Sausage and Shrimp Appetizer

(Prep + Cook Time: 15 minutes | **Serves:** 4)

Ingredients:
- 1 ½-pound shrimp, heads removed
- 12-ounce sausage; cooked and chopped.
- 1 teaspoon red pepper flakes, crushed.
- 1 tablespoon old bay seasoning
- 16-ounce chicken stock
- 2 sweet onions, cut into wedges
- 8 garlic cloves; minced.
- Salt and black pepper to the taste

Directions:
1. In your instant pot, mix stock with old bay seasoning, pepper flakes, salt, black pepper, onions, garlic, sausage and shrimp; then stir well. seal the instant pot lid and cook on High for 5 minutes
2. Divide into small bowls and serve as an appetizer

Spicy Mussels Recipe

(Prep + Cook Time: 15 minutes | **Serves:** 4)

Ingredients:
- 2-pound mussels, scrubbed
- 1/2 cup chicken stock
- 1/2 teaspoon red pepper flakes
- 2 tablespoon olive oil
- 2 teaspoon garlic; minced.
- 2 teaspoon oregano; dried
- 1 yellow onion; chopped.
- 14-ounce tomatoes; chopped.

Directions:
1. Set your instant pot on Sauté mode; add oil, heat it up, add onions, stir and sauté for 3 minutes
2. Add pepper flakes, garlic, stock, tomatoes, oregano and mussels; then stir well. seal the instant pot lid and cook on Low for 3 minutes
3. Divide mussels into small bowls and serve as an appetizer.

English Chicken Wings

(Prep + Cook Time: 27 minutes | **Serves:** 6)

Ingredients:
- 6-pound chicken wings, cut into halves
- one egg
- 1/2 cup parmesan cheese, grated
- 1/2 teaspoon Italian seasoning
- 1 teaspoon garlic powder
- 2 tablespoon ghee
- 2 cups water
- Salt and black pepper to the taste
- A pinch of red pepper flakes, crushed.

Directions:
1. Pour the water in your instant pot, add the trivet, add chicken wings, seal the instant pot lid and cook on High for 7 minutes
2. Meanwhile, in your blender, mix ghee with cheese, egg, salt, pepper, pepper flakes, garlic powder and Italian seasoning and blend very well

3. Arrange chicken wings on a lined baking sheet, pour cheese sauce over them, introduce in preheated broiler and broil for 5 minutes.
4. Flip and broil for 5 minutes more, arrange them all on a platter and serve

Chili Balls

(Prep + Cook Time: 15 minutes | **Serves:** 3)

Ingredients:
- 3 bacon slices
- 1 cup water
- 3-ounce cream cheese
- 1/4 teaspoon onion powder
- 2 jalapeno peppers; chopped.
- 1/2 teaspoon parsley; dried
- 1/4 teaspoon garlic powder
- Salt and black pepper to the taste

Directions:
1. Set your instant pot on sauté mode; add bacon, cook for a couple of minutes, transfer to paper towels drain grease and crumble it
2. In a bowl, mix cream cheese with jalapenos, bacon, onion, garlic powder, parsley, salt and pepper, stir well and shape balls out of this mix.
3. Clean the pot, add the water, and the steamer basket, add spicy balls inside, seal the instant pot lid and cook on High for 2 minutes.
4. Arrange balls on a platter and serve as an appetizer

Spinach Dip Recipe

(Prep + Cook Time: 30 minutes | **Serves:** 6)

Ingredients:
- 6 bacon slices; cooked and crumbled.
- 1 tablespoon garlic; minced.
- 5-ounce spinach
- 1 ½ cups water
- 1/2 cup coconut cream
- 8-ounce cream cheese, soft
- 1 ½ tablespoon parsley; chopped
- 2.5-ounce parmesan, grated
- 1 tablespoon lemon juice
- A drizzle of olive oil
- Salt and black pepper to the taste

Directions:
1. Set your instant pot on sauté mode; add oil heat it up, add spinach; then stir well. cook for 1 minute and transfer to a bowl
2. Add cream cheese, garlic, salt, pepper, coconut cream, parsley, bacon, lemon juice and parmesan, stir well and divide this into 6 ramekins
3. Add the water to your instant pot, add steamer basket, add ramekins inside, seal the instant pot lid and cook on High for 15 minutes
4. Introduce in a preheated broiler for 4 minutes and serve right away.

Stuffed Clams

(Prep + Cook Time: 14 minutes | **Serves:** 4)

Ingredients:
- 24 clams, shucked
- 1/4 cup parsley; chopped.
- 1/4 cup parmesan cheese, grated
- 2 cups water
- 3 garlic cloves; minced.
- 1 teaspoon oregano; dried
- 1 cup almonds, crushed.
- 4 tablespoon ghee
- Lemon wedges

Directions:
1. In a bowl, mix crushed almonds with parmesan, oregano, parsley, butter and garlic, stir and divide this into exposed clams
2. Add the water to your instant pot, add steamer basket, add clams inside, seal the instant pot lid and cook on High for 4 minutes.
3. Arrange clams on a platter and serve them as an appetizer with lemon wedges on the side.

Mushrooms and Mustard Dip

(Prep + Cook Time: 20 minutes | **Serves:** 4)

Ingredients:
- 6-ounce mushrooms; chopped.
- 3 tablespoon olive oil
- 1 thyme sprigs
- 1 garlic clove; minced.
- 4-ounce beef stock
- 1 tablespoon mustard
- 2 tablespoon coconut cream
- 2 tablespoon parsley; finely chopped.
- 1 tablespoon balsamic vinegar

Directions:
1. Set your instant pot on Sauté mode; add oil, heat it up, add thyme, mushrooms and garlic, stir and sauté for 4 minutes.
2. Add vinegar and stock; then stir well. close the lid, cook on High for 3 minutes, discard thyme, add mustard, coconut cream and parsley; then stir well. set the pot on simmer mode and cook for 3 minutes more.
3. Divide into bowls and serve as a snack

Stuffed Mushrooms and Shrimp

(Prep + Cook Time: 25 minutes | **Serves:** 5)

Ingredients:
- 24-ounce white mushroom caps
- 1 teaspoon curry powder
- 4-ounce cream cheese, soft
- 1 cup shrimp, cooked, peeled, deveined and chopped.
- 1/4 cup mayo
- 1 teaspoon garlic powder
- 1 small yellow onion; chopped.
- 1/4 cup coconut cream
- 1/2 cup Mexican cheese, shredded.
- 1 ½ cups water
- Salt and black pepper to the taste

Directions:
1. In a bowl, mix mayo with garlic powder, onion, curry powder, cream cheese, cream, Mexican cheese, shrimp, salt and pepper, stir and stuff mushrooms with this mix
2. Add the water to your instant pot, add steamer basket, add mushrooms inside, close the lid and cook on High for 14 minutes
3. Arrange mushrooms on a platter and serve as an appetizer.

Appetizing Cranberry Dip

(Prep + Cook Time: 15 minutes | **Serves:** 4)

Ingredients:
- 2 ½ teaspoon lemon zest, grated
- 3 tablespoon lemon juice
- 12-ounce cranberries
- 4 tablespoon stevia

Directions:
1. In your instant pot, mix lemon juice with stevia, lemon zest and cranberries; then stir well. seal the instant pot lid and cook on High for 2 minutes
2. Set the pot on simmer mode, stir your dip for a couple more minutes, transfer to a bowl and serve with some biscuits as a snack.

Avocado Dip Recipe

(Prep + Cook Time: 12 minutes | **Serves:** 4)

Ingredients:

- 1/4 cup erythritol powder
- 2 avocados, pitted, peeled and halved
- Juice from 2 limes
- 1/4 teaspoon stevia
- 1 cup coconut milk
- 1 cup water
- 1/2 cup cilantro; chopped.
- Zest of 2 limes, grated

Directions:

1. Add the water to your instant pot, add the steamer basket, add avocado halves, seal the instant pot lid and cook on High for 2 minutes
2. Transfer to your blender, add lime juice and cilantro and pulse well.
3. Add coconut milk, lime zest, stevia and erythritol powder, pulse again, divide into bowls and serve

Mussels Appetizer

(Prep + Cook Time: 17 minutes | **Serves:** 4)

Ingredients:

- 2-pound mussels, cleaned and scrubbed
- 1/2 cup water
- 1 white onion; chopped.
- 1/2 cup veggie stock
- 2 garlic cloves; minced.
- A drizzle of extra virgin olive oil

Directions:

1. Set instant pot on Sauté mode; add oil, heat it up, garlic and onion, stir and cook for 4 minutes.
2. Add stock, stir and cook for 1 minute
3. Add the steamer basket, add mussels inside, seal the instant pot lid and cook on High for 2 minutes.
4. Arrange mussels on a platter and serve with some of the cooking juices drizzled all over

Mussels and Clams

(Prep + Cook Time: 23 minutes | **Serves:** 4)

Ingredients:

- 30 mussels, scrubbed
- 2 chorizo links, sliced
- 1 yellow onion; chopped.
- 15 small clams
- 10-ounce veggie stock
- 2 tablespoon parsley; chopped.
- 1 teaspoon olive oil
- Lemon wedges for serving

Directions:

1. Set your instant pot on Sauté mode; add oil, heat it up, add onion and chorizo, stir and cook for 3 minutes.
2. Add clams, mussels and stock; then stir well. close the lid, cook on High for 10 minutes, add parsley; then stir well. divide into bowls and serve as an appetizer with lemon wedges on the side

Tuna Patties Appetizer

(Prep + Cook Time: 18 minutes | **Serves:** 12)

Ingredients:

- 15-ounce canned tuna, drained and flaked
- 1/2 cup red onion; chopped.
- 1 teaspoon parsley; dried
- 1 teaspoon garlic powder
- 1 ½ cups water
- 3 eggs
- 1/2 teaspoon dill; chopped.
- Salt and black pepper to the taste
- A drizzle of olive oil

Directions:

1. In a bowl, mix tuna with salt, pepper, dill, parsley, onion, garlic powder and eggs, stir and shape medium patties out of this mix
2. Set your instant pot on sauté mode; add a drizzle of oil, heat it up, add tuna patties, cook them for 2 minutes on each side and transfer to a plate.
3. Clean the pot, add the water, add steamer basket, add tuna cakes, close the lid and cook on High for 4 minutes
4. Arrange patties on a platter and serve.

Vegetable Recipes

Scalloped Potatoes.

(Prep + Cook Time: 25 minutes | **Serves:** 2 - 3)

Ingredients:

- 6 medium potatoes, peeled and thinly-sliced
- 1 cup chicken broth
- 1/3 cup sour cream
- 1/3 cup milk
- 2 tablespoon potato starch
- 1/4 teaspoon paprika
- 1 tablespoon chives, chopped.
- 1/2 teaspoon kosher salt
- 1/4 teaspoon ground black pepper

Directions:

1. Add the potatoes, chives, salt and pepper to the Instant Pot
2. Pour in the broth and stir. Close and lock the lid.
3. Select MANUAL and cook at HIGH pressure for 5 minutes.
4. Once pressure cooking is complete, select CANCEL and use a Quick Release
5. Carefully unlock the lid, Transfer the potatoes to the baking sheet. Preheat the oven to broil.
6. In the Instant Pot, combine the remaining liquid, sour cream, milk and potato starch
7. Select SAUTÉ and cook the mixture for 1 minute, until thickened
8. Pour the mixture over the potatoes and stir. Sprinkle with paprika and place under the broiler for 3 to 5 minutes for a browned top, serve and enjoy

Crisped Gold Potatoes

(Prep + Cook Time: 50 minutes | **Serves:** 4)

Ingredients:

- 1 ½ pounds' Yukon gold potatoes, cut in half
- 1 teaspoon ground black pepper
- 1/2 cup water or broth
- 2 tablespoon olive oil
- 2 tablespoon butter
- 1 teaspoon sea salt

Directions:

1. Select the SAUTÉ setting on the Instant Pot and heat the oil. Add the butter and melt it.
2. Add the potatoes and sauté, stirring occasionally, for 10 minutes until the halves have turned slightly golden.
3. Season with salt and pepper, stir well
4. Pour in the water. Close and lock the lid
5. Press the CANCEL button to reset the cooking program, then press the MANUAL button and set the cooking time for 6 minutes at HIGH pressure
6. Once cooking is complete, select CANCEL and let Naturally Release for 20 minutes. Release any remaining steam manually
7. Uncover the pot, Taste for seasoning and add more salt if needed and serve

Coconut Butter Garlic Potatoes

(Prep + Cook Time: 20 minutes | **Serves:** 2)

Ingredients:

- 1-pound new potatoes
- 3 tablespoon coconut butter
- 2/3 cup water
- Handful fresh herbs
- 2 cloves garlic, diced
- Salt and ground black pepper to taste

Directions:

1. Prepare the Instant Pot by adding the water to the pot and placing the steamer basket in it.
2. Place the new potatoes in the basket

3. Add the garlic, coconut butter, herbs and season with salt and pepper.
4. Close and lock the lid. Select MANUAL and cook at HIGH pressure for 4 minutes
5. Once pressure cooking is complete, turn off the Instant Pot and allow 5 minutes' rest time and then do a Quick Release
6. Carefully unlock the lid Transfer the potatoes to a serving bowl and serve

Mushrooms and Broccoli

(Prep + Cook Time: 20 minutes | **Serves:** 2 - 3)

Ingredients:
- 1 cup mushrooms, sliced
- 2 cups broccoli florets
- 1 cup vegetable broth
- 2 tablespoon coconut oil
- 1 tablespoon soy sauce

Directions:
1. To preheat the Instant Pot, select SAUTÉ. Once hot, add the coconut oil to the pot
2. Add the mushrooms and sauté for 5 minutes.
3. Add the soy sauce and broccoli and cook for another 1 minute
4. Pour in the broth and stir. Close and lock the lid.
5. Press the CANCEL button to reset the cooking program, then press the MANUAL button and set the cooking time for 2 minutes at HIGH pressure
6. When the timer beeps, use a Quick Release.
7. Carefully unlock the lid, let it cool a few minutes before serving

Spicy and Sweet Cabbage

(Prep + Cook Time: 25 minutes | **Serves:** 4)

Ingredients:
- 1 cabbage (3 pound), cut into 6 to 8 wedges
- 1 ½ cups + 2 teaspoon water
- 1 tablespoon olive oil
- 1/4 cup apple cider vinegar
- 1/2 teaspoon cayenne pepper
- 1 big carrot, grated
- 2 teaspoon cornstarch
- 1 teaspoon brown sugar
- 1/2 teaspoon red pepper flakes

Directions:
1. Preheat the Instant Pot by selecting SAUTÉ. Add and heat the oil
2. Add the cabbage and sauté for 3 minutes on one side.
3. Add 1 ½ cups of water, vinegar, sugar, pepper flakes, cayenne pepper and carrot. Mix well.
4. Press the CANCEL key to stop the SAUTÉ function.
5. Close and lock the lid. Select MANUAL and cook at HIGH pressure for 5 minutes
6. Once timer goes off, use a Quick Release. Carefully unlock the lid,
7. Transfer the cabbage and carrot to a serving bowl.
8. Mix together the cornstarch and 2 teaspoon of water. Add the mixture to the pot
9. Select SAUTÉ and cook the sauce until thickened enough. Pour the sauce over cabbage and Serve.

Special Potato Hash

(Prep + Cook Time: 25 minutes | **Serves:** 4-5)

Ingredients:
- 5 medium potatoes, peeled and roughly chopped.
- 5 eggs, whisked
- 1 cup ham, chopped.
- 1 cup cheddar cheese, shredded
- 1 tablespoon olive oil
- 1/4 cup water
- Salt and ground black pepper to the taste

Directions:

1. Select the SAUTÉ setting on the Instant Pot and heat the oil.
2. Add the potatoes and sauté for 3 to 4 minutes, until slightly brown.
3. Add eggs, cheese, ham, water, salt and pepper, Stir well. Close and lock the lid
4. Press the CANCEL button to stop the SAUTE function, then select the MANUAL setting and set the cooking time for 5 minutes at HIGH pressure.
5. Once pressure cooking is complete, select CANCEL and use a Quick Release.
6. Carefully unlock the lid, Serve warm

Brussels Sprouts with Bacon.

(Prep + Cook Time: 15 minutes | **Serves:** 2 - 3)

Ingredients:

- 1-pound Brussels sprouts, trimmed and cut into halves
- 1/2 cup bacon, chopped.
- 1 cup chicken broth
- 1 tablespoon butter
- 1 tablespoon mustard
- 2 tablespoon dill, chopped.
- Salt and ground black pepper to taste

Directions:

1. Select the SAUTÉ setting on the Instant Pot and add the bacon. Sauté until it is crispy
2. Add the Brussels sprouts and cook, stirring occasionally, for 2 minutes more
3. Add the mustard and broth. Season with salt and pepper, stir.
4. Press the CANCEL key to stop the SAUTÉ function.
5. Close and lock the lid. Select MANUAL and cook at HIGH pressure for 4 minutes
6. When the timer beeps, use a Quick Release.
7. Carefully unlock the lid, Add the butter and sprinkle with dill, stir
8. Select SAUTÉ again and cook for 1 minute more and Serve.

Potatoes Au Gratin.

(Prep + Cook Time: 35 minutes | **Serves:** 4-5)

Ingredients:

- 6 potatoes, peeled and sliced
- 1/2 cup sour cream
- 1 cup Monterey jack cheese, shredded
- 2 tablespoon butter
- 1/2 cup yellow onion, chopped.
- 1 cup chicken stock
- Salt and ground black pepper to taste

For the topping:

- 1 cup bread crumbs
- 3 tablespoon melted butter

Directions:

1. To preheat the Instant Pot, select SAUTÉ. Once hot, add the butter and melt it.
2. Add the onion and sauté for about 5 minutes, until softened
3. Pour in the stock and put a steam rack in the pot.
4. Place the potatoes on the rack. Close and lock the lid.
5. Press the CANCEL button to stop the SAUTE function, then select the MANUAL setting and set the cooking time for 5 minutes at HIGH pressure.
6. In a small bowl, combine the bread crumbs and 3 tablespoon butter. Mix well
7. When the timer goes off, use a Quick Release.
8. Carefully open the lid, Remove the potatoes and steam rack from the pot
9. Add the cream and cheese to the pot and stir well. Return the potatoes, season with salt and pepper and gently stir
10. Preheat the oven to broil.
11. Pour the mixture in a baking dish, top with bread crumbs mix and broil for 7 minutes, and Serve

IP Steamed Broccoli

(Prep + Cook Time: 10 minutes | **Serves:** 2 - 3)

Ingredients:
- 3 cups broccoli florets
- 1/4 cup water
- Bowl with iced water
- Salt and ground black pepper to taste

Directions:
1. Prepare the Instant Pot by adding the water to the pot and placing the steamer basket in it
2. Put the broccoli in the basket. Close and lock the lid.
3. Select MANUAL and cook at HIGH pressure for 0 minutes.
4. Prepare the bowl with very cold water
5. When the timer goes off, use a Quick Release.
6. Carefully open the lid, immediately transfer the broccoli to the bowl with cold water to keep bright green color.
7. Season the chilled broccoli with salt and pepper and serve

Potato with Cheese

(Prep + Cook Time: 60 minutes | **Serves:** 2 - 3)

Ingredients:
- 1-pound red potatoes, cut into 1 inch cubes
- 1/2 cup parmesan cheese, shredded
- 1 cup chicken broth
- 1 teaspoon dried rosemary
- 1 tablespoon butter
- 1 teaspoon dried oregano
- 1 teaspoon dried parsley
- 1/4 teaspoon salt

Directions:
1. Add the butter to the Instant Pot and select SAUTÉ. Once the butter has melted, add the potatoes. Stir until well coated and sauté for 5 minutes
2. Add the broth, rosemary, oregano and parsley. Close and lock the lid.
3. Press the CANCEL button to reset the cooking program, then press the MANUAL button and set the cooking time for 5 minutes at HIGH pressure
4. When the timer beeps, use a Natural Release for 10 minutes.
5. Uncover the pot, Season with salt and cheese and gently stir and serve

Sweet Potato Wedges

(Prep + Cook Time: 35 minutes | **Serves:** 4)

Ingredients:
- 3 large sweet potatoes, peeled
- 1 teaspoon paprika
- 1 tablespoon dry mango powder
- 1 cup water
- 2 tablespoon vegetable oil
- 1/2 teaspoon kosher salt

Directions:
1. Cut the potatoes into medium-sized wedges
2. Prepare the Instant Pot by adding the water to the pot and placing the steam rack in it.
3. Place the sweet potatoes on the rack. Close and lock the lid.
4. Select MANUAL and cook at HIGH pressure for 15 minutes
5. Once timer goes off, use a Quick Release. Carefully unlock the lid,
6. Drain the liquid from the pot.
7. Preheat the Instant Pot by selecting SAUTÉ. Add and heat the oil
8. Add the cooked sweet potatoes and sauté the wedges for 3-5 minutes, until they turn brown.
9. Season with salt, paprika and mango powder, Stir well, and Serve.

Simple Baked Potatoes

(Prep + Cook Time: 30 minutes | **Serves:** 8)

Ingredients:

- 5 pounds' potatoes, peeled and cut into half
- Salt to taste
- 1 ½ cups water

Directions:

1. Prepare the Instant Pot by adding the water to the pot and placing the steamer basket in it
2. Place the potatoes in the basket. Close and secure the lid
3. Select the MANUAL setting and set the cooking time for 10 minutes at HIGH pressure.
4. Once cooking is complete, let the pressure Release Naturally for 15 minutes. Release any remaining steam manually
5. Uncover the pot, Season with salt and serve.

Parmesan and Garlic Asparagus

(Prep + Cook Time: 20 minutes | **Serves:** 2 - 3)

Ingredients:

- 1-pound asparagus, trimmed (1 inch of the bottom)
- 2 cloves garlic, chopped.
- 3 tablespoon parmesan cheese, grated
- 1 cup water
- 3 tablespoon butter
- Salt and ground black pepper to taste

Directions:

1. Pour the water into the Instant Pot and set a steam rack in the pot
2. Place the asparagus on a tin foil, add butter and garlic. Sprinkle with salt and pepper.
3. Fold over the foil and seal the asparagus inside so the foil doesn't come open
4. Put the asparagus on the rack. Close and lock the lid.
5. Select MANUAL and cook at HIGH pressure for 8 minutes.
6. When the timer beeps, use a Quick Release.
7. Carefully unlock the lid, Unwrap the foil packet and transfer the asparagus to a serving plate. Sprinkle with cheese and serve

Pumpkin Puree Recipe

(Prep + Cook Time: 30 minutes | **Serves:** 4-5)

Ingredients:

- 2 pounds' small-sized sugar pumpkin, halved and seeds scooped out
- 1 + 1/4 cup water
- Salt to taste, optional

Directions:

1. Prepare the Instant Pot by adding 1 cup of water to the pot and placing the steam rack in it
2. Place the pumpkin halves on the rack. Close and lock the lid.
3. Select MANUAL and cook at HIGH pressure for 14 minutes.
4. When the timer goes off, use a Quick Release. Carefully unlock the lid
5. Transfer the pumpkin to a plate and let it cool. Then scoop out the flesh into a bowl.
6. Add ¼ cup of water. Using an immersion blender or food processor, blend until puree.
7. Season with salt and serve

Squash Porridge Recipe

(Prep + Cook Time: 20 minutes | **Serves:** 2 - 3)

Ingredients:

- 1 squash, peeled and chopped.
- 3 apples, cored and chopped.
- 2 tablespoon maple syrup
- 2 tablespoon cinnamon powder
- 3/4 cup water
- Salt to taste

Directions:

1. Combine all of the ingredients in the Instant Pot and stir to mix
2. Close and lock the lid. Select the MANUAL setting and set the cooking time for 8 minutes at HIGH pressure.
3. Once pressure cooking is complete, select CANCEL and use a Quick Release
4. Carefully unlock the lid, Stir the porridge and serve.

Potato and Bacon Salad

(Prep + Cook Time: 25 minutes | **Serves:** 6-7)

Ingredients:

- 1/2-pound cooked bacon, sliced into 1-inch-thick pieces
- 3 pounds' red potatoes, peeled and cut into 1 ½ inch cubes
- 2 celery stalks, chopped.
- 1 bunch green onions
- 1 ½ cups water
- 6 eggs
- 2 cups mayonnaise
- Salt and ground black pepper to taste

Directions:

1. Pour the water into the Instant Pot and insert a steamer basket
2. Place the eggs and potatoes in the basket.
3. Select MANUAL and cook at HIGH pressure for 5 minutes
4. When the timer goes off, use a Quick Release.
5. Carefully unlock the lid, Transfer the eggs to the bowl of cold water. Wait 2 to 3 minutes
6. In the large bowl, combine the cooked potatoes, mayonnaise, bacon, celery and green onion
7. Peel eggs, chop and add to the salad, Stir well.
8. Season with salt and pepper, stir and serve

Pumpkin Chili Recipe

(Prep + Cook Time: 25 minutes | **Serves:** 4-5)

Ingredients:

- 3 cups pumpkin, peeled and chopped into small pieces
- 1 teaspoon cumin
- 1 tablespoon nutritional yeasts
- 1 tablespoon chili powder
- 1 can white beans, drained and rinsed
- 2 cups tomatoes, diced
- Salt and ground black pepper to taste

Directions:

1. Combine all of the ingredients in the Instant Pot and stir well
2. Close and lock the lid. Select the MANUAL setting and set the cooking time for 10 minutes at HIGH pressure.
3. Once pressure cooking is complete, select CANCEL and use a Quick Release.
4. Carefully unlock the lid, serve with chopped green onions, avocado and cilantro

Tasty Potatoes

(Prep + Cook Time: 30 minutes | **Serves:** 2)

Ingredients:

- 4 gold potatoes, washed and peeled
- 1 cup chives, chopped for serving
- 1 tablespoon bacon fat or butter
- Water as needed
- 2 teaspoon Italian seasoning
- Salt and pepper to taste

Directions:

1. Place the potatoes in the Instant Pot and pour the water to cover them. Close and lock the lid.
2. Select MANUAL and cook at HIGH pressure for 10 minutes
3. Once cooking is complete, select CANCEL and let Naturally Release for 10 minutes. Release any remaining steam manually. Uncover the pot.
4. Transfer the potatoes to a bowl and mash them a bit with a fork
5. Select the SAUTÉ setting on the Instant Pot, add the bacon fat and heat up.
6. Return the mashed potatoes to the pot, add the Italian seasoning, salt and pepper, stir well
7. Close and lock the lid. Select MANUAL and cook at HIGH pressure for 1 minute
8. When the timer goes off, use a Quick Release.
9. Carefully unlock the lid, Stir the potatoes and top with chives and serve

IP Steamed Artichokes

(Prep + Cook Time: 40 minutes | **Serves:** 2 - 3)

Ingredients:

- 2 medium whole artichokes (about 6 ounces each)
- 1 lemon wedge
- 1 cup water

Directions:

1. Wash the artichokes and remove any damaged outer leaves.
2. Trim off the stem and top edge. Rub the top with lemon wedge
3. Prepare the Instant Pot by adding the water to the pot and placing the steamer basket in it.
4. Close and lock the lid. Select MANUAL and cook at HIGH pressure for 20 minutes
5. Once cooking is complete, let the pressure Release Naturally for 10 minutes. Release any remaining steam manually. Uncover the pot.
6. Transfer the artichokes to a serving plate and serve warm with your favorite sauce

Roasted Garlic Potatoes

(Prep + Cook Time: 30 minutes | **Serves:** 4-5)

Ingredients:

- 2 pounds' baby potatoes
- 1 rosemary spring
- 5 tablespoon vegetable oil
- 5 cloves garlic
- 1/2 cup stock
- Salt and ground black pepper to taste

Directions:

1. Select the SAUTÉ setting on the Instant Pot and heat the oil
2. Add the garlic, potatoes and rosemary.
3. Cook, stirring occasionally, for 10 minutes or until the potatoes start to brown.
4. Using a fork, pierce the middle of each potato.
5. Pour in the stock. Season with salt and pepper, Stir well
6. Press the CANCEL key to stop the SAUTÉ function.
7. Close and lock the lid. Select MANUAL and cook at HIGH pressure for 7 minutes.
8. When the timer beeps, use a Quick Release.
9. Carefully unlock the lid, and Serve

IP Hole Baked Potatoes

(Prep + Cook Time: 25 minutes | **Serves:** 4-5)

Ingredients:

- 6 to 8 medium Russet potatoes
- 2 tablespoon olive oil
- 1 cup water
- 1/2 teaspoon kosher salt
- 1/2 teaspoon ground black pepper

Directions:

1. Wash the potatoes and pat dry
2. Using a fork, pierce the middle of each potato
3. In a bowl; combine the salt, pepper and oil. Mix well.
4. Add the potatoes to the bowl and brush them well with the mixture.
5. Pour the water into the Instant Pot and set a steam rack in the pot
6. Place the potatoes on the steam rack. Close and lock the lid.
7. Select MANUAL and cook at HIGH pressure for 10 minutes.
8. Once timer goes off, use a Quick Release.
9. Carefully unlock the lid, Transfer the potatoes to a serving bowl. Serve with butter and fresh dill

Cauliflower Patties Recipe

(Prep + Cook Time: 30 minutes | **Serves:** 4)

Ingredients:

- 1 cauliflower head, chopped.
- 1 cup ground almonds
- 1 cup vegan cheese, shredded
- 1 ½ cups water
- 2 tablespoon olive oil
- Salt and ground black pepper to taste

Directions:

1. Pour the water into the Instant Pot and insert a steamer basket
2. Put the cauliflower in to the basket.
3. Close and lock the lid. Select MANUAL and cook at HIGH pressure for 5 minutes
4. Once timer goes off, use a Quick Release.
5. Carefully unlock the lid, Place the cauliflower in a food processor and ground it.
6. Add the almonds and cheese. Season with salt and pepper. Mix well
7. Shape the mixture into oval patties each 1/2 inch thick.
8. Carefully pour the water out of the pot and completely dry the pot before replacing it.
9. Select the SAUTÉ setting on the Instant Pot and heat the oil
10. Add the patties and cook on both sides until golden. You may have to do it in two batches and Serve.

Sweet Potatoes with Pecans.

(Prep + Cook Time: 30 minutes | **Serves:** 4-5)

Ingredients:

- 4 large sweet potatoes, peeled and sliced
- 1 cup pecans, chopped.
- 1/2 cup brown sugar
- 1/4 cup butter
- 1/4 cup maple syrup
- 1 tablespoon lemon zest
- 1/2 teaspoon sea salt
- 1 ¼ cup water
- 1 tablespoon cornstarch

Directions:

1. In the Instant Pot, combine the sugar, lemon zest, salt and water, Stir well
2. Add the potatoes to the pot. Close and lock the lid.
3. Select MANUAL and cook at HIGH pressure for 15 minutes.
4. Once timer goes off, use a Quick Release
5. Carefully unlock the lid, Transfer the potatoes to a serving bowl.
6. Select the SAUTÉ setting on the Instant Pot, add the butter and melt it.

7. Add the maple syrup, cornstarch and chopped pecans. Stir to combine and sauté the sauce for 2 minutes
8. Serve the potatoes with sauce and whole pecans.

Healthy Asparagus

(Prep + Cook Time: 15 minutes | **Serves:** 2 - 3)

Ingredients:
- 1-pound asparagus
- 10-ounce prosciutto, sliced
- 1 ½ cups water

Directions:
1. Wash asparagus and trim off bottom of stems by about 1 inch
2. Prepare the Instant Pot by adding the water to the pot and placing the steam rack in it.
3. Wrap the prosciutto slices around the asparagus spears
4. Place the un-wrapped asparagus on the rack and then place the prosciutto-wrapped spears on top.
5. Close and lock the lid. Select MANUAL and cook at HIGH pressure for 3 minutes.
6. When the timer goes off, let the pressure Release Naturally for 5 minutes, then release any remaining steam manually. Open the lid and Serve

Pumpkin Stew Recipe

(Prep + Cook Time: 25 minutes | **Serves:** 4)

Ingredients:
- 3 cups pumpkin, peeled and cubed (1 inch thick)
- 3 cups mixed greens
- 1 large can diced tomatoes
- 5 cups vegetable stock
- Salt and ground black pepper to taste

Directions:
1. Combine all of the ingredients in the Instant Pot and stir to mix.
2. Close and lock the lid. Select MANUAL and cook at HIGH pressure for 10 minutes
3. When the timer beeps, use a Quick Release
4. Carefully unlock the lid, Taste for seasoning and add more salt if needed and serve

Awesome Ratatouille

(Prep + Cook Time: 30 minutes | **Serves:** 4-5)

Ingredients:
- 1 jar (12 oz.) roasted red bell peppers, drained and sliced
- 1 can (28 oz.) tomatoes, chopped.
- 2 small eggplants, peeled and sliced thin
- 1 medium onion, sliced
- 4 small zucchinis, sliced thin
- 1 tablespoon olive oil
- 2 cloves garlic, chopped.
- 1/2 cup water
- 1 teaspoon kosher salt

Directions:
1. Select the SAUTÉ setting on the Instant Pot and heat the oil
2. Add the onion, garlic, eggplant, zucchini and bell peppers. Sauté for 3 to 4 minutes until softened
3. Add the tomatoes and water and sprinkle with salt, stir well. Close and lock the lid
4. Press the CANCEL button to stop the SAUTE function, then select the MANUAL setting and set the cooking time for 4 minutes at HIGH pressure.
5. When the timer beeps, use a Quick Release
6. Carefully unlock the lid, serve warm or chilled

Potatoes, Cheese and Bacon

(Prep + Cook Time: 25 minutes | **Serves:** 4-5)

Ingredients:
- 2 pounds' red potatoes, quartered
- 1/3 cup Ranch dressing
- 5-ounce cheddar cheese, shredded
- 3 bacon strips, cut into small pieces
- 3 tablespoon water
- 1 teaspoon garlic powder
- 2 teaspoon dried parsley
- 1 teaspoon kosher salt

Directions:
1. In the Instant Pot, combine the water, potatoes and bacon
2. Season with garlic powder, parsley and salt, Stir well.
3. Close and lock the lid. Select MANUAL and cook at HIGH pressure for 7 minutes
4. Once timer goes off, use a Quick Release.
5. Carefully unlock the lid, Add the ranch dressing and cheese. Mix well. Serve warm

Carrot Puree Recipe

(Prep + Cook Time: 25 minutes | **Serves:** 2 - 3)

Ingredients:
- 1 ½ pounds' carrots, peeled and sliced into 1 inch pieces
- 1 cup water
- 1 tablespoon honey
- 1 tablespoon soy butter, softened
- Brown sugar, optional
- 1/2 teaspoon kosher salt

Directions:
1. Prepare the Instant Pot by adding the water to the pot and placing a steamer basket in it
2. Put the carrots in the basket. Close and lock the lid.
3. Select the MANUAL setting and set the cooking time for 4 minutes at HIGH pressure
4. Once timer goes off, use a Quick Release.
5. Carefully unlock the lid, using a potato masher or electric beater, slowly blend the carrots until smooth and creamy
6. Add the honey and butter and stir well. Season with salt and stir. If desired, add sugar to taste and Serve

Onion Potato Pie

(Prep + Cook Time: 40 minutes | **Serves:** 4)

Ingredients:
- 1-pound onions, finely sliced
- 1 cup cheddar cheese, grated
- 2 tablespoon chives, chopped.
- Salad, optional
- 1 ½ cups water
- 2 tablespoon butter
- 1 ½-pound potato, peeled and thinly sliced
- Salt and ground black pepper to taste

Directions:
1. Pour the water into the Instant Pot and set a steam rack in the pot.
2. Butter 6- to 7-inch baking pan and start by putting the bottom layer of potatoes
3. Then layer the onion above the potatoes and the cheese; then place a layer of potatoes on top and sprinkle with cheese. Sprinkle with salt and pepper.
4. Cover the pan tightly with aluminum foil and place on the steam rack.
5. Close and lock the lid. Select MANUAL and cook at HIGH pressure for 20 minutes
6. Once timer goes off, use a Quick Release.
7. Carefully unlock the lid, Top with chives and serve with salad

Savory Ranch Yellow Potatoes

(Prep + Cook Time: 25 minutes | **Serves:** 2 - 3)

Ingredients:

- 3 large yellow potatoes, cubed
- 2 tablespoon Ranch dressing or seasoning mix
- 2 tablespoon butter
- 1/2 cup water
- Salt and ground black pepper to taste

Directions:

1. Preheat the Instant Pot by selecting Sauté. Once hot, add the butter and melt it
2. Add the potatoes and stir well.
3. Sprinkle with Ranch seasoning and stir. Add the water. Close and lock the lid
4. Press the CANCEL button to reset the cooking program, then press the MANUAL button and set the cooking time for 6 minutes at HIGH pressure.
5. When the timer beeps, use a Quick Release
6. Carefully unlock the lid, Season with salt and pepper and serve.

Roasted Potatoes

(Prep + Cook Time: 30 minutes | **Serves:** 4)

Ingredients:

- 1 ½ - 2 pounds' small Yukon gold or red potatoes
- 1/2 teaspoon garlic powder
- 1/2 teaspoon dried oregano
- 1/4 teaspoon dried rosemary
- 1/2 teaspoon dried marjoram
- 1/2 teaspoon dried thyme
- 3 tablespoon olive oil
- 1/2 cup chicken broth or water
- 1 teaspoon sea salt
- 1/2 teaspoon ground black pepper

Directions:

1. Rinse the potatoes and pat dry with a kitchen paper.
2. Preheat the Instant Pot by selecting SAUTÉ. Add and heat the oil
3. Add the potatoes and cook, stirring occasionally, for 6-7 minutes until the potatoes have turned light brown and crisp. Poke some holes using a fork. You may have to cook the potatoes in two batches
4. In a bowl; combine the garlic powder, marjoram, thyme, oregano, rosemary, salt and pepper
5. Add the herb mix to the pot and stir well
6. Pour in the water. Close and lock the lid.
7. Press the CANCEL button to stop the SAUTE function, then select the MANUAL setting and set the cooking time for 7 minutes at HIGH pressure.
8. Once timer goes off, use a Quick Release
9. Carefully unlock the lid, Taste for seasoning and add more salt if needed and serve

Mashed Potatoes with Rosemary and Garlic

(Prep + Cook Time: 25 minutes | **Serves:** 4-5)

Ingredients:

- 6 large potatoes, peeled and cubed
- 1 cup chicken broth
- 1/4 cup milk
- 2 tablespoon butter
- 3 cloves garlic
- 1 sprig rosemary
- Salt to taste

Directions:

1. In the Instant pot, combine the potatoes, garlic, rosemary and broth, Stir well
2. Close and lock the lid. Select MANUAL and cook at HIGH pressure for 15 minutes
3. Once timer goes off, use a Quick Release.
4. Carefully unlock the lid, Drain the potatoes. Using a potato masher or electric beater, slowly blend milk and butter into potatoes until smooth and creamy. Season with salt and serve

Brussels Sprouts and Pomegranate.

(Prep + Cook Time: 20 minutes | **Serves:** 2 - 3)

Ingredients:

- 1-pound Brussels sprouts, trimmed and cut into half
- 1/4 cup pine nuts, toasted
- 1 pomegranate, seeds separated
- 1 teaspoon olive oil
- 1 cup water
- Salt and ground black pepper to taste

Directions:

1. Pour the water into the Instant Pot and insert a steamer basket
2. Place the Brussels sprouts in the basket.
3. Close and lock the lid. Select MANUAL and cook at HIGH pressure for 4 minutes
4. When the timer beeps, use a Quick Release.
5. Carefully unlock the lid, Transfer the sprouts to a serving plate
6. Season with salt, pepper and pine nuts. Add the pomegranate seeds and stir. Drizzle with oil and stir well and serve

Zucchini Casserole

(Prep + Cook Time: 30 minutes | **Serves:** 2 - 3)

Ingredients:

- 2 zucchinis, cut into ½-inch slices
- 4 stalks celery, chopped.
- 1 large onions, chopped.
- 4 eggs, beaten
- 1 package Italian seasoning
- 1/2 cup vegetable stock
- Salt and ground black pepper to taste

Directions:

1. Add the stock, zucchinis, celery, onion and eggs to the Instant Pot
2. Sprinkle with Italian seasoning, salt and pepper. Stir. Close and lock the lid
3. Select MANUAL and cook at HIGH pressure for 4 minutes
4. Once cooking is complete, select CANCEL and let Naturally Release for 10 minutes
5. Release any remaining steam manually. Uncover the pot and Serve

Cauliflower Curry Recipe

(Prep + Cook Time: 10 minutes | **Serves:** 2 - 3)

Ingredients:

- 16-ounce cauliflower florets
- 6 teaspoon garam masala
- 1 can full-fat coconut milk
- 2 cups water
- Salt and ground black pepper to taste

Directions:

1. In the Instant Pot, combine the cauliflower, coconut milk, garam masala and water.
2. Season with salt and pepper, stir well
3. Close and lock the lid. Select MANUAL and cook at HIGH pressure for 4 minutes.
4. When the timer goes off, use a Quick Release. Carefully open the lid, and Serve

Brussels Sprouts and Potatoes.

(Prep + Cook Time: 20 minutes | **Serves:** 2 - 3)

Ingredients:
- 1 ½ pounds' Brussels sprouts
- 1 cup new potatoes cut into 1 inch cubes
- 1 ½ tablespoon butter
- 1/2 cup chicken stock
- 1 ½ tablespoon bread crumbs
- Salt and ground black pepper to taste

Directions:
1. Wash the Brussels sprouts and remove the outer leaves, then cut into halves
2. In the Instant pot, combine the potatoes, sprouts, stock, salt and pepper, Stir well.
3. Select MANUAL and cook at HIGH pressure for 5 minutes.
4. When the timer goes off, use a Quick Release
5. Carefully open the lid, Select the SAUTÉ setting, add the butter and bread crumbs to the pot. Mix well and serve.

Sweet Potato Recipe

(Prep + Cook Time: 20 minutes | **Serves:** 4-5)

Ingredients:
- 6 medium sweet potatoes
- 2 cups water

Directions:
1. Pour the water into the Instant Pot and set a steam rack in the pot
2. Wash the sweet potatoes and place on the steam rack.
3. Close and lock the lid. Select MANUAL and cook at HIGH pressure for 12 minutes.
4. When the timer goes off, use a Quick Release
5. Carefully open the lid, Serve or store in an airtight container in the refrigerator for up to 3 days.

Spaghetti Squash Recipe

(Prep + Cook Time: 20 minutes | **Serves:** 4)

Ingredients:
- 1 whole winter squash, cut in half lengthwise and remove seeds
- 1 teaspoon olive oil
- 1 cup water
- Salt to taste

Directions:
1. Pour the water into the Instant Pot and insert a steamer basket
2. Put the squash in the basket. Close and lock the lid.
3. Select the MANUAL setting and set the cooking time for 7 minutes at HIGH pressure
4. Once timer goes off, use a Quick Release.
5. Carefully unlock the lid, transfer squash to a plate and using a fork make spaghetti noodles out of the squash.
6. Season with salt and oil and serve

Potato Hash

(Prep + Cook Time: 20 minutes | **Serves:** 4)

Ingredients:
- 2 large sweet potato, diced into 1 inch pieces
- 2 large potato, diced into 1/2 inch pieces
- 4 bell peppers, chopped.
- 2 medium onion, chopped.
- 2 cloves garlic, minced
- 2 tablespoon olive oil
- 1 teaspoon kosher salt
- 1/2 teaspoon black pepper
- 1 ½ teaspoon of paprika
- 1 cup water
- 1 ½ teaspoon cumin
- 1/4 teaspoon cayenne pepper

Directions:

1. In the Instant Pot, combine the onion, garlic, sweet potato, potato, bell peppers and oil
2. Season with salt, pepper, paprika, cumin and cayenne pepper. Mix well
3. Pour in the water. Close and lock the lid.
4. Select MANUAL and cook at HIGH pressure for 1 minutes.
5. When the timer beeps, use a Quick Release. Carefully unlock the lid
6. Select SAUTÉ and cook the mixture for about 7 minutes, until the potatoes start to brown.
7. Press the CANCEL key to stop the SAUTÉ function and Serve warm

Cauliflower Mash

(Prep + Cook Time: 20 minutes | **Serves:** 2 - 3)

Ingredients:

- 1 cauliflower, florets separated
- 1 tablespoon butter
- 1/2 teaspoon turmeric
- 2 chives, finely chopped.
- 1 ½ cups water
- Salt and ground black pepper to taste

Directions:

1. Prepare the Instant Pot by adding the water to the pot and placing the steamer basket in it
2. Put the cauliflower in the basket. Close and lock the lid.
3. Select MANUAL and cook at HIGH pressure for 6 minutes
4. Once cooking is complete, let the pressure Release Naturally for 2 minutes. Release any remaining steam manually.
5. Uncover the pot. Using a potato masher or fork, mash the cauliflower
6. Season with salt and pepper. Add in the butter and turmeric and mix well. Top with chopped chives and serve.

IP Steamed Asparagus

(Prep + Cook Time: 15 minutes | **Serves:** 2 - 3)

Ingredients:

- 1-pound asparagus
- 4 teaspoon olive oil
- 1 tablespoon onion, chopped.
- 1 cup water
- Salt and fresh ground pepper to taste

Directions:

1. Wash asparagus and trim off bottom of stems by about 1 ½ inches
2. Prepare the Instant Pot by adding the water to the pot and placing the steam rack in it
3. Place the asparagus on the steam rack. Brush the asparagus with the olive oil.
4. Sprinkle with the onion. Close and secure the lid.
5. Select the STEAM setting and set the cooking time for 2 minutes.
6. Once timer goes off, use a Quick Release
7. Carefully unlock the lid, Season with salt and pepper and serve.

IP Mashed Potatoes

(Prep + Cook Time: 35 minutes | **Serves:** 4-5)

Ingredients:

- 2 pounds' potatoes, peeled and quartered
- 3 tablespoon butter
- 1 cup milk
- 1 cup water
- Salt and ground black pepper to taste

Directions:

1. Pour the water into the Instant Pot and insert a steamer basket.
2. Put the potatoes in the basket

3. Close and lock the lid. Select the MANUAL setting and set the cooking time for 15 minutes at HIGH pressure.
4. Once cooking is complete, use a Natural Release for 15 minutes, then release any remaining pressure manually
5. Open the lid, Transfer the potatoes to a bowl.
6. Add the milk and butter. Mash until creamy and smooth
7. Season with salt and pepper and serve.

Delicious Broccoli Salad

(**Prep + Cook Time:** 25 minutes | **Serves:** 2 - 3)

Ingredients:
- 1-pound broccoli florets
- 1 onion, sliced
- 1 tablespoon lemon juice
- 1/2 cup chicken stock
- 3 tablespoon raisins
- 2 tablespoon walnuts, crushed
- 1 teaspoon garlic powder
- 1 teaspoon oregano
- 1 teaspoon olive oil
- Bowl with iced water
- 1 tablespoon kosher salt

Directions:
1. Pour the stock into the Instant Pot and insert a steamer basket
2. Put the broccoli in the basket. Close and lock the lid.
3. Select MANUAL and cook at HIGH pressure for 0 minutes.
4. Prepare the bowl with very cold water.
5. Once pressure cooking is complete, select CANCEL and use a Quick Release
6. Carefully unlock the lid, immediately transfer the broccoli to the bowl with cold water to keep bright green color
7. Transfer the chilled broccoli to a serving bowl.
8. Add the onion, raisins, crushed walnuts and season with lemon juice, oregano, garlic powder, salt and oil. Gently stir to combine and Serve

Glazed Baby Carrots

(**Prep + Cook Time:** 20 minutes | **Serves:** 2 - 3)

Ingredients:
- 1 ½-pound baby carrots
- 4 tablespoon butter
- 1/2 cup honey
- 1 ½ teaspoon dry dill
- 2/3 cup water
- 1 teaspoon dry thyme
- Salt to taste

Directions:
1. Pour the water into the Instant Pot and insert a steamer basket
2. Put the carrots in the basket. Close and lock the lid.
3. Select MANUAL and cook at HIGH pressure for 4 minutes
4. When the timer goes off, use a Quick Release.
5. Carefully unlock the lid, Transfer the carrots to a plate.
6. Carefully pour the water out of the pot and completely dry the pot before replacing it
7. Select the SAUTÉ setting on the Instant Pot and add the butter, melt it.
8. Add the honey, dill and thyme. Mix well.
9. Return the carrots to the pot and stir until well coated. Sauté for 1 minute more
10. Taste for seasoning and add more salt if needed and Serve

Tasty French Fries

(Prep + Cook Time: 25 minutes | **Serves:** 4)

Ingredients:
- 8 medium potatoes, peeled, cut into 1/2 inch sticks
- 3-4 tablespoon olive oil
- 1 ¼ cups water
- 1/4 teaspoon baking soda
- Salt to taste

Directions:
1. In the Instant Pot, combine the water, baking soda and salt. Mix well
2. Put the steam rack in the pot and place the potatoes on the rack.
3. Close and lock the lid. Select MANUAL and cook at HIGH pressure for 3 minutes
4. When the timer beeps, use a Quick Release.
5. Carefully unlock the lid, Transfer the potatoes to a serving bowl. Pat dry with paper towels
6. Carefully pour the water out of the pot and completely dry the pot before replacing it.
7. Preheat the Instant Pot by selecting SAUTÉ on high heat. Add the oil and heat it up
8. Put the potato sticks in the pot and sauté, stirring occasionally, until the potatoes turn golden brown, Season with salt and serve

Creamy Artichoke and Zucchini

(Prep + Cook Time: 25 minutes | **Serves:** 6-7)

Ingredients:
- 1 large artichoke hearts, cleaned and sliced
- 2 tablespoon olive oil
- 8 cloves garlic, minced
- 2 medium zucchinis, sliced thin
- 1/2 cup whipping cream
- 1/2 cup vegetable broth
- Salt and ground black pepper to taste

Directions:
1. Preheat the Instant Pot by selecting SAUTÉ. Add and heat the oil
2. Add the garlic and sauté for 2 minutes, until fragrant.
3. Add the zucchinis, artichoke hearts, broth and cream.
4. Season with salt and pepper, Stir well. Close and lock the lid
5. Press the CANCEL button to stop the SAUTE function, then select the MANUAL setting and set the cooking time for 10 minutes at high pressure. Once pressure cooking is complete, select CANCEL and use a Quick Release. Carefully unlock the lid and serve

Aweosme Potatoes Salad

(Prep + Cook Time: 25 minutes | **Serves:** 4-5)

Ingredients:
- 6 medium potatoes, peeled and cut into 1 ½ inch cubes
- 1 cup homemade mayonnaise
- 2 tablespoon parsley, finely chopped.
- 1/4 cup onion, finely chopped.
- 1 ½ cups water
- 4 eggs
- 1 tablespoon mustard
- 1 tablespoon dill pickle juice
- Salt and ground black pepper to taste

Directions:
1. Pour the water into the Instant Pot and insert a steamer basket
2. Place the eggs and potatoes in the basket.
3. Select MANUAL and cook at HIGH pressure for 5 minutes.
4. When the timer goes off, use a Quick Release.
5. Carefully unlock the lid, Transfer the eggs to the bowl of cold water. Wait 2 to 3 minutes
6. In another bowl, combine the dill pickle juice, mayo, parsley, onion and mustard. Mix well.
7. Add the potatoes and gently stir to coat with the sauce.
8. Peel eggs, chop and add to the salad, Stir well.
9. Season with salt and pepper, stir and serve

Cheesy Beets

(Prep + Cook Time: 30 minutes | **Serves:** 4-5)

Ingredients:

- 6 medium beets, trimmed
- 1/4 cup cheese (by choice), crumbled
- 1 cup water
- Salt and ground black pepper to taste

Directions:

1. Pour the water into the Instant Pot and insert a steamer basket
2. Place the beets in the basket. Close and lock the lid.
3. Select MANUAL and cook at HIGH pressure for 20 minutes
4. Once cooking is complete, let the pressure Release Naturally for 10 minutes. Release any remaining steam manually. Uncover the pot.
5. Transfer the beets to a bowl and let them cool.
6. Season with salt and pepper and add the blue cheese then Serve

Turnips and Carrots

(Prep + Cook Time: 25 minutes | **Serves:** 2 - 3)

Ingredients:

- 3 medium carrots, sliced
- 1 small onion, chopped.
- 2 medium turnips, peeled and sliced
- 1 teaspoon ground cumin
- 1 tablespoon olive oil
- 1 cup water
- 1 teaspoon lemon juice
- Salt and ground black pepper to the taste

Directions:

1. Press the SAUTÉ button on the Instant Pot and heat the oil
2. Add the onion and sauté for 2 minutes until fragrant.
3. Add the carrots, turnips, cumin and lemon juice. Sauté for 1 minute more
4. Season with salt and pepper, stir well.
5. Pour in the water. Close and lock the lid
6. Press the CANCEL key to stop the SAUTÉ function.
7. Select MANUAL and cook at HIGH pressure for 7 minutes
8. Once timer goes off, use a Quick Release.
9. Carefully unlock the lid, Taste for seasoning and Serve

Carrot and Sweet Potato Medley Recipe

(Prep + Cook Time: 20 minutes | **Serves:** 6-7)

Ingredients:

- 2 pounds' baby carrots, halved
- 2 pounds' sweet potatoes, peeled and cubed
- 1 cup veggie broth
- 2 tablespoon extra-virgin olive oil
- 1 medium onion, chopped.
- Salt and ground black pepper to taste

Directions:

1. Select the SAUTÉ setting on the Instant Pot and heat the oil
2. Add the onion and sauté for 5 minutes, until softened.
3. Add the carrots, sweet potatoes and broth.
4. Season with salt and pepper, Stir well. Close and lock the lid
5. Press the CANCEL button to stop the SAUTE function, then select the MANUAL setting and set the cooking time for 8 minutes at HIGH pressure.
6. When the timer beeps, use a Quick Release.
7. Carefully unlock the lid and Serve

Mashed Potatoes & Parsnips

(Prep + Cook Time: 20 minutes | **Serves:** 4-5)

Ingredients:

- 2 pounds' Yukon gold potatoes, peeled and cubed
- 3/4-pound parsnips, cut into 1-inch-thick pieces
- 5 tablespoon half and half
- 2 tablespoon butter, melted
- 2 cups water
- 1 teaspoon sea salt
- 1 teaspoon ground black pepper

Directions:

1. Prepare the Instant Pot by adding the water to the pot and placing the steamer basket in it
2. Put the potatoes and parsnips in the basket.
3. Close and lock the lid. Select MANUAL and cook at HIGH pressure for 7 minutes.
4. When the timer goes off, use a Quick Release
5. Carefully unlock the lid, Transfer the potatoes and parsnips to the bowl. Season with salt and pepper, Stir well.
6. Using a potato masher or electric beater, slowly blend half and half and butter into vegetables until smooth and creamy. Serve warm

Special Vegetable Dish

(Prep + Cook Time: 25 minutes | **Serves:** 4)

Ingredients:

- 2 green bell pepper, sliced thinly
- 1 yellow bell peppers, sliced thinly
- 2 cloves garlic, chopped.
- 1 red onion, sliced
- 2 red bell peppers, sliced thinly
- 1 bunch parsley, finely chopped.
- 2 tomatoes, chopped
- 1 tablespoon extra virgin olive oil
- Salt and ground black pepper to taste

Directions:

1. Select the SAUTÉ setting on the Instant Pot and heat the oil.
2. Add the onion and sauté for 3 minutes.
3. Add the bell peppers, stir and sauté for another 5 minutes
4. Add the tomatoes and sprinkle with salt and pepper. Mix well. Close and lock the lid.
5. Press the CANCEL button to reset the cooking program, then press the MANUAL button and set the cooking time for 6 minutes at HIGH pressure
6. Once pressure cooking is complete, select CANCEL and use a Quick Release.
7. Carefully unlock the lid, Transfer the veggies to a serving bowl and add the garlic and parsley. Stir well and Serve

Tasty Buttery Beets

(Prep + Cook Time: 45 minutes | **Serves:** 4-5)

Ingredients:

- 1 ¾ pounds' medium beets, trimmed
- 2 tablespoon fresh parsley, chopped.
- 1 cup water
- 2 tablespoon butter, melted
- Salt and freshly ground black pepper to taste

Directions:

1. Prepare the Instant Pot by adding the water to the pot and placing the steamer basket in it
2. Place the beets in the basket. Close and lock the lid.
3. Select MANUAL and cook at HIGH pressure for 24 minutes
4. When the timer goes off, use a Quick Release.
5. Carefully unlock the lid, Transfer the beets to a plate and let them cool
6. Peel and into wedges the beets and put in the bowl.

7. Add the butter, salt and pepper. Gently stir to coat the beets with the butter.
8. Sprinkle with parsley then serve

Instant Pot Steamed Vegetables

(Prep + Cook Time: 15 minutes | **Serves:** 2 - 3)

Ingredients:
- 2 bell peppers, sliced (1 inch thick)
- 3 small zucchinis, sliced (1 inch thick)
- 1/2 cup garlic, peeled and minced
- 2 tablespoon olive oil
- 1 cup water
- 1 tablespoon Italian herb mix
- Salt to taste

Directions:
1. Prepare the Instant Pot by adding the water to the pot and placing the steam rack in it
2. In a large bowl, combine the zucchinis, peppers and garlic.
3. Season the veggies with Italian herb mix, salt and oil, Stir well
4. Place the vegetables on the rack. Close and lock the lid.
5. Select the STEAM setting and set the cooking time for 7 minutes.
6. When the timer beeps, use a Quick Release.
7. Carefully unlock the lid, and Serve

Brussels Sprouts.

(Prep + Cook Time: 10 minutes | **Serves:** 2 - 3)

Ingredients:
- 1-pound Brussels sprouts
- 1 teaspoon extra virgin olive oil
- 1/4 cup pine nuts
- 1 cup water
- Salt and ground black pepper to taste

Directions:
1. Wash the Brussels sprouts and remove the outer leaves, then cut into halves
2. Prepare the Instant Pot by adding the water to the pot and placing the steamer basket in it.
3. Place the Brussels sprouts in the basket
4. Close and lock the lid. Select MANUAL and cook at HIGH pressure for 4 minutes.
5. Once timer goes off, use a Quick Release.
6. Carefully unlock the lid, Transfer the Brussels sprouts to a serving bowl.
7. Season with salt, pepper and drizzle with oil. Top with the pine nuts and serve

Mashed Turnips Recipe

(Prep + Cook Time: 20 minutes | **Serves:** 4)

Ingredients:
- 4 turnips, peeled and cubed
- 1 yellow onion, chopped.
- 1/2 cup chicken stock
- 1/4 cup sour cream
- Salt and ground black pepper to the taste

Directions:
1. Add the turnips, onion and chicken stock to the Instant Pot
2. Close and lock the lid. Select the MANUAL setting and set the cooking time for 5 minutes at HIGH pressure.
3. Once cooking is complete, select CANCEL and let Naturally Release for 5 minutes. Release any remaining steam manually. Uncover the pot
4. Using a potato masher or electric beater, slowly blend sour cream into turnips until smooth and creamy.
5. Season with salt and pepper and serve

Mashed Sweet Potatoes

(Prep + Cook Time: 30 minutes | **Serves:** 4-5)

Ingredients:

- 1-pound sweet potatoes, peeled and cubed
- 2 cloves garlic
- 1/2 teaspoon dried parsley
- 1/4 cup milk
- 2 tablespoon butter
- 1/2 cup parmesan cheese, grated
- 1/4 teaspoon dried thyme
- 1/4 teaspoon dried sage
- 1/4 teaspoon dried rosemary
- 1 cup water
- Salt and ground black pepper to taste

Directions:

1. Pour the water into the Instant Pot and insert a steamer basket
2. Put the sweet potatoes and garlic in the basket.
3. Close and lock the lid. Select the MANUAL setting and set the cooking time for 15 minutes at HIGH pressure.
4. Once pressure cooking is complete, select CANCEL and use a Quick Release
5. Carefully unlock the lid, Transfer the potatoes to a serving bowl
6. Add the thyme, sage, rosemary and parsley, Stir well.
7. Using a potato masher or electric beater, slowly blend milk and butter into potatoes until smooth and creamy.
8. Add cheese and season with salt and pepper, stir well and serve

Mushroom Chili Recipe

(Prep + Cook Time: 15 minutes | **Serves:** 2 - 3)

Ingredients:

- 1 can (15 oz) baby Bella mushrooms, chopped.
- 2 stalks celery, chopped.
- 1 teaspoon Mexican spicy seasoning
- 1 tablespoon cumin
- 2 cups tomatoes, diced
- Salt to taste

Directions:

1. In the Instant Pot, combine the mushrooms, tomatoes, celery, spicy seasoning, cumin and salt
2. Close and lock the lid. Select MANUAL and cook at HIGH pressure for 10 minutes.
3. When the timer goes off, use a Quick Release
4. Carefully open the lid, Stir well and serve.

Cabbage with Bacon

(Prep + Cook Time: 25 minutes | **Serves:** 2 - 3)

Ingredients:

- 1 green cabbage head, chopped.
- 3 bacon slices, chopped.
- 2 cups chicken stock
- 1/4 cup butter
- Salt and ground black pepper to taste

Directions:

1. To preheat the Instant Pot, select SAUTÉ
2. Add the bacon and sauté for 5 minutes, until it begins to render some fat but is not yet crispy.
3. Add butter and cook until it melts
4. Add the cabbage, salt, pepper and stock. Stir. Close and lock the lid
5. Press the CANCEL button to stop the SAUTE function, then select the MANUAL setting and set the cooking time for 3 minutes at HIGH pressure.
6. When the timer beeps, use a Quick Release.
7. Carefully unlock the lid, and Serve

Beet Salad Recipe

(Prep + Cook Time: 55 minutes | **Serves:** 4)

Ingredients:

- 4 medium beets, trimmed
- 1 clove garlic, chopped.
- 1/3 cup parsley, chopped.
- 2 tablespoon capers
- 1 cup water
- 1 tablespoon extra-virgin olive oil
- 2 tablespoon balsamic vinegar
- Salt and ground black pepper to taste

Directions:

1. Pour the water into the Instant Pot and insert a steamer basket
2. Place the beets in the basket. Close and lock the lid.
3. Select MANUAL and cook at HIGH pressure for 20 minutes
4. Meanwhile, in a medium bowl, combine the garlic, parsley, salt, pepper, capers and olive oil.
5. Once cooking is complete, let the pressure Release Naturally for 10 minutes. Release any remaining steam manually
6. Uncover the pot. Transfer the beets to a plate and let them cool
7. Peel and slice the beets, arrange them on a platter.
8. Drizzle with the vinegar and sprinkle with parsley and Serve

Farro and Cherry Salad

(Prep + Cook Time: 40 minutes | **Serves:** 4)

Ingredients:

- 1 ½ cup faro, rinsed
- 8 mint leaves, minced
- 1/4 cup chives, minced
- 1 ½ tablespoon extra-virgin olive oil
- 3 cups water
- 1/2 cup dried cherries, chopped.
- 2 cups fresh cherries, pitted and halved
- 1 teaspoon lemon juice
- 1 tablespoon apple cider vinegar
- 1/4 teaspoon kosher salt

Directions:

1. In the Instant Pot, combine the farro and water.
2. Select MANUAL and cook at HIGH pressure for 10 minutes
3. Once cooking is complete, select CANCEL and let Naturally Release for 10 minutes. Release any remaining steam manually. Uncover the pot
4. Transfer the farro to a salad bowl and let it cool for a few minutes.
5. Add the remaining ingredients, except for the fresh cherries and stir to combine
6. Allow the faro totally cool; add the fresh cherries, stir and then serve

Spicy Eggplant

(Prep + Cook Time: 25 minutes | **Serves:** 4)

Ingredients:

- 3 cups eggplant, peeled and cubed
- 1 cup fresh spinach, torn
- 1/2 teaspoon ground black pepper
- 1 tablespoon olive oil
- 1 tablespoon five spice powder
- 1/2 cup coconut milk
- 3/4 cup vegetable stock
- Fresh scallions, chopped.
- 1 teaspoon sea salt

Directions:

1. Preheat the Instant Pot by selecting SAUTÉ. Add and heat the oil
2. Add the eggplant and cook for 2 minutes, stirring occasionally.
3. Add the spinach, stir. Sprinkle with salt, pepper and five spice powder
4. Add the coconut milk and stock. Stir to combine.
5. Press the CANCEL key to stop the SAUTÉ function.
6. Close and lock the lid. Select MANUAL and cook at HIGH pressure for 4 minutes

7. When the timer goes off, let the pressure Release Naturally for 5 minutes, then release any remaining steam manually
8. Open the lid, Top with fresh scallions and serve.

Curried Squash Stew Recipe

(Prep + Cook Time: 20 minutes | **Serves:** 6-7)

Ingredients:
- 2 cups squash, chopped.
- 2 tablespoon garam masala
- 1 can full-fat coconut milk
- 1 bag baby spinach, rinsed
- Salt and ground black pepper to taste

Directions:
1. In the Instant Pot, combine the squash, garam masala and coconut milk
2. Season with salt and pepper, Stir well.
3. Close and lock the lid. Select MANUAL and cook at HIGH pressure for 10 minutes
4. When the timer goes off, use a Quick Release. Carefully unlock the lid,
5. Select the SAUTÉ setting and add the spinach.
6. Sauté until the spinach has wilted and serve

Maple Glazed Carrots Recipe

(Prep + Cook Time: 40 minutes | **Serves:** 4-5)

Ingredients:
- 2 pounds' carrots, sliced into ½ inch diagonal pieces
- 1/4 cup raisins
- 1 tablespoon maple syrup
- 2/3 cup water
- 1 tablespoon butter
- Salt and ground black pepper to taste

Directions:
1. Add the water, carrots and raisins to the Instant Pot.
2. Secure the lid. Select the MANUAL setting and set the cooking time for 4 minutes at HIGH pressure
3. Once pressure cooking is complete, select CANCEL and use a Quick Release
4. Carefully unlock the lid, Transfer the carrots to a bowl.
5. Carefully pour the water out of the pot and completely dry the pot before replacing it
6. Select SAUTÉ; add the butter and maple syrup.
7. Return the carrots to the pot and stir well until fully coated with butter
8. Press the CANCEL key to stop the SAUTÉ function. Season with salt and pepper and Serve

Savoy Cabbage and Cream

(Prep + Cook Time: 25 minutes | **Serves:** 2 - 3)

Ingredients:
- 1 medium savoy cabbage head, chopped.
- 1 bay leaf
- 1 cup coconut milk
- 1 medium onion, chopped.
- 1 cup bacon, chopped.
- 2 tablespoon parsley, chopped.
- 1/4 teaspoon nutmeg
- 2 cups bone stock
- Salt and ground black pepper to taste

Directions:
1. Select the SAUTÉ setting on the Instant Pot and add the onion and bacon. Sauté a few minutes until the bacon is crispy
2. Add the cabbage, nutmeg, stock, salt, pepper and bay leaf. Mix well. Close and lock the lid.
3. Press the CANCEL button to stop the SAUTE function, then select the MANUAL setting and set the cooking time for 5 minutes at HIGH pressure
4. Once timer goes off, use a Quick Release. Carefully unlock the lid,

5. Press the SAUTE button. Add the milk and parsley. Cook for 4 to 5 minutes
6. Taste for seasoning and add more salt if needed and Serve

Turnip Alfredo Sauce

(Prep + Cook Time: 15 minutes | **Serves:** 4)

Ingredients:
- 3 medium turnips, peeled and cubed
- 1/2 teaspoon garlic salt
- 1/3 cup chives, chopped.
- 1 cup water
- 1 cup vegan alfredo sauce

Directions:
1. Add the water and turnip to the Instant Pot
2. Close and lock the lid. Select MANUAL and cook at HIGH pressure for 5 minutes
3. Once timer goes off, use a Quick Release.
4. Carefully unlock the lid, Use a potato masher to mash the turnips.
5. Add the alfredo sauce, garlic salt and chives. Mix well.
6. Serve with veggies or pasta

Corn On the Cob.

(Prep + Cook Time: 14 minutes | **Serves:** 3-5)

Ingredients:
- 6 ears corn
- 6 tablespoon butter
- 1 cup water
- Salt to taste

Directions:
1. Shuck the corn husks and rinse off the corn. Cut off the pointy ends
2. Add the water to the Instant Pot.
3. Arrange the corn vertically, with the larger end in the water. If the ear is too tall break it in half
4. Close and lock the lid. Select MANUAL and cook at HIGH pressure for 3 minutes.
5. Once timer goes off, use a Quick Release
6. Carefully unlock the lid, Transfer the corn to a serving bowl. Serve with butter and salt

Bok Choy

(Prep + Cook Time: 25 minutes | **Serves:** 2-4

Ingredients:
- 2 pounds' bok choy, trimmed tough ends
- 1 teaspoon extra virgin olive oil
- 1 tablespoon olive oil
- 1/2 teaspoon ginger, grated
- 1 teaspoon soy sauce
- 1 clove garlic, minced
- 3/4 cup water
- Salt and ground black pepper to taste

Directions:
1. Set your instant pot on SAUTÉ mode, add the olive oil and heat it up
2. Add the ginger and garlic and sauté for 3 to 4 minutes, until start to brown
3. Add the bok choy and water. Close and lock the lid.
4. Press the CANCEL button to stop the SAUTE function, then select the MANUAL setting and set the cooking time for 5 minutes at HIGH pressure.
5. When the timer beeps, use a Quick Release
6. Carefully unlock the lid, Transfer to a serving plate.
7. In a small bowl, whisk together the liquid from the pot, extra virgin olive oil, soy sauce, salt and pepper.
8. Drizzle the bok choy with the sauce and serve

Cabbage with Garlic

(Prep + Cook Time: 30 minutes **| Serves:** 2 - 3)

Ingredients:

- 6 cups red cabbage, chopped.
- 1/2 cup yellow onion, chopped.
- 1 tablespoon olive oil
- 3 cloves garlic, chopped.
- 1 cup water
- 1 tablespoon apple cider vinegar
- 1 cup applesauce
- Salt and ground black pepper to taste

Directions:

1. Preheat the Instant Pot by selecting SAUTÉ. Add and heat the oil
2. Add the onion and sauté for about 4 minutes, until softened
3. Add the garlic and sauté for 1 minute more.
4. Add the cabbage, apple cider vinegar, applesauce, salt, pepper and water.
5. Press the CANCEL key to stop the SAUTÉ function.
6. Close and lock the lid. Select MANUAL and cook at HIGH pressure for 10 minutes
7. Once timer goes off, use a Quick Release. Carefully unlock the lid
8. Stir the dish, taste for seasoning and add more salt, pepper or vinegar, if needed. Serve and enjoy

Barbeque Tofu

(Prep + Cook Time: 25 minutes **| Serves:** 4-5)

Ingredients:

- 28-ounce firm tofu, cubed
- 3 cloves garlic, minced
- 1 celery stalk, chopped.
- 1 green bell pepper, chopped.
- 2 tablespoon olive oil
- 1/8 teaspoon curry powder
- 1 ½ cups bbq sauce
- 1 medium yellow onion, chopped.
- 1 red bell pepper, chopped.
- Salt to taste

Directions:

1. Select the SAUTÉ setting on the Instant Pot and heat the oil
2. Sauté the onion, garlic, celery and bell peppers for 1 minute.
3. Season with salt and curry powder, stir well and sauté the veggies for 1 minutes more.
4. Add the tofu and cook, stirring occasionally, for another 4 minutes
5. Pour in bbq sauce and stir to combine.
6. Press the CANCEL key to stop the SAUTÉ function.
7. Close and lock the lid. Select MANUAL and cook at HIGH pressure for 5 minutes.
8. Once timer goes off, use a Quick Release
9. Carefully unlock the lid and Serve

Tomato with Tofu

(Prep + Cook Time: 15 minutes **| Serves:** 4)

Ingredients:

- 14-ounce firm tofu, cubed
- 1/2 cup vegetable or chicken broth
- 2 teaspoon Italian seasoning
- 1 cup diced tomatoes
- 2 tablespoon jarred banana pepper rings
- 1 tablespoon olive oil

Directions:

1. In the Instant Pot, combine the tofu, tomatoes, banana pepper rings and broth
2. Season with Italian seasoning and oil. Mix well.
3. Close and lock the lid. Select MANUAL and cook at HIGH pressure for 4 minutes
4. When the timer beeps, use a Quick Release.
5. Carefully unlock the lid and Serve

Garlic Eggplant Dish

(**Prep + Cook Time:** 25 minutes | **Serves:** 2 - 3)

Ingredients:

- 4 cups eggplant, cubed
- 1 tablespoon olive oil
- 3 cloves garlic, minced
- 1 tablespoon garlic powder
- 1 cup marinara sauce
- 1/2 cup water
- Salt and ground black pepper to taste

Directions:

1. Select the SAUTÉ setting on the Instant Pot and heat the oil
2. Add the garlic and sauté for 2 minutes
3. Add the eggplant, salt, pepper, marinara sauce and garlic powder. Stir to combine.
4. Pour in the water and stir. Close and lock the lid
5. Press the CANCEL button to reset the cooking program, then press the MANUAL button and set the cooking time for 8 minutes at HIGH pressure.
6. Once pressure cooking is complete, select CANCEL and use a Quick Release
7. Carefully unlock the lid, Serve with pasta

Mushroom Scramble Mug

(**Prep + Cook Time:** 20 minutes | **Serves:** 2 - 3)

Ingredients:

- 3 large eggs
- 1/2 teaspoon ground red pepper
- 1/2 cup mushrooms, chopped.
- 1-ounce deli ham, sliced and chopped.
- 1 tablespoon parsley, minced
- 1/8 teaspoon cumin
- 1 teaspoon extra virgin olive oil
- 1 cup + 1 tablespoon water
- 2 tablespoon Swiss cheese, shredded
- Salt and ground black pepper to taste

Directions:

1. In a bowl; whisk together the eggs, oil, 1 tablespoon of water and red pepper
2. Add the mushrooms and ham, mix well
3. Add the parsley, cumin, salt, pepper and cheese. Stir to combine.
4. Pour the mixture into three heatproof ramekins. Top with cheese.
5. Pour 1 cup of water into the Instant Pot and insert a steamer basket
6. Put the ramekins in the basket.
7. Close and lock the lid. Select MANUAL and cook at HIGH pressure for 5 minutes.
8. When the timer beeps, use a Quick Release.
9. Carefully unlock the lid and Serve

Apple and Butternut Mash

(**Prep + Cook Time:** 30 minutes | **Serves:** 4-5)

Ingredients:

- 2 apples, peeled and sliced
- 1 butternut squash, peeled, deseeded and cut into medium chunks
- 1/2 teaspoon apple pie spice
- 1 cup water
- 1 yellow onion, thinly sliced
- 2 tablespoon brown butter
- Salt to taste

Directions:

1. Pour the water into the Instant Pot and insert a steamer basket
2. Place the squash, onion and apples in the basket.
3. Close and lock the lid. Select MANUAL and cook at HIGH pressure for 8 minutes.
4. When the timer goes off, use a Quick Release. Carefully unlock the lid
5. Transfer the squash, onion and apples to a bowl. Using a potato masher or electric beater, mash them until smooth
6. Add the butter, salt and apple pie spice. Mix well and serve

Zucchini and Tomatoes

(Prep + Cook Time: 25 minutes | **Serves:** 2 - 3)

Ingredients:

- 6 zucchinis, roughly chopped.
- 1-pound cherry tomatoes, cut into halves
- 1 bunch basil, chopped.
- 2 - 3 cloves garlic, minced
- 1 teaspoon extra virgin olive oil, optional
- 1 tablespoon olive oil
- 2 yellow onions, chopped.
- 1 cup tomato puree
- Salt and ground black pepper to taste

Directions:

1. Preheat the Instant Pot by selecting SAUTÉ. Add and heat the oil
2. Add the onion and sauté for 5 minutes, until softened.
3. Add the zucchinis, tomatoes, tomato puree, salt and pepper. Stir. Close and lock the lid
4. Select the MANUAL setting and set the cooking time for 5 minutes at HIGH pressure
5. Once timer goes off, use a Quick Release. Carefully unlock the lid,
6. Add the basil and garlic, stir well. If desired, drizzle with extra virgin olive oil and serve

Mushroom Stroganoff.

(Prep + Cook Time: 25 minutes | **Serves:** 2)

Ingredients:

- 2 cups baby Bella mushrooms, quartered
- 1 cup vegetable or chicken stock
- 1 tablespoon butter
- 1/2 cup sour cream
- 4 cloves garlic, chopped.
- 1 ½ teaspoon flour
- 1 teaspoon Dijon mustard
- Salt and ground black pepper to taste

Directions:

1. Preheat the Instant Pot by selecting SAUTÉ. Once hot, add the butter and melt it
2. Add the garlic and mushrooms, stir. Sauté for 4 to 5 minutes, until softened.
3. Add the stock, flour, Dijon mustard, salt and pepper. Mix well. Close and lock the lid
4. Press the CANCEL button to reset the cooking program, then press the MANUAL button and set the cooking time for 2 minutes at HIGH pressure.
5. When the timer beeps, use a Quick Release. Carefully unlock the lid
6. Select the SAUTÉ setting, pour in the sour cream and cook, stirring occasionally, for 2 minutes and then Serve

Stuffed Bell Peppers

(Prep + Cook Time: 30 minutes | **Serves:** 2 - 3)

Ingredients:

- 4 bell peppers, tops and seeds removed
- 10-ounce canned tomato soup
- 1 cup water
- 1 cup white rice, cooked
- 1/2 cup milk
- 1 egg, beaten
- 1-pound ground beef
- 2 onions, chopped.
- Salt and ground black pepper to the taste

Directions:

1. In a large bowl, combine the rice, milk, egg, beef, onions, salt and pepper. Mix well
2. Fill each bell pepper to the top of the meat mixture.
3. Pour the water and tomato soup into the Instant Pot and set a steam rack in the pot
4. Place the peppers on the rack. Close and lock the lid.
5. Close and lock the lid. Select MANUAL and cook at HIGH pressure for 15 minutes
6. Once cooking is complete, select CANCEL and let Naturally Release for 7 minutes. Release any remaining steam manually. Uncover the pot, Transfer the stuffed peppers to a serving bowl and drizzle with tomato sauce and Serve

Sweet Potatoes and Kale with Tofu

(Prep + Cook Time: 35 minutes | **Serves:** 4-5)

Ingredients:
- 2 cups kale, chopped.
- 2 medium sweet potatoes, cubed
- 1 tablespoon tamari sauce
- 1 cup vegetable broth
- 14-ounce tofu, cubed

Directions:
1. Select the SAUTÉ setting on the Instant Pot and add the 1/2 tablespoon of tamari sauce and 2 tablespoon of broth
2. Add the tofu and sauté for 3 minutes.
3. Add the kale, sweet potatoes and the remaining tamari sauce and broth. Mix well
4. Close and lock the lid. Press the CANCEL button to reset the cooking program, then press the MANUAL button and set the cooking time for 4 minutes at HIGH pressure.
5. Once cooking is complete, let the pressure Release Naturally for 10 minutes
6. Release any remaining steam manually. Uncover the pot, Serve and enjoy

Cabbage with Carrot

(Prep + Cook Time: 35 minutes | **Serves:** 2 - 3)

Ingredients:
- 1 head cabbage, shredded
- 2 carrots, sliced
- 2 tablespoon coconut oil
- 2 small onions, sliced
- 1 tablespoon curry powder
- 1 jalapeño pepper, deseeded and chopped.
- 1 cup water
- 2 tablespoon fresh lemon juice
- 1/2 cup desiccated unsweetened coconut
- 2 cloves garlic, chopped.
- Salt to taste

Directions:
1. Select the SAUTÉ setting on the Instant Pot and heat the oil
2. Add the onion and sauté for about 4 minutes, until softened
3. Add the garlic, salt, curry powder and jalapeño pepper, stir and sauté for 1 minute more.
4. Add the cabbage, carrots, water, lemon juice and coconut.
5. Press the CANCEL key to stop the SAUTÉ function.
6. Close and lock the lid. Select MANUAL and cook at HIGH pressure for 5 minutes
7. Once cooking is complete, use a Natural Release for 10 minutes, then release any remaining pressure manually.
8. Open the lid, taste for seasoning and add more salt if needed then Serve

Eggplant Spread

(Prep + Cook Time: 30 minutes | **Serves:** 4-5)

Ingredients:
- 2 pounds' eggplant, sliced
- 1 lemon, juiced
- 1 tablespoon tahini
- 1 teaspoon extra virgin olive oil
- 4 tablespoon olive oil
- 1/4 cup black olives, pitted and sliced
- 2 sprigs of thyme
- 4 cloves garlic, sliced
- 1 teaspoon kosher salt
- 1 cup water

Directions:
1. Preheat the Instant Pot by selecting SAUTÉ. Add and heat the oil
2. Put the eggplant in the pot and sauté for 3 minutes on both sides
3. Add the garlic and cook for 1 to 2 minutes more, until fragrant
4. Sprinkle with salt and pour in the water.
5. Press the CANCEL key to stop the SAUTÉ function.

6. Close and lock the lid. Select MANUAL and cook at HIGH pressure for 6 minutes
7. Once cooking is complete, let the pressure Release Naturally for 5 minutes. Release any remaining steam manually
8. Uncover the pot. Place the mixture in a blender or food processor; add the lemon juice and tahini. Blend until the texture is smooth
9. Transfer to a serving bowl and drizzle with extra virgin olive oil. Serve with olives and thyme.

Vegan Pizza

(Prep + Cook Time: 20 minutes | **Serves:** 2)

Ingredients:
- 1/2 cup vegan cheese, shredded
- 1 pizza crust, store-bought
- 1 teaspoon oregano, chopped.
- 1/4 cup vegan Alfred sauce
- 1 ½ cups water

Directions:
1. Prepare the Instant Pot by adding the water to the pot and placing the steam rack in it
2. Line a baking dish that can fit into the pot with parchment paper
3. Place the pizza crust inside the baking dish and spread the Alfredo sauce over.
4. Sprinkle the cheese over the crust and top with oregano
5. Put the baking dish on the rack. Secure the lid.
6. Select MANUAL and cook at HIGH pressure for 5 minutes.
7. When the timer beeps, use a Quick Release.
8. Carefully unlock the lid and Serve

Spiced Okra Recipe

(Prep + Cook Time: 25 minutes | **Serves:** 4-5)

Ingredients:
- 2 pounds' okra, cut into 1 inch pieces
- 2 medium tomatoes, chopped.
- 2 tablespoon olive oil
- 1 teaspoon cumin seeds
- 6 cloves garlic, chopped.
- 2 medium onions, sliced
- 1/2 teaspoon ground turmeric
- 1/2 teaspoon red chili powder
- 1 teaspoon ground coriander
- 1 teaspoon lemon juice
- 1/2 cup vegetable broth
- Salt and ground black pepper to taste

Directions:
1. Select the SAUTÉ setting on the Instant Pot and heat the oil.
2. Add the cumin and garlic and sauté for 1 minute
3. Add the onion and sauté for 4 minutes more.
4. Add the broth, okra, tomatoes, salt, pepper, turmeric, chili powder, coriander and lemon juice. Stir to combine and cook for another 1 minute
5. Press the CANCEL key to stop the SAUTÉ function.
6. Close and lock the lid. Select MANUAL and cook at HIGH pressure for 2 minutes
7. Once timer goes off, use a Quick Release
8. Carefully unlock the lid and Serve warm

Pasta & Side Dishes

Alfredo Chicken Pasta

(Prep + Cook Time: 15 minutes | **Serves:** 2)

Ingredients:

- 8-ounce fettuccine, halved
- 1 jar (15 oz) Alfredo sauce
- 1 cup cooked and diced chicken
- 2 cups water
- 2 teaspoon chicken seasoning
- Salt and ground black pepper to taste

Directions:

1. Pout the water in the Instant Pot and add the pasta and chicken seasoning, Stir well
2. Close and lock the lid. Select MANUAL and cook at HIGH pressure for 3 minutes
3. Once pressure cooking is complete, use a Quick Release.
4. Unlock and carefully open the lid. Drain the pasta and add to serving bowl.
5. Add the sauce and cooked chicken. Season with salt and pepper to taste.
6. Stir well and serve

Instant Pesto Farfalle

(Prep + Cook Time: 20 minutes | **Serves:** 2 - 3)

Ingredients:

- 1 ½ cup farfalle
- 3/4 cup vegan pesto sauce
- 1 cup cherry tomatoes, quartered
- 4 cups water

Directions:

1. Add the farfalle and water to the Instant Pot
2. Close and lock the lid. Select MANUAL and cook at HIGH pressure for 7 minutes.
3. When the timer beeps, use a Quick Release
4. Carefully unlock the lid, Drain the pasta and return to the pot.
5. Add the sauce and stir. Select SAUTÉ and cook for 1 - 2 minutes
6. Add the tomatoes and stir well and serve.

Turkey Spaghetti

(Prep + Cook Time: 30 minutes | **Serves:** 4-5)

Ingredients:

- 1 jar (25 oz) Delallo Pomodoro Tomato-Basil Sauce (or of your choice)
- 2 cups water
- 8-ounce whole wheat spaghetti, halved
- 1 teaspoon olive oil
- 1-pound ground turkey
- 3/4 teaspoon kosher salt
- 1/4 onion, diced
- 1 clove garlic, minced
- Parmesan cheese, grated, optional

Directions:

1. Select the SAUTÉ setting on the Instant Pot and heat the oil
2. Add the ground turkey and cook for 3 minutes, stirring occasionally.
3. Add the garlic and onion. Sauté for 4 minutes more, stirring occasionally
4. Add the spaghetti, sauce and salt. Pour the water in the pot and stir well. Close and lock the lid.
5. Press the CANCEL button to stop the SAUTE function, then select the MANUAL setting and set the cooking time for 9 minutes at HIGH pressure
6. When the timer beeps, use a Quick Release.
7. Carefully unlock the lid, Top with grated cheese and serve

Macaroni and Cheese

(Prep + Cook Time: 20 minutes | **Serves:** 4-5)

Ingredients:

- 1-pound elbow macaroni
- 4 cups chicken broth or vegetable broth, low sodium
- 3 cups Cheddar cheese shredded, about 12-ounce
- 1 ½ teaspoon yellow mustard
- 3 tablespoon unsalted butter
- 1/2 cup Parmesan cheese shredded, about 2-ounce
- 1/2 cup sour cream
- 1/8 teaspoon cayenne pepper

Directions:

1. In the Instant Pot, combine the macaroni, butter and broth
2. Close and lock the lid. Select MANUAL and cook at HIGH pressure for 6 minutes.
3. When the timer goes off, use a Quick Release.
4. Carefully unlock the lid, Add the cheese, sour cream, cayenne pepper and mustard. Mix well.
5. Let sit for 5 minutes, then stir and serve.

Pepper Jack Mac and Cheese

(Prep + Cook Time: 20 minutes | **Serves:** 4-5)

Ingredients:

- 1 ½ cups mozzarella cheese, shredded
- 2 ½ cups elbow macaroni
- 1 ½ cups pepper jack cheese, shredded
- 1 cup heavy cream
- 2 cups chicken stock
- 1 teaspoon salt
- 1 teaspoon ground black pepper
- 1 tablespoon butter
- 1/2 cup whole milk

Directions:

1. Add the macaroni, heavy cream and stock to the Instant Pot.
2. Season with salt and pepper, stir well. Close and lock the lid
3. Select the MANUAL setting and set the cooking time for 7 minutes at HIGH pressure.
4. When the timer beeps, use a Quick Release.
5. Carefully unlock the lid, Add the butter, milk and cheese. Stir well and let sit for 5 minutes then Serve

Veggie Pasta

(Prep + Cook Time: 25 minutes | **Serves:** 4-5)

Ingredients:

- 2 cups dried pasta
- 1/2 can black olives, rinsed and drained
- 1/2 cup frozen spinach
- 1/2 zucchini, sliced
- 1/2 squash, shredded
- 1/2 teaspoon garlic powder
- 1/2 teaspoon cumin
- 1/2 tablespoon Italian seasoning
- 1 cup water
- 1/2 jar spaghetti sauce
- 1/2 can chickpeas, rinsed and drained
- 1/2 cup frozen lima beans

Directions:

1. Combine all of the ingredients in the Instant Pot and stir to mix
2. Select MANUAL and cook at HIGH pressure for 7 minutes.
3. Once timer goes off, allow to Naturally Release for 10 minutes, then release any remaining pressure manually.
4. Uncover the pot and Serve

Pasta with Meat Sauce

(Prep + Cook Time: 25 minutes | Serves: 4)

Ingredients:

- 1-pound ground beef
- 24-ounce pasta sauce
- 8-ounce dried pasta
- 1 teaspoon olive oil
- 1 ½ cup water
- Italian seasoning to taste
- Salt and ground black pepper to taste

Directions:

1. Preheat the Instant Pot by selecting SAUTÉ. Add and heat the oil.
2. Add the ground beef and cook until all the meat is browned, stirring occasionally
3. Add the pasta, water and sauce, stir well.
4. Press the CANCEL key to stop the SAUTÉ function.
5. Close and lock the lid. Select MANUAL and cook at HIGH pressure for 7 minutes
6. When the timer beeps, use a Quick Release.
7. Carefully unlock the lid, Sprinkle with Italian seasoning, salt and pepper to taste. Stir and serve.

Seafood Pasta Recipe

(Prep + Cook Time: 30 minutes | Serves: 4-5)

Ingredients:

- 1/2 cup dry white wine
- 2 cups vegetable stock
- 2 cups macaroni
- 1/2 cup parmesan cheese, grated
- 1 ½ cups frozen mixed seafood
- 1 medium onion, chopped.
- 2 cloves garlic, chopped.
- 1 teaspoon mixed herbs
- 1 tablespoon olive oil
- 2 tomatoes, chopped.
- 1 red bell pepper, chopped.
- 1 tablespoon tomato purée
- 1/2 teaspoon salt
- 1/2 teaspoon ground black pepper

Directions:

1. Preheat the Instant Pot by selecting SAUTÉ. Add and heat the oil
2. Add the onion and garlic and sauté for 2 minutes.
3. Add the tomatoes and bell pepper and cook for 2 minutes more.
4. Pour in the wine and stir well. Simmer for 5 minutes.
5. Add the stock, macaroni, seafood, herbs and tomato purée. Season with salt and pepper. Stir well to combine
6. Press the CANCEL button to reset the cooking program, then press the MANUAL button and set the cooking time for 5 minutes at HIGH pressure.
7. Once pressure cooking is complete, select CANCEL and use a Quick Release
8. Carefully unlock the lid, Top with cheese and serve.

Tomato Pasta with Capers and Tuna

(Prep + Cook Time: 25 minutes | Serves: 4-5)

Ingredients:

- 1 ½ cups tomatoes, diced
- 1/8 teaspoon chili pepper
- 1/8 teaspoon oregano
- 2 cups water
- 2 cups pasta of your choice
- 2 tablespoon olive oil
- 2 cloves garlic, sliced
- 1 small can tuna in oil
- 2 tablespoon capers
- 1/2 cup parmesan cheese, grated
- 3/4 cup red wine
- Salt and ground black pepper to taste

Directions:
1. Select the SAUTÉ setting on the Instant Pot and heat the oil.
2. Add the garlic and sauté for 1 minute.
3. Add the tomatoes and pasta, stir. Sprinkle with chilies and oregano
4. Add the water and red wine. Sprinkle with salt and pepper, Stir well.
5. Close and lock the lid. Press the CANCEL button to stop the SAUTE function, then select the MANUAL setting and set the cooking time for 6 minutes at HIGH pressure.
6. Once pressure cooking is complete, use a Quick Release
7. Carefully unlock the lid, set your instant pot on SAUTÉ mode, add the tuna and capers.
8. Stir and cook for 3 to 4 minutes. Top with cheese and serve

Easy Cheesy Beef Pasta

(Prep + Cook Time: 30 minutes | **Serves:** 4-5)

Ingredients:
- 1 ¼ pounds' ground beef
- 1-pound elbow macaroni
- 3 beef bouillon cubes
- 8-ounce sharp cheddar cheese, shredded
- 1 teaspoon olive oil
- 3 ½ cups hot water
- 1 packet onion soup mix
- Salt and ground black pepper to taste

Directions:
1. Preheat the Instant Pot by selecting SAUTÉ. Add and heat the oil
2. Add the ground beef and cook until all the meat is browned, stirring occasionally.
3. In a bowl; combine the water, onion soup mix and bouillon cubes
4. Add the mixture and macaroni to the pot, Stir well.
5. Press the CANCEL button to reset the cooking program, then press the MANUAL button and set the cooking time for 7 minutes at HIGH pressure.
6. Once pressure cooking is complete, select Cancel and use a Quick Release.
7. Sprinkle with cheddar cheese, stir and let sit for 5 minutes
8. Taste and season with salt and pepper if necessary and serve.

Ip Carbonara

(Prep + Cook Time: 25 minutes | **Serves:** 4)

Ingredients:
- 1-pound pasta dry, rigatoni, penne or cavatappi are great
- 8-ounce bacon pancetta or guanciale
- 4 tablespoon heavy cream
- 4 large eggs, beaten
- 1 cup Parmesan cheese, grated
- Ground black pepper to taste
- 4 cups water
- 1/4 teaspoon kosher salt

Directions:
1. Add the pasta, water and salt to the Instant Pot.
2. Close and lock the lid. Select MANUAL and cook at HIGH pressure for 5 minutes
3. Meanwhile, in a bowl, whisk together the eggs, cheese and black pepper until combined.
4. In a frying pan, cook the bacon on medium heat for 3 minutes, or until it's crispy
5. When the timer goes off, use a Quick Release.
6. Carefully unlock the lid, Set your instant pot on SAUTÉ mode.
7. Add the bacon to the pot and cook for 30 second.
8. Pour in the egg mixture and heavy cream. Stir well to combine
9. Press the CANCEL key to stop the SAUTÉ function.
10. Close the lid and let it sit for 5 minutes and serve.

Spinach and Fusilli

(Prep + Cook Time: 25 minutes | **Serves:** 4-5)

Ingredients:
- 1-pound fusilli pasta
- 4 cloves garlic, minced
- 1/2 cup parmesan cheese, shredded
- 4 tablespoon butter
- Water as needed, to cover the pasta
- 4 cups spinach, chopped.
- Salt and ground black pepper to taste

Directions:
1. Add the pasta and water to the Instant Pot.
2. Add the spinach and garlic. Close and lock the lid.
3. Select the MANUAL setting and set the cooking time for 6 minutes at HIGH pressure
4. Once pressure cooking is complete, select Cancel and use a Quick Release.
5. Carefully unlock the lid, Add the cheese and butter. Sprinkle with salt and pepper, Stir well
6. Close and lock the lid. Select MANUAL and cook at HIGH pressure for 5 minutes.
7. When the timer beeps, use a Quick Release.
8. Carefully unlock the lid, and Serve

Pasta with Broccoli.

(Prep + Cook Time: 20 minutes | **Serves:** 4)

Ingredients:
- 1/2-pound pasta
- 1/2 cup broccoli
- 8-ounce cheddar cheese, grated
- 1/2 cup half and half
- 2 cups water
- Salt to taste

Directions:
1. Add pasta and water to the Instant Pot.
2. Place a steamer basket on top and Put the broccoli in the basket. Close and lock the lid.
3. Select MANUAL and cook at HIGH pressure for 4 minutes.
4. When the timer goes off, use a Quick Release. Carefully unlock the lid. Take out the broccoli and drain the pasta.
5. Set your Instant Pot on SAUTÉ mode. Add the cooked pasta, broccoli, cheese and half and half, stir well. Season with salt to taste. Cook the dish for 2 minutes then Serve

Parmesan Chicken Pasta

(Prep + Cook Time: 40 minutes | **Serves:** 2 - 3)

Ingredients:
- 8-ounce linguine noodles, halved
- 3 cloves garlic, chopped.
- 8-ounce cherry tomatoes, halved
- 1/2 teaspoon Italian seasoning
- 1/4 cup parsley, chopped.
- 1 cup water
- 1 tablespoon butter
- 1/2 cup Italian breadcrumbs
- 1 cup Parmesan cheese, grated
- 1/2 jar spaghetti sauce
- 2 chicken breasts, skinless and boneless
- Salt and crushed red pepper to taste

Directions:
1. Add the water, noodles and jar of spaghetti sauce to the Instant Pot, Stir well.
2. Add the jar chicken breasts, garlic, tomatoes, Italian seasoning, parsley, salt and pepper
3. Close and lock the lid. Select the MANUAL setting and set the cooking time for 20 minutes at HIGH pressure.
4. Meanwhile, melt the butter in a pan and toast breadcrumbs. Once pressure cooking is complete, use a Quick Release
5. Unlock and carefully open the lid, Stir the dish. Top with breadcrumbs and cheese; let it sit for 5 minutes and serve.

Egg Recipes

Egg and Ham Casserole

(Prep + Cook Time: 35 minutes | **Serves:** 3)

Ingredients:
- 1/2 cup plain Greek yogurt
- 1 cup ham, diced
- 1 cup cheddar cheese, shredded
- 1 cup water
- 6 beaten eggs
- 1/4 cup chives, chopped.
- 1/2 teaspoon black pepper

Directions:
1. In a medium bowl, whisk together eggs and yogurt until combined.
2. Add the cheese, ham, chives, and pepper. Stir well.
3. Prepare the Instant Pot by adding the water to the pot and placing the steam rack in it
4. Pour the mixture into the heatproof bowl or cup.
5. Place the bowl on the steam rack and secure the lid.
6. Close and lock the lid. Select the MANUAL setting and set the cooking time for 20 minutes at HIGH pressure.
7. When the timer beeps, use a Quick Release. Carefully unlock the lid, Serve the dish warm.

Simple French Eggs

(Prep + Cook Time: 20 minutes | **Serves:** 4)

Ingredients:
- 4 eggs
- 4 slices bacon
- 1/2 teaspoon olive oil
- 4 tablespoon chives, chopped.
- 1 cup water
- Salt to taste

Directions:
1. Prepare the ramekins by adding a drop of olive oil in each and rubbing the bottom and sides
2. Crack an egg in each, add a bacon slice on top, season with salt and top each with chives
3. Pour the water into the Instant Pot and insert a steamer basket.
4. Place the ramekins in the basket. Close and lock the lid. Select MANUAL and cook at HIGH pressure for 8 minutes. Once pressure cooking is complete, use a Quick Release. Serve immediately

Spinach and Tomato Breakfast

(Prep + Cook Time: 35 minutes | **Serves:** 5)

Ingredients:
- 3 cups baby spinach, chopped.
- 1 cup tomato, diced
- 1 ½ cups water
- 3 green onions, sliced
- 4 tomato, sliced
- 1/4 cup parmesan, grated
- 12 beaten eggs
- Salt and ground black pepper to the taste
- 1/2 cup milk

Directions:
1. Prepare the Instant Pot by adding the water to the pot and placing the steam rack in it
2. In a bowl, mix the eggs with salt, pepper and milk. Stir to combine.
3. In a baking dish, mix diced tomato, spinach, and green onions
4. Pour the eggs mix over veggies, spread tomato slices on top. Sprinkle with parmesan.
5. Place the dish on the steam rack.
6. Close and lock the lid. Select MANUAL and cook at HIGH pressure for 20 minutes.
7. Once pressure cooking is complete, use a Quick Release
8. Carefully uncover the pot. If you want a crisp top, slide under the broiler for a few minutes at the end.

Eggs Dish

(Prep + Cook Time: 20 minutes **| Serves:** 5)

Ingredients:

- 1 cup water
- 1/4 cup cream
- 8 eggs
- 1/4 cup dill, chopped.
- 1 teaspoon mayo sauce
- 1 teaspoon minced garlic
- 1 tablespoon mustard
- 1 teaspoon ground white pepper
- 1/2 teaspoon sea salt

Directions:

1. Pour the water into the Instant Pot and insert a steamer basket
2. Place the eggs in the basket.
3. Close and lock the lid. Select MANUAL and cook at HIGH pressure for 5 minutes
4. When the timer beeps, use a Quick Release. Carefully unlock the lid.
5. Transfer the eggs to the bowl of cold water and cool for 2 - 3 minutes
6. Peel the eggs, remove the egg yolks and mash them.
7. In a medium bowl, combine the cream, mayo sauce, mustard, pepper, garlic, salt and mashed egg yolks.
8. Sprinkle the mixture with the dill. Mix well.
9. Transfer the egg yolk mixture to the pastry bag.
10. Fill the egg whites with the yolk mixture, Serve

Soft Eggs and Ham

(Prep + Cook Time: 10 minutes **| Serves:** 4)

Ingredients:

- 3 eggs
- 6-ounce ham
- 2 tablespoon chives
- 1 cup water
- 1/4 teaspoon ground ginger
- 1 teaspoon paprika
- 1 teaspoon salt
- 1/2 teaspoon ground white pepper

Directions:

1. Beat the eggs into the small ramekins.
2. Season with the salt, pepper, and paprika.
3. Prepare the Instant Pot by adding the water to the pot and placing the steam rack on top
4. Place the ramekins on the steam rack and secure the lid.
5. Select the STEAM setting and set the cooking time for 4 minutes.
6. Meanwhile, chop the ham and chives and combine the ingredients together. Add ground ginger and stir the mixture
7. Transfer the mixture to the serving plates.
8. When the timer beeps, use a Quick Release.
9. Carefully unlock the lid. Serve the eggs over the ham mixture

Cheesy Hash Brown Bake

(Prep + Cook Time: 15 minutes **| Serves:** 4)

Ingredients:

- 6 slices bacon, chopped.
- 1 cup shredded cheddar cheese
- 2 cups frozen hash browns
- 1/4 cup milk
- 8 beaten eggs
- 1/2 teaspoon salt
- 1/2 teaspoon ground black pepper

Directions:

1. Preheat the Instant Pot by selecting SAUTÉ.
2. Sauté the bacon until lightly crispy.
3. Add hash brown. Cook, stirring occasionally, for 2 minutes or until they start to thaw

4. Press the CANCEL button to stop the cooking program.
5. In a medium bowl, whisk together the eggs, cheese, milk, salt and pepper
6. Pour the mixture over the hash browns.
7. Close and lock the lid. Select MANUAL and cook at HIGH pressure for 5 minutes.
8. Once pressure cooking is complete, use a Quick Release. Slice and serve

Sausage Frittata

(Prep + Cook Time: 45 minutes | **Serves:** 3)

Ingredients:
- 1/4 cup cheddar cheese, grated
- 1/2 cup cooked ground sausage
- 4 beaten eggs
- 1 ½ cups water
- 1 tablespoon butter
- 2 tablespoon sour cream
- Salt and ground black pepper to taste

Directions:
1. Prepare the Instant Pot by adding the water to the pot and placing the steam rack on top
2. Grease 6-7-inch soufflé dish with butter.
3. In a bowl, whisk together the eggs and sour cream until combined.
4. Add the cheese, sausage, salt and pepper, stir well.
5. Pour into the dish and wrap tightly with foil all over.
6. Place the dish on the steam rack, close and secure the lid
7. Select the MANUAL setting and set the cooking time for 17 minutes at LOW pressure.
8. When the timer goes off, use a Quick Release. Carefully unlock the lid, Serve

Cheese and Bacon Quiche

(Prep + Cook Time: 50 minutes | **Serves:** 4)

Ingredients:
- 1 cup water
- 6 large eggs, beaten
- 1 cup ground sausage, cooked
- 1 cup parmesan Cheese
- 2 large green onions, chopped.
- 1/2 cup almond or coconut milk
- 1/2 cup diced ham
- 4 slices cooked and crumbled bacon
- 1/4 teaspoon salt
- 1/8 teaspoon black pepper, ground

Directions:
1. Pour the water into the Instant Pot and insert a steam rack
2. In a bowl, whisk together the eggs, milk, salt and pepper until combined
3. Add the ham, sausage, bacon, cheese and green onion and stir well.
4. Cover the dish with foil and place on the steam rack.
5. Close and lock the lid. Select MANUAL and cook at HIGH pressure for 30 minutes.
6. Once cooking is complete, use a Natural Release for 10 minutes, then release any remaining pressure manually
7. Uncover the pot, Remove the foil, Serve.
8. If you like a crisp top, you can sprinkle the dish with some additional cheese then slide under the broiler for a few minutes at the end

Scrambled Eggs & Bacon.

(Prep + Cook Time: 15 minutes | **Serves:** 4)

Ingredients:
- 7 eggs
- 1/2 cup. milk
- 1 teaspoon basil
- 1 teaspoon paprika
- 1 tablespoon butter
- 1/4 cup. fresh parsley
- 4-ounce bacon
- 1 teaspoon salt
- 1 tablespoon cilantro

Directions:

1. Beat the eggs in the mixing bowl and whisk them well.
2. Then add milk, basil, salt, paprika, and cilantro. Stir the mixture. Chop the bacon and parsley.
3. Set the Instant Pot mode "Sauté" and transfer the chopped bacon. Cook it for 3 minutes
4. Then add whisked egg mixture and cook the dish for 5 minutes more.
5. After this, mix up the eggs carefully with the help of the wooden spoon
6. Then sprinkle the dish with the chopped parsley and cook it for 4 minutes more.
7. When the eggs are cooked - remove them from the Instant Pot.
8. Serve the dish immediately. Enjoy!

IP Hard Boiled Eggs

(Prep + Cook Time: 15 minutes | **Serves:** 4-8)

Ingredients:

- 5 to 10 eggs
- 1 cup water

Directions:

1. Pour the water into the Instant Pot and insert a steamer basket.
2. Put the eggs in the basket
3. Close and lock the lid. Select MANUAL and cook at HIGH pressure for 5 minutes.
4. Once timer goes off, allow to Naturally Release for 5 minutes. Then use a Quick Release.
5. Transfer the eggs to the bowl of cold water. Wait 2 - 3 minutes. If you like, you can peel immediately

Omelet Cups

(Prep + Cook Time: 25 minutes | **Serves:** 2)

Ingredients:

- 1 onion, chopped.
- 1 jalapeño pepper, chopped.
- 3 eggs, beaten
- 1/2 teaspoon olive oil
- 1 cup water
- Salt and freshly ground black pepper to taste

Directions:

1. Prepare two ramekins by adding a drop of olive oil in each and rubbing the bottom and sides
2. In a medium bowl, whisk together the eggs, water, salt and black pepper until combined.
3. Add the onion and jalapeño, stir.
4. Transfer egg mixture to the ramekins.
5. Prepare the Instant Pot by adding the water to the pot and placing the steam rack in it
6. Place the ramekins on the steam rack and secure the lid.
7. Close and lock the lid. Select MANUAL and cook at HIGH pressure for 5 minutes.
8. When the timer goes off, use a Quick Release.
9. Carefully unlock the lid. Serve hot

Mexican Style Egg Casserole

(Prep + Cook Time: 50 minutes | **Serves:** 5)

Ingredients:

- 1 pound' mild sausages, ground
- 1 cup Cotija cheese (or any semi-hard cheese)
- 1 cup mozzarella cheese
- 1 large red onion, chopped.
- Sour cream, optional to garnish
- Cilantro, optional to garnish
- 1/2 cup green onions
- 8 large eggs, beaten
- 1/2 teaspoon olive oil
- 1/2 cup flour
- 1 can black beans, rinsed

Directions:

1. Select the Sauté setting on the Instant Pot and heat the oil
2. Add the onion and sauté for 2 - 3 minutes. Add the sausages and cook until starting to brown on all sides.
3. In another bowl, combine the eggs and flour
4. Pour the mixture into the Instant Pot and stir well.
5. Add the beans, Cotija cheese and mozzarella cheese to the pot.
6. Press the Cancel button to reset the cooking program, then select the MANUAL setting and set the cooking time for 20 minutes at HIGH pressure
7. Once cooking is complete, let the pressure Release Naturally for 10 minutes. Release any remaining steam manually.
8. Uncover the pot, Top with sour cream, cilantro and green onion. Chill for a while and serve

Spinach Tomato Quiche

(Prep + Cook Time: 45 minutes | **Serves:** 5)

Ingredients:

- 10-12 large eggs, beaten
- 1 cup tomato, deseeded and roughly chopped.
- 4 medium green onions, chopped.
- 2 ½ cups baby spinach, diced
- 3 tomato slices

- 1/3 cup parmesan cheese, shredded
- 1/2 cup milk
- 2 cups water
- 1/2 teaspoon kosher salt
- Ground black pepper to taste

Directions:

1. In a large bowl, whisk together eggs, milk, salt, and pepper until combined
2. In a baking dish that can fit into the pot, combine the spinach, tomato and green onions.
3. Add the egg mixture to the baking dish and stir well.
4. Place 3 tomato slices on top and sprinkle with cheese.
5. Prepare the Instant Pot by adding the water to the pot and placing the steam rack in it
6. Put the baking dish on the rack. Close and lock the lid.
7. Select the MANUAL setting and set the cooking time for 20 minutes at HIGH pressure.
8. Once cooking is complete, let the pressure Release Naturally for 5 minutes. Release any remaining steam manually
9. Uncover the pot, Remove the dish from the pot.
10. If desired, broil in the oven for a few minutes for a browned top then Serve

Eggs, Sausage and Bacon Omelet

(Prep + Cook Time: 50 minutes | **Serves:** 6)

Ingredients:

- 6-12 beaten eggs
- 6 bacon slices, cooked
- 6 sausage links, sliced
- 1 onion, diced
- Garlic powder

- 1/2 cup milk
- Dried oregano, optional
- Olive oil cooking spray
- 2 cup water
- Salt and ground black pepper to taste

Equipment:

- 1 ½ quart ceramic baking dish or Pyrex glass bowl

Directions:

1. In a medium bowl, whisk together the eggs and milk, until well combined.
2. Add the sausages and onion. Season with garlic powder, salt, and pepper. Stir well
3. Grease Pyrex glass bowl with cooking spray
4. Pour the egg mixture into the Pyrex and wrap tightly with foil all over.
5. Prepare the Instant Pot by adding the water to the pot and placing the steam rack in it.

6. Place the bowl on the steam rack and secure the lid.
7. Close and lock the lid. Select MANUAL and cook at HIGH pressure for 25 minutes
8. Once cooking is complete, select CANCEL and let Naturally Release for 10 minutes. Open the lid,
9. Remove the foil. The egg may pop-out of the bowl; just push it back.
10. Lay the cooked bacon on top and cover with shredded cheese
11. Close and lock the lid. Select the MANUAL setting and set the cooking time for 5 minutes at HIGH pressure.
12. When the timer beeps, use a Quick Release.
13. Carefully unlock the lid. Take the dish out from the Instant Pot. If you like, top with dried oregano and serve

Fresh Mushroom Frittata

(Prep + Cook Time: 20 minutes | **Serves:** 3)

Ingredients:

- 1 cup fresh mushrooms, chopped.
- 4 beaten eggs
- 1 cup sharp cheddar cheese, shredded and divided
- 1 cup water
- 1/4 cup half-and-half
- Salt and freshly ground black pepper to taste

Directions:

1. In a medium bowl, combine the eggs, mushrooms, half-and-half, salt and pepper, and 1/2 cup cheese. Mix well
2. Divide mixture into 1/2-pint wide mouth jars evenly and sprinkle with remaining cheese. Cover the jars with lids loosely.
3. Pour the water into the Instant Pot and insert a steamer trivet. Place the jars on top of trivet
4. Close and lock the lid. Select the MANUAL setting and set the cooking time for 3 minutes at HIGH pressure.
5. Once pressure cooking is complete, use a Quick Release. Carefully unlock the lid, Serve

IP Soft Boiled Eggs

(Prep + Cook Time: 10 minutes | **Serves:** 2)

Ingredients:

- 2 English muffins, toasted
- 4 eggs
- 1 cup water
- Salt and ground black pepper to taste

Directions:

1. Prepare the Instant Pot by adding the water to the pot and insert a steamer basket.
2. Put the eggs in the basket
3. Close and lock the lid. Select the STEAM setting and set the cooking time for 4 minutes
4. When the timer goes off, use a Quick Release.
5. Carefully unlock the lid. Transfer the eggs to the bowl of cold water. Wait 2 - 3 minutes
6. Peel the eggs. Serve one egg per half of toasted English muffin. Sprinkle with salt and pepper to taste.

Savory Egg Porridge Breakfast.

(Prep + Cook Time: 50 minutes | **Serves:** 4)

Ingredients:

- 4 eggs
- 2 cups. chicken broth
- 1 tablespoon olive oil
- 2 teaspoon soy sauce
- 4 chopped scallions
- 1/2 cup. rinsed and drained white rice
- 1 tablespoon sugar
- 1/2 teaspoon salt
- 2 cups. water
- Black pepper to taste

Directions:

1. Pour water, broth, sugar, salt, and rice into the Instant Pot. Close the lid
2. Hit "Porridge" and 30 minutes on "High" pressure
3. While that cooks, heat oil in a saucepan
4. Crack in the eggs one at a time, so they aren't touching each other
5. Cook until the whites become crispy on the edges, but the yolks are still runny. Sprinkle on salt and pepper.
6. When the Instant Pot timer goes off, hit "Cancel" and wait for the pressure to go down on its own.
7. If the porridge isn't thick enough, hit "Sauté" and cook uncovered for 5 - 10 minutes.
8. Serve with scallions, soy sauce, and an egg per bowl

Easy Egg Muffins

(Prep + Cook Time: 15 minutes | **Serves:** 2)

Ingredients:

- 4 beaten eggs
- 1 green onion, chopped.
- 4 bacon slices, cooked and crumbled
- 4 tablespoon cheddar cheese, shredded
- 1 ½ cups water
- A pinch of salt

Directions:

1. In a medium bowl, whisk together eggs, bacon, cheese, onion and salt until combined
2. Divide the mixture into muffin cups.
3. Pour the water into the Instant Pot and insert a steamer basket. Place the muffin cups in the basket
4. Close and lock the lid. Select MANUAL and cook at HIGH pressure for 8 minutes.
5. When the timer goes off, allow a 2 minutes rest time and then do a Quick Release.
6. Carefully unlock the lid. Remove the steamer basket with muffins from the pot, Serve

Pepper Egg Cups

(Prep + Cook Time: 20 minutes | **Serves:** 4)

Ingredients:

- 4 bell peppers
- 2 tablespoon mozzarella cheese, grated freshly
- Chopped fresh herbs
- 2/3 cup water
- 4 eggs
- Salt and ground black pepper to taste

Directions:

1. Cut the bell peppers ends to form about 1 ½-inch high cup. Remove the seeds
2. Crack 1 egg into each pepper. Season with salt and black pepper. Cover each bell pepper with a piece of foil.
3. Pour the water into the Instant Pot and insert a steamer basket.
4. Place the bell peppers in the basket. Close and lock the lid.
5. Select MANUAL and cook at HIGH pressure for 4 minutes.
6. When the timer goes off, use a Quick Release. Carefully unlock the lid. Transfer the bell pepper cups onto serving plates.
7. Sprinkle with mozzarella cheese and chopped fresh herbs of your choice, Serve

Cheesy Spinach Egg Cups

(Prep + Cook Time: 20 minutes | **Serves:** 4)

Ingredients:

- 1 cup chopped baby spinach
- 1/2 cup mozzarella cheese, shredded
- 1/4 cup feta cheese, cubed
- 6 beaten eggs
- 1 cup water
- 1 chopped tomato
- 1 teaspoon black pepper
- 1/2 teaspoon salt

Directions:

1. Pour the water into the Instant Pot and insert a steam rack
2. Lay the spinach in two heatproof cups.
3. In a bowl, whisk together the eggs, mozzarella cheese, feta cheese, tomato, salt and pepper until combined.
4. Pour the mixture into the cups, leaving 1/4-inch of head room
5. Place the cups on the steam rack and secure the lid.
6. Select the MANUAL setting and set the cooking time for 8 minutes at HIGH pressure
7. Once pressure cooking is complete, use a Quick Release
8. Carefully unlock the lid. Serve the dish warm.

Cheesy Egg Bake

(Prep + Cook Time: 20 minutes | **Serves:** 4)

Ingredients:

- 2 cups frozen hash browns
- 1 cup cheddar cheese, shredded
- 6 slices of turkey bacon, cubed
- 8 beaten eggs
- 1 teaspoon olive oil
- 1/2 cup half and half or milk
- Salt to taste

Directions:

1. Select the SAUTÉ setting on the Instant Pot and heat the oil.
2. Add the slices of turkey bacon. Sauté for about 1 - 2 minutes until the bacon is browned
3. Press the CANCEL button to stop the cooking program.
4. Layer the hash brown potatoes over the top of the bacon.
5. Sprinkle one half of the cheddar cheese over the potatoes.
6. In a medium bowl, whisk together the eggs, milk and salt until well combined
7. Pour the mixture into the Instant Pot and sprinkle with the remaining half of the cheddar cheese.
8. Close and lock the lid. Select the MANUAL setting and set the cooking time for 7 minutes at HIGH pressure.
9. When the timer beeps, use a Quick Release
10. Carefully unlock the lid. Taste and season more if necessary.

Potato and Egg Mayo Salad

(Prep + Cook Time: 20 minutes | **Serves:** 3)

Ingredients:

- 1 ½ cups water
- 1/4 cup onion, chopped.
- 1 cup mayonnaise
- 6 russet potatoes, peeled and diced
- 4 large eggs
- 1 tablespoon dill pickle juice
- 1 tablespoon mustard
- 2 tablespoon fresh parsley, chopped.
- Pinch of salt
- Pinch of ground black pepper

Directions:

1. Pour the water into the Instant Pot and insert a steamer basket
2. Place the potatoes and eggs in the basket
3. Close and lock the lid. Select the MANUAL setting and set the cooking time for 5 minutes at HIGH pressure.
4. Once pressure cooking is complete, use a Quick Release. Carefully unlock the lid
5. Transfer the eggs to the bowl of cold water and cool for 2 - 3 minutes.
6. In a medium bowl, combine the mayonnaise, parsley, onion, dill pickle juice, and mustard. Mix well. Add salt and pepper
7. Peel and slice the eggs. Toss the potatoes and eggs in the bowl. Stir and serve.

Grains Recipes

Pearl Barley Salad

(Prep + Cook Time: 30 minutes | **Serves:** 3)

Ingredients:

- 1 cup pearl barley
- 1 green apple, chopped.
- 3/4 cup jarred spinach pesto
- 2 ½ cups water
- 1/4 cup celery, chopped.
- Salt and white pepper to taste

Directions:

1. Rinse the barley well.
2. Add the barley, water, salt and pepper to the Instant Pot, stir well
3. Close and secure the lid. Select MANUAL and cook at HIGH pressure for 20 minutes.
4. Once pressure cooking is complete, use a Quick Release
5. Carefully open the pot, strain barley and move to a bowl.
6. Add celery, apple and spinach pesto, toss to coat and serve

Cheesy Ground Grits

(Prep + Cook Time: 30 minutes | **Serves:** 6)

Ingredients:

- 4-ounce cheddar cheese
- 2 cup stone-ground grits
- 3 cups water
- 2 - 3 tablespoon butter
- 2 tablespoon olive oil
- 1 cup half and half
- 1 ½ teaspoon salt

Directions:

1. To preheat the Instant Pot, select SAUTÉ. Once hot, add the oil to the pot
2. Add grits, stir and cook for 3 minutes until fragrant.
3. Add the water, half and half, cheese, butter and salt, stir well.
4. Close and secure the lid. Select MANUAL and cook at HIGH pressure for 10 minutes
5. Once cooking is complete, use a Natural Release for 15 minutes, then release any remaining pressure. Open the lid and serve hot!

Vegan Polenta

(Prep + Cook Time: 35 minutes | **Serves:** 2)

Ingredients:

- 2 cups veggie stock
- 1/4 cup cilantro, minced
- 1 bunch green onion, chopped.
- 1 cup polenta
- 2 teaspoon garlic, chopped.
- 1/8 teaspoon cayenne pepper
- 1 ½ cups hot water
- 1 tablespoon chili powder
- 1 teaspoon olive oil
- 1/2 teaspoon cumin
- 1/2 teaspoon smoked paprika
- 1/2 teaspoon dried oregano
- Salt and ground black pepper to taste

Directions:

1. Set your instant pot on SAUTÉ mode, add the oil and heat it up
2. Add the garlic and green onion and cook for 2 minutes.
3. Add the cilantro, chili powder, cumin, paprika, oregano, salt, black pepper, cayenne pepper, and stock. Stir well.
4. Press the CANCEL key to stop the SAUTÉ function
5. In a bowl, whisk together the polenta and hot water until combined.
6. Pour the mixture in the pot and mix well. Close and lock the lid

7. Select MANUAL and cook at HIGH pressure for 10 minutes.
8. When the timer goes off, let the pressure Release Naturally for 10 minutes, then release any remaining steam manually. Open the lid, Serve warm

Pumpkin Oats Granola

(Prep + Cook Time: 30 minutes | **Serves:** 5)

Ingredients:
- 1 cup steel cut oats
- 1/4 cup maple syrup
- 1 teaspoon pumpkin pie spice
- 2 teaspoon cinnamon
- 1 tablespoon soft butter
- 1 cup pumpkin puree
- 3 cups water
- A pinch of salt

Directions:
1. To preheat the Instant Pot, select SAUTÉ. Once hot, add the butter and melt it
2. Add the oats and stir, cooking for 3 minutes.
3. Add pumpkin puree, water, cinnamon, salt, maple syrup and pumpkin spice, stir.
4. Close and secure the lid. Select MANUAL and cook at HIGH pressure for 10 minutes
5. Once pressure cooking is complete, use a Natural Release for 10 minutes, then release any remaining pressure and uncover the pot.
6. Stir oats granola and leave it aside for 10 minutes. Serve

Couscous and Vegetable Medley

(Prep + Cook Time: 30 minutes | **Serves:** 5)

Ingredients:
- 1 cup carrot grated
- 1 large red bell pepper chopped.
- 1/2 large onion, chopped.
- 2 bay leaves
- 1 ¾ cups couscous Israeli
- 1 tablespoon olive oil
- 1/2 teaspoon garam masala
- 2 teaspoon salt or to taste
- 1 tablespoon lemon juice
- Cilantro to garnish
- 1 ¾ cups water

Directions:
1. Preheat the Instant Pot by selecting SAUTÉ. Once hot, add the oil to the pot
2. Add the onion and bay leaves. Sauté for 2 minutes.
3. Add the carrots and bell pepper. Sauté for 1 minute more. Add the couscous, garam masala, water and salt. Stir well
4. Close and secure the lid. Select MANUAL and cook at HIGH pressure for 2 minutes.
5. Once cooking is complete, use a Natural Release for 10 minutes, then release any remaining pressure.
6. Fluff the couscous and add the lemon juice. Garnish with cilantro and serve hot

Millet Pudding

(Prep + Cook Time: 25 minutes | **Serves:** 3)

Ingredients:
- 7 ounces' water
- 2/3 cup millet
- 1 ⅔ cups coconut milk
- 4 dates, pitted
- Salt to taste
- Honey for serving

Directions:
1. Add the millet, milk, dates and a pinch of salt to the Instant Pot and stir well.
2. Add the water and stir again.
3. Close and secure the lid. Select MANUAL and cook at HIGH pressure for 10 minutes
4. Once cooking is complete, use a Natural Release for 10 minutes, then release any remaining pressure.
5. Uncover the pot and fluff the dish with a fork. Top with honey in the serving bowls

Buckwheat Porridge

(Prep + Cook Time: 30 minutes | **Serves:** 4)

Ingredients:
- 1 cup raw buckwheat groats
- 1 banana, sliced
- 1/4 cup raisins
- 3 cups rice milk
- 1 teaspoon ground cinnamon
- 1/2 teaspoon vanilla
- Chopped nuts, optional

Directions:
1. Rinse the buckwheat well and put in the Instant Pot
2. Add the rice milk, banana, raisins, cinnamon and vanilla.
3. Close and secure the lid. Select MANUAL and cook at HIGH pressure for 6 minutes
4. Once cooking is complete, use a Natural Release for 20 minutes, then release any remaining pressure.
5. Open the lid and stir the porridge. If you like, you can sprinkle with chopped nuts

Dried-Fig Millet

(Prep + Cook Time: 25 minutes | **Serves:** 5)

Ingredients:
- 1 ¾ cups millet
- 1/3 cup chopped dried figs
- 1 cup almond milk
- 2 cups water
- 2 tablespoon coconut oil

Directions:
1. Add the millet, milk, water, figs and coconut oil to the Instant Pot and stir.
2. Close and secure the lid. Select the SOUP setting and set the cooking time for 10 minutes
3. When the timer goes off, let the pressure Release Naturally for 10 minutes, then release any remaining steam. Fluff the dish with a fork. and Serve

Creamy Strawberry Oats

(Prep + Cook Time: 20 minutes | **Serves:** 3)

Ingredients:
- 1/3 cup rolled oats
- 2 tablespoon strawberries, freeze-dried (or your favorite dried or frozen fruit)
- 2 cups water
- 1/2 teaspoon white sugar (or to taste)
- 2/3 cup whole milk
- 1 pinch of salt

Directions:
1. Add 2 cups of water to the Instant Pot and place the steam rack in the pot
2. In a small-sized, heat-safe mug or bowl, add the oats, strawberries, milk, and salt
3. Close and secure the lid. Select MANUAL and cook at HIGH pressure for 10 minutes.
4. When the timer beeps, use a Natural Release for 7-10 minutes, then release any remaining pressure.
5. Carefully remove the bowl from the pot.
6. Mix the contents vigorously and then sprinkle with sugar to taste. Serve

Tomato Polenta

(Prep + Cook Time: 30 minutes | **Serves:** 7)

Ingredients:

- 2 teaspoon fresh oregano, minced
- 2 tablespoon fresh parsley, minced
- 1 teaspoon fresh rosemary, minced
- 3 tablespoon fresh basil, minced
- 2 tablespoon olive oil
- 4 cups vegetable stock
- 1 cup polenta
- 1/2 cup onion, diced
- 2 cloves garlic, chopped.
- 1/3 cup sun-dried tomatoes, finely chopped.
- 1 bay leaf
- 1 teaspoon kosher salt

Directions:

1. Preheat the Instant Pot by selecting SAUTÉ. Add and heat the oil
2. Add the onion and garlic and cook for about 3 minutes until fragrant.
3. Add the tomatoes, oregano, parsley, rosemary, basil, bay leaf and salt
4. Pour in the stock and stir well.
5. Top the mixture with polenta. Secure the lid.
6. Press the CANCEL button to reset the cooking program, then press the MANUAL button and set the cooking time for 5 minutes at HIGH pressure
7. Once cooking is complete, let the pressure Release Naturally for 10 minutes. Release any remaining steam manually.
8. Uncover the pot, Serve warm

Delightful Farro

(Prep + Cook Time: 55 minutes | **Serves:** 5)

Ingredients:

- 1 cup whole grain farro
- 1/4 cup green onions, chopped.
- 1 tablespoon extra-virgin olive oil
- 1 teaspoon lemon juice
- 1 tablespoon apple cider vinegar
- 2 cups cherries, cut into halves
- 10 mint leaves, chopped.
- 3 cups water
- Salt to taste

Directions:

1. Rinse the farro well.
2. Pour the water in your instant pot, add farro and stir well
3. Close and secure the lid. Select the MANUAL setting and set the cooking time for 40 minutes at HIGH pressure.
4. When the timer goes off, use a Quick Release.
5. Open the lid, Drain farro, transfer to a bowl and mix with salt, oil, lemon juice, vinegar, cherries, green onions, and mint
6. Stir well and serve

Spinach and Tomato Couscous

(Prep + Cook Time: 18 minutes | **Serves:** 4)

Ingredients:

- 1/2 cup spinach, chopped.
- 1 ½ tomatoes, chopped.
- 1 cup couscous
- 1 ¼ cups vegetable broth
- 2 tablespoon vegan butter

Directions:

1. Preheat the Instant Pot by selecting SAUTÉ. Once hot, add the butter and melt it
2. Add the couscous and cook for a minute.
3. Pour the broth over and stir to combine

4. Close and secure the lid. Select MANUAL and cook at HIGH pressure for 5 minutes.
5. Once pressure cooking is complete, use a Quick Release
6. Open the lid, Transfer the couscous to a bowl. Add the tomatoes and spinach, and stir. and Serve.

Cornmeal-Porridge

(Prep + Cook Time: 20 minutes | **Serves:** 3)

Ingredients:
- 4 cups water
- 1 cup cornmeal
- 1/2 teaspoon nutmeg, ground
- 1/2 cup sweetened condensed milk
- 1 cup milk

Directions:
1. In a bowl, mix 1 cup of water with cornmeal and stir well.
2. Add the rest of the water with milk and cornmeal mix to the Instant Pot and stir
3. Add nutmeg and stir
4. Close and secure the lid. Select the MANUAL setting and set the cooking time for 6 minutes at HIGH pressure.
5. Once cooking is complete, use a Natural Release for 10 minutes, then release any remaining pressure
6. Open the lid, Add condensed milk and stir. and Serve.

Delicious Quinoa

(Prep + Cook Time: 15 minutes | **Serves:** 5)

Ingredients:
- 1 ½ cups quinoa, uncooked, well rinsed
- 2 ¼ cups water
- A pinch of salt
- 2 tablespoon maple syrup
- 1/4 teaspoon ground cinnamon
- 1/2 teaspoon vanilla

Optional toppings:
- Sliced almonds
- Milk
- Fresh berries

Directions:
1. Rinse the quinoa well
2. Combine all ingredients (except optional) in the Instant Pot and lock the lid
3. Select MANUAL and cook at HIGH pressure for 1 minute
4. When the timer goes off, use a Natural Release for 10 minutes, then move the pressure release to venting to release any remaining steam.
5. Unlock the lid, Fluff the cooked quinoa with a fork.
6. Serve with almonds, milk, and berries

Perfect Couscous

(Prep + Cook Time: 15 minutes | **Serves:** 4)

Ingredients:
- 2 cups couscous
- 2 ½ cups chicken stock
- 2 tablespoon butter
- Parsley leaves, chopped for serving
- Salt and ground black pepper to taste

Directions:
1. Select the SAUTÉ setting on the Instant Pot, add the butter and melt it
2. Add couscous and stock and stir.
3. Close and secure the lid. Select the MANUAL setting and set the cooking time for 5 minutes at HIGH pressure.
4. Once pressure cooking is complete, use a Quick Release
5. Open the pot. Fluff couscous with a fork, season with salt and pepper. Top with parsley and serve.

Quinoa Pilaf

(Prep + Cook Time: 15 minutes | **Serves:** 3)

Ingredients:
- 2 cups quinoa
- 1 handful parsley, chopped
- 3 cups water
- 2 tablespoon extra-virgin olive oil
- 2 cloves garlic, minced
- 2 teaspoon ground cumin
- 2 teaspoon turmeric
- Salt to taste

Directions:
1. Rinse the quinoa well.
2. Preheat the Instant Pot by selecting SAUTÉ. Once hot, add the oil to the pot
3. Add garlic, stir and cook for 1 minute.
4. Add water, quinoa, cumin, turmeric and salt, stir well.
5. Close and secure the lid. Select MANUAL and cook at HIGH pressure for 1 minute
6. Once pressure cooking is complete, use a Natural Release for 10 minutes, then release any remaining pressure.
7. Carefully unlock the lid and fluff quinoa with a fork. Season with more salt if needed. Sprinkle parsley on top and serve

Quinoa with Sausage Meat

(Prep + Cook Time: 20 minutes | **Serves:** 3)

Ingredients:
- 1 cup quinoa
- 1/2 pound' sausage meat, casings removed
- 1 cup chicken stock
- 1 red bell pepper, chopped.
- 1-ounce Bella mushrooms, halved
- 1 tablespoon olive oil
- 1/2 small broccoli head, florets separated
- 1 small yellow onion, chopped.
- A pinch of turmeric powder
- 1/2 teaspoon sweet paprika

Directions:
1. Preheat the Instant Pot by selecting SAUTÉ. Add the oil, sausage and onion, stir and brown for a few minutes
2. Add turmeric and paprika, stir well
3. Add stock, quinoa, bell pepper, mushrooms and bell pepper, stir.
4. Close and secure the lid. Select MANUAL and cook at HIGH pressure for 1 minute
5. Once cooking is complete, use a Natural Release for 10 minutes, then release any remaining pressure.
6. Open the lid and fluff the cooked quinoa with a fork. Serve

Blueberry Quinoa

(Prep + Cook Time: 15 minutes | **Serves:** 3)

Ingredients:
- 1 ½ cups quinoa
- 1 cup apple juice
- 1 ½ cups water
- 3 tablespoon blueberries
- 1 tablespoon honey

Directions:
1. Rinse the quinoa well.
2. In the instant pot, add quinoa and water, stir until well combined
3. Close and secure the lid. Select MANUAL and cook at HIGH pressure for 1 minute.
4. Once cooking is complete, use a Natural Release for 10 minutes, then release any remaining pressure
5. Open the pot. Add honey, apple juice and blueberries, stir well. Serve

Quinoa and Veggies

(Prep + Cook Time: 15 minutes | **Serves:** 4)

Ingredients:
- 1 ½ cups quinoa, rinsed
- 4 cups spinach
- 1 ½ cups chicken broth
- 1/2 cup feta cheese
- 3 stalks of celery, chopped.
- 1 bell pepper, chopped.
- 1/4 teaspoon salt

Directions:
1. Rinse the quinoa well.
2. Combine all ingredients (except the feta cheese) in the Instant Pot
3. Close and secure the lid. Select the MANUAL setting and set the cooking time for 2 minutes at HIGH pressure
4. Once cooking is complete, use a Natural Release for 10 minutes, then release any remaining pressure.
5. Carefully unlock the lid, garnish with feta cheese on top. and Serve

Creamy Peaches Oats

(Prep + Cook Time: 15 minutes | **Serves:** 3)

Ingredients:
- 2 peaches, diced
- 1 cup steel cut oats
- 1/2 vanilla bean, scraped, seeds and pod
- 1 cup coconut milk, full fat
- 2 cups water

Directions:
1. Combine all the ingredients into the bowl of the Instant Pot
2. Close and secure the lid. Select MANUAL and cook at HIGH pressure for 3 minutes.
3. When the timer beeps, use a Natural Release for 10 minutes, then release any remaining pressure.
4. Sweeten the oats, if desired. Serve

Simple Quinoa

(Prep + Cook Time: 15 minutes | **Serves:** 3)

Ingredients:
- 3 cups water or vegetable broth
- 2 cups quinoa
- Juice of 1 lemon
- Handful your choice of fresh herbs, minced
- 1/2 teaspoon salt

Directions:
1. Rinse the quinoa well
2. Add the quinoa, broth, lemon juice, salt, and, if using, herbs into the Instant Pot
3. Close and secure the lid. Select MANUAL and set the cooking time for 1 minute at HIGH pressure
4. When the timer goes off, use a Natural Release for 10 minutes, then release any remaining pressure.
5. Carefully unlock the lid and fluff the cooked quinoa with a fork. Serve

Millet Porridge

(Prep + Cook Time: 15 minutes | **Serves:** 2)

Ingredients:
- 1/2 cup millet
- Butter to taste
- 1 cup water
- Salt to taste

Directions:
1. Add the millet and water to the Instant Pot and stir. Add salt to taste
2. Close and secure the lid. Select the MANUAL setting and set the cooking time for 8 minutes at HIGH pressure

3. When the timer goes off, let the pressure Release Naturally for 10 minutes, then release any remaining steam.
4. Open the lid and fluff the millet with a fork before serving. If you like, you can add butter to taste

Cranberry Almond Quinoa

(Prep + Cook Time: 15 minutes | **Serves:** 3)

Ingredients:
- 1 cup quinoa
- 1 cup dried cranberries
- 1/2 cup slivered almonds
- 1/4 cup salted sunflower seeds
- 2 cups water

Directions:
1. Rinse the quinoa well.
2. Combine water and quinoa in the Instant Pot.
3. Close and secure the lid. Select MANUAL and cook at HIGH pressure for 10 minutes
4. When the timer goes off, use a Quick Release method.
5. Unlock the lid, add sunflower seeds, almonds, and dried cranberries and gently mix until well combined. Serve

Cinnamon Oats

(Prep + Cook Time: 20 minutes | **Serves:** 3)

Ingredients:
- 2-ounce cream cheese, soft
- 1 cup steel oats
- 1 tablespoon butter
- 3 ½ cups water
- 3/4 cup raisins
- 2 tablespoon white sugar
- 1 teaspoon milk
- 1 teaspoon cinnamon
- 1/4 cup brown sugar
- A pinch of salt

Directions:
1. Preheat the Instant Pot by selecting SAUTÉ. Add butter and melt it
2. Add oats, stir and toast for 3 minutes. Add a pinch of salt and water.
3. Close and secure the lid. Select MANUAL and cook at HIGH pressure for 10 minutes
4. Once cooking is complete, use a Natural Release for 5 minutes, then release any remaining pressure and uncover the pot
5. Add raisins, stir and set aside.
6. Meanwhile, mix white sugar with cream cheese and milk and stir well
7. In another bowl, mix cinnamon with brown sugar and stir.
8. Transfer oats mix to breakfast bowls and top each with cinnamon mix and cream cheese. Serve

Pearl Barley

(Prep + Cook Time: 30 minutes | **Serves:** 4)

Ingredients:
- 1 ½ cups pearl barley
- 3 cups chicken broth
- Butter to taste, optional
- Salt to taste

Directions:
1. Rinse the barley well.
2. Combine the barley, broth, and salt in the Instant Pot. Mix well
3. Close and secure the lid. Select the MANUAL setting and set the cooking time for 25 minutes at HIGH pressure.
4. When the timer goes off, let the pressure Release Naturally for 15 minutes, then release any remaining steam.
5. Open the lid and serve, if you like, you can add the butter to taste

Polenta with Pine Nuts

(Prep + Cook Time: 25 minutes | **Serves:** 5)

Ingredients:

- 1/4 cup pine nuts, toasted
- 1/2 cup heavy cream
- 1/2 cup honey
- 5 cups water
- 1 cup polenta
- Salt to taste

Directions:

1. In the Instant Pot, combine the honey and water.
2. Select SAUTÉ and bring the mixture to a boil, stirring occasionally.
3. Add the polenta and stir to combine
4. Press the CANCEL key to stop the SAUTÉ function.
5. Close and lock the lid. Select MANUAL and cook at HIGH pressure for 12 minutes.
6. When the timer beeps, use a Quick Release
7. Carefully unlock the lid, Add the heavy cream and stir well. Let the dish sit for 1 minute.
8. Sprinkle with salt and stir. Top with pine nuts and serve

Beans Recipes

Steamed Black Beans

(Prep + Cook Time: 30 minutes **| Serves:** 6)

Ingredients:

- 1 cup black beans, soaked overnight, drained and rinsed
- 2 cloves garlic, minced
- 1-piece kombu seaweed
- 1 spring epazote
- 1/2 teaspoon cumin seeds
- 1 ½ cups water
- Salt to taste

Directions:

1. Add the beans, water, garlic, kombu, epazote and cumin to the Instant Pot, stir to combine
2. Close and secure the lid. Select MANUAL and cook at HIGH pressure for 7 minutes.
3. Once cooking is complete, let the pressure Release Naturally for 10 minutes. Release any remaining steam manually
4. Carefully Open the lid, Take out kombu and epazote. Season with salt, Serve.

Green-Bean Casserole

(Prep + Cook Time: 30 minutes **| Serves:** 4)

Ingredients:

- 3 cups green beans (I used Frozen)
- 1/2 cup French's onions, for garnishing
- 1 ½ cups mushroom, sliced
- 3 tablespoon butter
- 1 onion, chopped.
- 1/2 cup heavy cream
- 1/2 cup chicken broth

Directions:

1. Preheat the Instant Pot by selecting SAUTÉ. Once hot, add the butter and melt it
2. Add the onion and mushrooms. Sauté for about 3-4 minutes or until the onion is translucent.
3. Add the green beans, heavy cream and chicken broth, stir.
4. Press the CANCEL button to reset the cooking program, close and secure the lid. Then select the MANUAL setting and set the cooking time for 15 minutes at HIGH pressure
5. When the timer goes off, use a Quick Release.
6. Unlock and carefully Open the lid, Top with French's onions and serve

Tasty Hummus

(Prep + Cook Time: 1 hour 40 minutes **| Serves:** 4)

Ingredients:

- 1 cup dried chickpeas
- 1/3 cup lemon juice
- 1/4 cup plus 1 tablespoon olive oil
- 1/3 cup tahini
- 8 cups water
- 1 teaspoon garlic
- 2 teaspoon cumin
- 3/4 teaspoon salt
- 3/4 teaspoon pepper

Directions:

1. Add the chickpeas and 4 cups water to the Instant Pot.
2. Close and lock the lid. Select MANUAL and cook at HIGH pressure for 1 minute.
3. When the timer beeps, use a Quick Release. Unlock the lid
4. Drain the chickpeas. Return to the Instant Pot, add the remaining 4 cups water and let soak for 1 hour.
5. Add 1 tablespoon of olive oil
6. Close and lock the lid. Select the MANUAL setting and set the cooking time for 20 minutes at HIGH pressure.
7. Once cooking is complete, select Cancel and let Naturally Release for 10 minutes

8. Uncover the pot, Drain the chickpeas and reserve 1 cup of cooking liquid.
9. Add the chickpeas, 1/4 cup olive oil, garlic, cumin, lemon juice, tahini, salt and pepper to the food processor blend until the texture is smooth. Add more liquid as needed to reach the desired consistency, Serve

Green-Beans Salad

(Prep + Cook Time: 20 minutes | Serves: 5)

Ingredients:
- 2-pound green beans, trimmed and cleaned
- 1-ounce dried porcini mushrooms, soaked overnight and rinsed
- 2-pound potatoes, sliced to 1 inch thick
- Boiling water as needed
- 1 tablespoon olive oil
- 1 tablespoon balsamic vinegar
- Salt and ground black pepper to taste

Directions:
1. Add the mushrooms, potatoes, and beans to the Instant Pot.
2. Add water to cover the vegetables
3. Close and secure the lid. Select the MANUAL setting and set the cooking time for 6 minutes at HIGH pressure.
4. Once pressure cooking is complete, use a Quick Release.
5. Transfer the vegetables into a salad bowl and drain the water
6. Add the salt, pepper, olive oil and balsamic vinegar. Stir well until fully coated, Serve.

Pinto Beans

(Prep + Cook Time: 60 minutes | Serves: 3)

Ingredients:
- 1 cup dried Pinto beans
- 2 tablespoon garlic powder
- 1 tablespoon onion powder
- 5 cups water
- 1 tablespoon chili powder
- 1 teaspoon oregano
- 1/2 teaspoon salt

Directions:
1. Add the beans, onion powder, garlic powder, chili powder, oregano and salt to the Instant Pot
2. Add the water and stir well.
3. Close and secure the lid. Select the MANUAL setting and set the cooking time for 25 minutes at HIGH pressure.
4. Once cooking is complete, select Cancel and let Naturally Release for about 30 minutes
5. Open the lid. Add salt to taste and serve.

Instant Pot Lima beans

(Prep + Cook Time: 1 hour 30 minutes | Serves: 4)

Ingredients:
- 1 cup dried lima beans
- 4 cups vegetable stock
- 1 tablespoon vegetable oil
- 4 cups water
- Salt to taste

Directions:
1. Add the beans and water to the Instant Pot.
2. Close and lock the lid. Select MANUAL and cook at HIGH pressure for 1 minute.
3. When the timer goes off, use a Quick Release. Carefully unlock the lid
4. Drain the water, rinse the beans, and add to the Instant Pot again. Pour in the vegetable stock. Let soak for 1 hour.

5. Add the vegetable oil. Close and lock the lid. Select the MANUAL setting and set the cooking time for 6 minutes at HIGH pressure
6. Once cooking is complete, use a Natural Release for 10 minutes, then release any remaining pressure manually.
7. Uncover the pot, Taste and season with salt more if necessary, Serve

Black Beans and Bacon

(Prep + Cook Time: 1 hour 10 minutes | Serves: 4)

Ingredients:
- 1 pound' dried black beans
- 2 quarts' chicken stock
- 3 strips bacon, cut into halves
- 6 cloves garlic, crushed
- 1 small onion, cut in half
- 1 orange, cut in half
- 2 bay leaves
- 2 teaspoon kosher salt

Directions:
1. Preheat the Instant Pot by selecting Sauté.
2. Add the bacon and SAUTÉ for 2 - 3 minutes or until crisp
3. Add the beans, chicken stock, garlic, onion, orange, bay leaves and salt, stir.
4. Close and secure the lid. Select the MANUAL setting and set the cooking time for 40 minutes at HIGH pressure
5. Once pressure cooking is complete, use a Quick Release. If you want a creamier and tender bean let the pressure release naturally for 10-15 minutes.
6. Uncover the pot, Remove the bay leaves, orange and onion. Season with salt to taste, Serve

Notes: If you want texture and flavor in your dish, serve with orange zest, green onions, and orange slices.

Cannellini Beans

(Prep + Cook Time: 40 minutes | Serves: 4)

Ingredients:
- 1 cup cannellini beans, soaked overnight
- 1 clove garlic, smashed
- 1 bay leaf
- 1 sprig mint fresh
- 1 dash vinegar
- 4 cups water
- 1 tablespoon olive oil
- Salt and ground black pepper to taste

Directions:
1. Add soaked beans, water, clove garlic and bay leaf to the Instant Pot
2. Close and secure the lid. Select the MANUAL setting and set the cooking time for 8 minutes at HIGH pressure.
3. When the timer goes off, let the pressure Release Naturally for 15 to 20 minutes, then release any remaining steam manually
4. Strain the beans and add the oil, vinegar, mint, salt and pepper to taste. Mix well, Serve.

Lentils Chili

(Prep + Cook Time: 40 minutes | Serves: 7)

Ingredients:
- 28 ounces' canned diced tomatoes, undrained
- 2 cups lentils
- 1 onion, diced
- 6 cups vegetable broth
- 1 tablespoon olive oil

Directions:
1. Select the SAUTÉ setting on the Instant Pot and heat the oil
2. Add the onion and sauté for about 5 minutes, until softened.
3. Add the tomatoes and sauté for 1 minute more.
4. Add the lentils and broth and stir.

5. Close and lock the lid. Select MANUAL and cook at HIGH pressure for 18 minutes
6. Once cooking is complete, let the pressure Release Naturally for 15 minutes. Release any remaining steam manually. Open the lid and gently stir, Serve.

Pinto Beans Recipe

(Prep + Cook Time: 45 minutes | **Serves:** 7)

Ingredients:
- 2 cups pinto beans
- 3 cups veggie broth (or water)
- 1 onion, quartered
- 1 teaspoon cumin
- 1 teaspoon salt
- 1/2 cup cilantro salsa

Directions:
1. Add the beans, broth (or water), onion, cumin and salt to the Instant Pot and stir
2. Close and secure the lid. Select the MANUAL setting and set the cooking time for 25 minutes at HIGH pressure.
3. Once cooking is complete, select CANCEL and let Naturally Release for 10 minutes.
4. Uncover the pot, Transfer the mixture and cilantro salsa to a food processor and pulse until the dish is chopped up, Serve

Northern Bean Dip

(Prep + Cook Time: 30 minutes | **Serves:** 4)

Ingredients:
- 1 cup soaked overnight Great Northern white beans
- 1 ½ teaspoon chili powder
- 2 teaspoon ground cumin
- Water as needed
- 2 cloves garlic
- 3 tablespoon extra-virgin olive oil
- 3 tablespoon lemon juice
- 3 tablespoon cilantro, minced
- Pinch of red pepper flakes
- Salt and ground black pepper to taste

Directions:
1. Drain the beans and put in the Instant Pot. Cover with 1 inch of water
2. Close and secure the lid. Select MANUAL and cook at HIGH pressure for 13 minutes.
3. Once cooking is complete, select CANCEL and let Naturally Release for 10 minutes. Release any remaining steam manually
4. Uncover the pot, Drain the beans and run under cold water.
5. In a food processor, chop up the garlic.
6. Add the oil, cooked beans, chili powder, lemon juice, cumin, red pepper flakes, salt and pepper to taste and pulse until the mixture is chopped up.
7. Transfer the dish to a serving bowl. Top with cilantro and serve

Brown Lentil Tacos

(Prep + Cook Time: 20 minutes | **Serves:** 7)

Ingredients:
- 2 cups dry brown lentils
- 4-ounce tomato sauce
- 4 cups water
- 1/2 teaspoon cumin
- 1 teaspoon onion powder
- 1 teaspoon garlic powder
- 1 teaspoon chili powder
- 1 teaspoon salt

Directions:
1. Add the water, lentils, tomato sauce, chili powder, garlic powder, onion powder, cumin and salt to the Instant Pot. Stir well
2. Close and lock the lid. Select MANUAL and cook at HIGH pressure for 16 minutes.
3. Once pressure cooking is complete, use a Quick Release

4. Carefully unlock the lid. Let it cool for a few minutes, Serve.
5. This dish is great as part of a taco or burrito salad. It's great with soft or crunchy tacos.

Green Lentil Sloppy Joe's

(Prep + Cook Time: 55 minutes | **Serves:** 6)

Ingredients:
- 2 cups green lentils
- 1 chopped yellow onion
- 1 red bell pepper, stemmed and chopped.
- 3 cups veggie broth
- 1 can (14 oz) crushed tomatoes
- 1 tablespoon olive oil
- 2 tablespoon soy sauce
- 1 tablespoon Dijon mustard
- 1 tablespoon brown sugar
- 1 teaspoon black pepper

Directions:
1. Select the SAUTÉ setting on the Instant Pot and heat the oil
2. Add the onion and bell pepper and sauté for about 5 minutes, until softened.
3. Add the broth, soy sauce, lentils, tomatoes, mustard, brown sugar and black pepper. Stir until the sugar has dissolved
4. Close and lock the lid. Select the MANUAL setting and set the cooking time for 27 minutes at HIGH pressure.
5. Once cooking is complete, let the pressure Release Naturally for 15 minutes. Release any remaining steam manually
6. Uncover the pot, Stir and serve the mixture on toasted buns.

Pot Steamed Green Beans

(Prep + Cook Time: 20 minutes | **Serves:** 3)

Ingredients:
- 1 pound' green beans, washed
- 2 tablespoon fresh parsley, chopped, for garnish
- 1 cup water

For the dressing:
- 2 tablespoon white wine vinegar
- 3 cloves garlic, sliced
- 3 tablespoon olive oil
- 1 pinch of ground black pepper
- 1 pinch of salt

Directions:
1. Pour the water into the Instant Pot and insert a steamer basket. Put the green beans in the basket
2. Close and secure the lid. Select the MANUAL setting and set the cooking time for 1 minute at HIGH pressure.
3. When the timer goes off, use a Quick Release
4. Carefully Open the lid, Transfer the beans into a serving bowl.
5. Stir in the dressing ingredients and let stand for 10 minutes
6. Remove the slices of garlic, then garnish with the parsley, Serve.

Mushrooms and Green Beans

(Prep + Cook Time: 25 minutes | **Serves:** 4)

Ingredients:
- 1 pound' fresh green beans, trimmed
- 6-ounce bacon, chopped.
- 8-ounce mushrooms, sliced
- 1 clove garlic, minced
- 1 small yellow onion, chopped.
- A splash of balsamic vinegar
- Water as needed
- Salt and ground black pepper to taste

Directions:
1. Add the beans to the Instant Pot. Add water to cover the beans
2. Close and secure the lid. Select MANUAL and cook at HIGH pressure for 3 minutes.
3. Once cooking is complete, select Cancel and let Naturally Release for 10 minutes.
4. Unlock the pot, Drain the beans and leave them aside for now
5. Select the SAUTÉ setting on the Instant Pot. Add the bacon and sauté for 1 or 2 minutes stirring often.
6. Add the garlic and onion, stir and cook for 2 minutes
7. Add the mushrooms, stir and cook until they are soft
8. Add cooked beans, salt, pepper and a splash of vinegar, stir well
9. Press the CANCEL button to stop the cooking program, Serve.

Instant Pot Kidney Beans

(Prep + Cook Time: 55 minutes | **Serves:** 4)

Ingredients:
- 1 cup dried white kidney beans
- 1/2 teaspoon salt
- 6 cups water

Directions:
1. Add the beans, water and salt to the Instant Pot
2. Close and secure the lid. Select the MANUAL setting and set the cooking time for 40 minutes at HIGH pressure
3. Once timer goes off, allow to Naturally Release for 10 minutes. Release any remaining pressure manually.
4. Open the lid, Serve as side dish

Black Eyed Peas and Ham

(Prep + Cook Time: 50 minutes | **Serves:** 8-10

Ingredients:
- 3 ½ cups stock (vegetable, chicken or 3 ¼ cups water mixed with 2 tablespoon chicken bouillon)
- 2 cups dried peas, use black-eyed (rinse, but do not pre-soak)
- 3 ounces' ham, diced
- Salt and ground black pepper to taste

Directions:
1. Add the peas, ham and stock to the Instant Pot and stir.
2. Close and lock the lid. Select the MANUAL setting and set the cooking time for 30 minutes at HIGH pressure
3. When the timer goes off, let the pressure Release Naturally for 10 minutes, then release any remaining steam manually.
4. Carefully unlock the lid. Add salt and pepper to taste if needed. Serve

Notes: If you want the peas to be more firm, then reduce the cooking time for a couple of minutes.

Stewed Green Beans and Tomatoes

(Prep + Cook Time: 15 minutes | **Serves:** 5)

Ingredients:

- 1 pound' trimmed green beans
- 2 cups fresh, chopped tomatoes
- 1 teaspoon olive oil
- 1 clove garlic, crushed
- 1/2 cup water
- Salt to taste

Directions:

1. Select the SAUTÉ setting on the Instant Pot and heat the oil
2. Add the garlic and sauté until fragrant and golden. Add tomatoes and stir. If the tomatoes are dry, add 1/2 cup water.
3. Put the green beans in the Instant Pot and sprinkle with salt.
4. Close and secure the lid. Select MANUAL and cook at HIGH pressure for 5 minutes.
5. Once pressure cooking is complete, use a Quick Release
6. If the beans aren't quite tender enough, sauté in sauce for a few minutes, Serve.

Red Lentil Breakfast

(Prep + Cook Time: 40 minutes | **Serves:** 4)

Ingredients:

- 1 cup red lentils, soaked for 4 hours and drained
- 2 apples, diced
- Maple syrup to taste
- Coconut milk for serving
- 3 cups rooibos tea
- 1 tablespoon cinnamon, ground
- 1 teaspoon turmeric, ground
- 1 teaspoon cloves, ground

Directions:

1. Add the lentils and tea to the Instant Pot. Stir well.
2. Close and lock the lid. Select MANUAL and cook at HIGH pressure for 15 minutes
3. When the timer goes off, use a Quick Release.
4. Carefully uncover the pot. Add the cinnamon, apples, turmeric, and cloves, stir.
5. Close and lock the lid. Select MANUAL and cook at HIGH pressure for 15 more minutes.
6. When the timer beeps, use a Quick Release.
7. Transfer the lentils to a serving bowl. Add the maple syrup and coconut milk, Serve

Sweet Potato and Black Bean Hash

(Prep + Cook Time: 15 minutes | **Serves:** 4)

Ingredients:

- 2 cups peeled, chopped sweet potatoes
- 1 cup onion, chopped.
- 1 cup cooked and drained black beans
- 1/3 cup veggie broth
- 1/4 cup scallions, chopped.
- 1/2 tablespoon olive oil
- 1 clove garlic, minced
- 2 teaspoon hot chili powder
- Salt to taste

Directions:

1. Select the SAUTÉ setting on the Instant Pot and heat the oil.
2. Add the onion and sauté for 2 - 3 minutes, stirring so it doesn't burn
3. Add the garlic and stir until fragrant. Add the sweet potatoes and chili powder. Stir to coat the sweet potatoes with the chili powder.
4. Pour in the broth and stir
5. Close and secure the lid. Select the MANUAL setting and set the cooking time for 3 minutes at HIGH pressure.
6. When the timer beeps, use a Quick Release.
7. Add the black beans, scallions and salt, stir well. Season with more chili powder if desired

Red Beans Stew

(Prep + Cook Time: 1 hour 25 minutes **| Serves:** 7)

Ingredients:

- 1 pound' red beans, dry
- 1 small yellow onion, diced
- 1 tomato, chopped.
- 2 green onions stalks, chopped.
- 1 plantain, chopped.
- 2 carrots, chopped.
- Salt and ground black pepper to taste
- 2 tablespoon vegetable oil
- 1/4 cup cilantro leaves, chopped.
- 6 cups water

Directions:

1. Add the beans and water to the Instant Pot
2. Close and secure the lid. Select the MANUAL setting and set the cooking time for 35 minutes at HIGH pressure.
3. When the timer goes off, let the pressure Release Naturally for 5 minutes, then release any remaining steam manually. Uncover the pot,
4. Add the plantain, carrots, salt and pepper to taste.
5. Close and secure the lid. Select MANUAL and cook at HIGH pressure for 30 more minutes
6. Meanwhile, heat up a pan with the vegetable oil over medium high heat, add yellow onion, stir and cook for 2 minutes.
7. Add tomatoes, green onions, some salt and pepper, stir again, cook for 3 minutes more and take off the heat.
8. Once pressure cooking is complete, use a Quick Release
9. Open the lid, Top with tomatoes and onions mix, sprinkle with cilantro, Serve.

Peas and Ham

(Prep + Cook Time: 55 minutes **| Serves:** 5)

Ingredients:

- 1/2 pound' dried black-eyed peas
- 3-ounce ham, diced
- 3 ½ cups chicken stock
- Salt and ground black pepper to taste

Directions:

1. Add the peas, chicken stock and ham to the Instant Pot
2. Close and secure the lid. Select MANUAL and cook at HIGH pressure for 30 minutes.
3. Once cooking is complete, select CANCEL and let Naturally Release for 20 minutes
4. Open the lid, Add salt and pepper to taste if needed, Serve.

Black Rice and Black Beans

(Prep + Cook Time: 50 minutes | **Serves:** 4)

Ingredients:

- 1/2 cup black rice
- 1/2 cup dry black beans
- 1 clove garlic, crushed and then minced
- 1/4 onion, diced
- 1 teaspoon olive oil
- 1/2 lime, optional
- Avocado, optional
- 2 cups water
- 1/2 teaspoon salt

Directions:

1. Select the SAUTÉ setting on the Instant Pot and heat the oil.
2. Add the garlic and onion to the Instant Pot and sauté for 2 minutes
3. Add the rice and black beans, stir.
4. Pour in the water and sprinkle with salt. Close and secure the lid
5. Press the CANCEL button to reset the cooking program, then select the MANUAL setting and set the cooking time for 25 minutes at HIGH pressure.
6. Once cooking is complete, let the pressure Release Naturally for 10 minutes. Release any remaining steam manually
7. Uncover the pot, if you like, you can squeeze a lime wedge over the dish. Serve with a couple of avocado slices

Creamy Heirloom Beans

(Prep + Cook Time: 60 minutes | **Serves:** 4)

Ingredients:

- 2 cups mixed dried heirloom beans, soaked overnight
- 4 sprigs thyme
- 8 cups chicken stock
- 1/2 cup heavy cream
- Salt and ground black pepper to taste

Directions:

1. Add the beans, chicken stock, thyme and salt to the Instant Pot
2. Close and secure the lid. Select MANUAL and cook at HIGH pressure for 45 minutes.
3. When the timer beeps, use a Quick Release.
4. Carefully unlock the lid, Select the SAUTÉ setting and add the heavy cream, stir
5. Simmer the dish for 5 minutes. Press the CANCEL button. Serve

Rice Recipes

Beef and Basmati Rice Porridge

(Prep + Cook Time: 25 minutes | **Serves:** 4)

Ingredients:
- 1 pound' ground beef
- 1 ½ cups basmati rice, rinsed
- 1 ½ cups water (chicken or vegetable stock)
- 1 cup onion, diced
- 1 tablespoon olive oil
- 5 cloves garlic, minced
- Salt to taste

Directions:
1. Select the SAUTÉ setting on the Instant Pot and heat the oil
2. Add the garlic and cook for 30 seconds
3. Add the onion and ground beef to the pot. Sauté, stirring occasionally, until starting to brown.
4. Add the rice, water and salt and stir.
5. Close and secure the lid. Select MANUAL and cook at HIGH pressure for 5 minutes
6. Once cooking is complete, select CANCEL and let Naturally Release for 10 minutes. Unlock the pot and serve

Jasmine Rice and Chicken

(Prep + Cook Time: 50 minutes | **Serves:** 5)

Ingredients:
- 1 pound' boneless chicken thighs
- 3 carrots, diced
- 3 small shallots, diced
- 2 cloves garlic, minced
- 1 ½ cups white jasmine rice, rinsed and drained
- 1 ½ cups chicken stock
- 1 tablespoon olive oil
- 2 tablespoon thyme leaves
- Salt and ground black pepper to taste

Directions:
1. To preheat the Instant Pot, select SAUTÉ. Heat the oil.
2. Add the shallots and garlic and sauté until fragrant
3. Add in the chicken thighs, salt and pepper to taste
4. Continue stirring for 5 minutes, until chicken meat is starting to brown.
5. Add the carrots, rice, chicken stock and thyme leaves, stir
6. Close and secure the lid. Select the MANUAL setting and set the cooking time for 10 minutes at HIGH pressure.
7. Once timer goes off, allow to Naturally Release for 15 to 20 minutes. Then release any remaining steam manually
8. Open the lid, Fluff the dish with the rice spatula or fork, Serve

Peas and Parmesan Risotto

(Prep + Cook Time: 30 minutes | **Serves:** 4)

Ingredients:
- 1 ½ cups frozen peas, thawed
- 2 tablespoon parmesan, finely grated
- 2 tablespoon parsley, finely chopped.
- 1 teaspoon lemon zest, grated
- 2 tablespoon butter
- 1 tablespoon extra-virgin olive oil
- 1 yellow onion, chopped.
- 1 ½ cups Arborio rice
- 3 ½ cups chicken stock
- 2 tablespoon lemon juice
- Salt and ground black pepper to taste

Directions:
1. Select the SAUTÉ setting on the Instant Pot and heat the oil and 1 tablespoon butter.
2. Add the onion, stir and sauté for 5 minutes. Add the rice, stir and sauté for 3 more minutes
3. Pour 3 cups of stock and lemon juice in the Instant Pot, stir well.
4. Close and secure the lid. Select MANUAL and cook at HIGH pressure for 5 minutes.
5. When the timer goes off, use a Quick Release
6. Select the SAUTÉ setting again, add peas and the rest of the stock, stir and cook for 2 minutes.
7. Add parmesan, parsley, the rest of the butter, lemon zest, salt and pepper to the taste and stir, Serve

French Style Butter Rice

(Prep + Cook Time: 45 minutes | **Serves:** 5)

Ingredients:
- 1 ½ cups French onion soup
- 1 stick (½ cup) butter
- 2 cups brown rice
- 1 cups vegetable stock

Directions:
1. To preheat the Instant Pot, select SAUTÉ. Once hot, add the butter and melt it
2. Add the rice, vegetable stock, onion soup and stir to combine
3. Close and secure the lid. Select the MANUAL setting and set the cooking time for 22 minutes at HIGH pressure.
4. Once cooking is complete, let Naturally Release for 10 minutes. Release any remaining steam manually.
5. Open the lid, Serve. If you like, you can garnish the rice with parsley

Coconut Rice

(Prep + Cook Time: 30 minutes | **Serves:** 3)

Ingredients:
- 1 cup Thai sweet rice
- 1/2 can full-fat coconut milk
- 2 tablespoon sugar
- 1 ½ cups water
- 1/2 teaspoon salt

Directions:
1. Add the rice and water to the Instant Pot, stir
2. Close and secure the lid. Select MANUAL and cook at HIGH pressure for 3 minutes.
3. Once cooking is complete, use a Natural Release for 10 minutes, then release any remaining pressure manually
4. Meanwhile, heat coconut milk, sugar, and salt in a saucepan
5. When the sugar has melted, remove from the heat.
6. Open the pot and add the coconut milk mixture, stir to combine. Put the lid back on and let it rest 5-10 minutes, Serve

Basmati Rice

(Prep + Cook Time: 25 minutes | **Serves:** 4)

Ingredients:
- 1 cup white basmati rice
- 1/4 teaspoon salt
- 1 ¼ cups water
- Butter to taste, optional

Directions:
1. Rinse the rice well
2. Add the rice, water and salt to the Instant Pot and stir.
3. Close and secure the lid. Select the MANUAL setting and set the cooking time for 6 minutes at HIGH pressure
4. Once cooking is complete, use a Natural Release for 10 minutes, then release any remaining pressure.
5. Open the pot, Fluff the rice with a fork. If you like, you can add the butter, Serve

Chipotle Rice

(Prep + Cook Time: 40 minutes | **Serves:** 5)

Ingredients:
- 2 cups brown rice, rinsed
- 4 small bay leaves
- 1/2 cup chopped cilantro
- 1 ½ tablespoon olive oil
- 2 ¾ cups water
- 1 lime, juiced
- 1 teaspoon salt

Directions:
1. Add the rice, water and bay leaves to the Instant Pot.
2. Close and secure the lid. Select the RICE setting and let cook at default time
3. Once cooking is complete, let the pressure Release Naturally for 10 minutes. Release any remaining steam manually
4. Uncover the pot, Add the oil, lime juice, salt and cilantro and mix until combined, Serve.

Rice with Broccoli and Chicken

(Prep + Cook Time: 25 minutes | **Serves:** 5)

Ingredients:
- 1 cup broccoli florets
- 1/2 cup cheddar cheese, grated
- 1 ½-pound boneless chicken breasts, sliced
- 1 onion, chopped.
- 2 cloves garlic, minced
- 2 tablespoon butter
- 1 ⅓ cups long grain rice
- 1 ⅓ cups chicken broth
- 1/2 cup milk
- Salt and ground black pepper to taste

Directions:
1. Preheat the Instant Pot by selecting SAUTÉ. Once hot, add the butter and melt it
2. Add the chicken pieces, onion and garlic. Add salt and pepper to taste.
3. Cook, stirring occasionally, for 5 minutes or until the chicken has slightly browned
4. Add the rice, chicken broth and milk and stir. Add the broccoli florets and cheddar cheese.
5. Close and secure the lid. Select the MANUAL setting and set the cooking time for 15 minutes at HIGH pressure.
6. Once cooking is complete, let Naturally Release for 10 minutes. Release any remaining steam manually
7. Carefully Open the lid, Serve

Brown Rice Medley

(Prep + Cook Time: 50 minutes | **Serves:** 4)

Ingredients:
- 3/4 cup (or more) short grain brown rice
- 3-4 tablespoon red, wild or black rice
- 1/4 teaspoon sea salt
- 1 ½ cups water

Directions:
1. Rinse the rice well.
2. Add all kinds of rice, salt and water to the Instant Pot, stir well
3. Close and secure the lid. Select the MULTIGRAIN setting and set the cooking time for 23 minutes.
4. When the timer beeps, let the pressure Release Naturally for 15 minutes; then release any remaining pressure manually
5. Open the lid, Fluff with a fork and serve immediately.

Multi Grain Rice Millet Blend

(Prep + Cook Time: 15 minutes | **Serves:** 5)

Ingredients:

- 2 cups jasmine rice or long-grain white rice
- 1/2 cup millet
- 1/2 teaspoon sea salt (optional)
- 3 ¼ cups water

Directions:

1. Put the rice, millet, water and salt in the Instant Pot and stir
2. Close and secure the lid. Select the RICE setting and set the cooking time for 10 minutes.
3. When the timer goes off, use a Quick Release.
4. Carefully Open the lid, Fluff the dish with the rice spatula or fork, Serve

Spanish Rice V2

(Prep + Cook Time: 35 minutes | **Serves:** 5)

Ingredients:

- 2 tablespoon butter
- 1 ½ cups chicken stock or water
- 8-ounce tomato sauce
- 2 cups long grain rice
- 1/2 teaspoon garlic powder
- 1/2 teaspoon onion powder
- 1 teaspoon cumin
- 1 teaspoon chili powder
- 1/2 teaspoon salt

Directions:

1. To preheat the Instant Pot, select SAUTÉ. Once hot, add the butter and melt it
2. Add the rice and sauté, stirring occasionally, for 4 minutes.
3. Stir in chicken stock, tomato sauce, cumin, chili powder, garlic powder, onion powder and salt
4. Close and lock the lid. Select MANUAL and cook at HIGH pressure for 10 minutes.
5. Once cooking is complete, use a Natural Release for 10 minutes, then release any remaining pressure manually
6. Open the pot, Fluff the rice with the rice spatula or fork, Serve.

Pineapple and Cauliflower Rice

(Prep + Cook Time: 40 minutes | **Serves:** 5)

Ingredients:

- 2 teaspoon extra virgin olive oil
- 1 cauliflower, florets separated and chopped.
- 1/2 pineapple, peeled and chopped.
- 2 cups jasmine rice
- 4 cups water
- Salt and ground black pepper to taste

Directions:

1. Combine all of the ingredients in the Instant Pot and stir to combine
2. Close and secure the lid. Select the MANUAL setting and set the cooking time for 20 minutes at LOW pressure
3. Once pressure cooking is complete, let Naturally Release for 10 minutes, then quick release remaining pressure.
4. Carefully open the pot, Fluff the dish with the rice spatula or fork, Serve

Special Shawarma Rice

(Prep + Cook Time: 35 minutes | **Serves:** 7)

Ingredients:

- 1 pound' ground beef (chicken, fish, pork, etc. optional), cooked
- 1 ½ cups basmati rice, rinsed and drained
- 1/4 cup cilantro, chopped.
- 1 cup onion, chopped.
- 1 ½ cups water
- 4 cups cabbage, shredded
- 1 tablespoon olive oil
- 5 cloves garlic, minced
- 3 tablespoon shawarma spice
- 1 teaspoon salt

Directions:

1. Combine all of the ingredients in the Instant Pot, except for the cilantro, stir to mix
2. Close and secure the lid. Select the MANUAL setting and set the cooking time for 15 minutes at HIGH pressure
3. Once cooking is complete, let the pressure Release Naturally for 10 minutes. Release any remaining steam manually. Open the lid. Add cilantro and stir, Serve

Spinach Rice

(Prep + Cook Time: 45 minutes | **Serves:** 5)

Ingredients:

- 1 cup dill
- 2 cups basmati rice
- 3-ounce butter
- 1 tablespoon minced garlic
- 1 cup spinach
- 4 cups beef broth
- 1 tablespoon olive oil
- 1 teaspoon salt
- 1 teaspoon dried oregano

Directions:

1. Select the SAUTÉ setting on the Instant Pot and heat the oil.
2. Add rice, butter and minced garlic. Stir and sauté the mixture for 5 minutes
3. Meanwhile, wash the spinach and dill carefully. Chop the greens.
4. Transfer the chopped greens in the blender and blend them well
5. Pour the beef broth in the Instant Pot and stir.
6. Add the blended greens in the rice mixture. Add salt and dried oregano and mix just until combined.
7. Close and secure the lid. Select RICE and cook for 20 minutes
8. Once cooking is complete, use a Quick Release.
9. Open the lid, Transfer the rice to the serving bowl and serve

Asian Rice Bowl

(Prep + Cook Time: 35 minutes | **Serves:** 4)

Ingredients:

- 1 cup brown rice
- 1/2 cup coconut chips
- 1/4 cup almonds
- A pinch of cinnamon powder
- 1 cup water
- 1 cup coconut milk
- 1/2 cup maple syrup
- 1/4 cup raisins
- Salt to taste

Directions:

1. Put the rice in the Instant Pot and add the water, stir.
2. Close and secure the lid. Select MANUAL and cook at HIGH pressure for 15 minutes
3. Once pressure cooking is complete, use a Quick Release. Open the lid
4. Add milk, coconut chips, almonds, raisins, salt, cinnamon and maple syrup, stir well.
5. Close and secure the lid. Select MANUAL and cook at HIGH pressure for 5 more minutes
6. Use a Quick Release. Open the lid and transfer rice to breakfast bowls. Serve.

Simple Brown Rice

(Prep + Cook Time: 30 minutes | **Serves:** 5)

Ingredients:
- 2 cups brown rice
- 2 cups vegetable broth or water
- 1/2 teaspoon salt

Directions:
1. Add the rice, broth and salt to the Instant Pot and stir.
2. Close and secure the lid. Select MANUAL and cook at HIGH pressure for 21 minutes
3. When the timer goes off, let the pressure Release Naturally for 10 minutes, then release any remaining steam manually
4. Carefully Open the lid, Fluff the rice with the rice spatula or fork, Serve.

Jasmine Rice

(Prep + Cook Time: 25 minutes | **Serves:** 5)

Ingredients:
- 2 cups jasmine rice
- 2 teaspoon olive oil
- 2 cups water
- 1/2 teaspoon salt

Directions:
1. Rinse the rice well
2. Transfer the rice to the Instant Pot. Add the water, oil and salt and stir.
3. Close and secure the lid. Select MANUAL and cook at HIGH pressure for 4 minutes
4. Once timer goes off, allow to Naturally Release for 10 minutes, then release the remaining pressure manually.
5. Open the lid, Fluff the rice with a fork and serve

Arborio Risotto V2

(Prep + Cook Time: 40 minutes | **Serves:** 5)

Ingredients:
- 3 ½ cups chicken stock
- 1 ½ cups Arborio rice
- 1 finely chopped medium onion
- 1 ½ tablespoon olive oil
- 3 tablespoon romano or parmesan cheese
- Salt and ground black pepper to taste

Directions:
1. To preheat the Instant Pot, select SAUTÉ. Add the oil to the pot
2. Add the onion and sauté for several minutes, until the onion is translucent.
3. Add the rice and chicken stock.
4. Close and secure the lid. Select the RICE setting and set the cooking time for 15 minutes
5. Once timer goes off, let the pressure Release Naturally for 10-15 minutes, then release any remaining steam.
6. Open the lid, add salt and black pepper to taste. Add the Romano or Parmesan cheese and stir, Serve

Pink Rice

(Prep + Cook Time: 25 minutes | **Serves:** 5)

Ingredients:
- 1 cups pink rice
- 1/2 teaspoon salt
- 1 cups water

Directions:
1. Rinse the rice well
2. Add the rice, water and salt to the Instant Pot, stir.
3. Close and secure the lid. Select the MANUAL setting and set the cooking time for 5 minutes at HIGH pressure.
4. When the timer goes off, let the pressure Release Naturally for 10 minutes, then release any remaining steam manually
5. Open the pot, Fluff the rice with the rice spatula or fork, Serve.

Veg Rice

(Prep + Cook Time: 40 minutes | **Serves:** 5)

Ingredients:
- 2 cups chicken broth
- 1 cup frozen peas
- 1/4 cup shallots, chopped.
- 1 ½ cups basmati rice
- 1/2 cup carrots, chopped.
- 1 tablespoon olive oil
- 1 clove garlic, minced
- 2 teaspoon curry powder
- Salt and ground black pepper to taste

Directions:
1. Rinse the rice well.
2. Select the SAUTÉ setting on the Instant Pot and heat the oil
3. Cook the shallots and garlic until fragrant.
4. Add the rice, carrots, curry powder, chicken broth, pears, salt and pepper to taste. Stir to combine
5. Press the CANCEL button to reset the cooking program, then select the RICE setting and set the cooking time for 20 minutes.
6. When the timer goes off, let the pressure Release Naturally for 10 minutes, then release any remaining steam manually
7. Carefully open the lid, fluff the rice with the rice spatula or fork and serve.

Rice with Veggies

(Prep + Cook Time: 20 minutes | **Serves:** 7)

Ingredients:
- 3 cups chicken stock
- 2 cups basmati rice
- 1 cup sweet corn, frozen
- 1 cup garden peas, frozen
- 1 large onion, finely chopped.
- 3 cloves garlic, minced
- 3 tablespoon olive oil
- 3 tablespoon cilantro stalks, chopped.
- 1/4 teaspoon salt
- 1 teaspoon turmeric powder
- 2 tablespoon butter, optional

Directions:
1. Rinse the rice well. Select the SAUTÉ setting on the Instant Pot and heat the oil
2. Add the onion, garlic and cilantro. Stir and sauté for 5-6 minutes, until the onion is translucent.
3. Add the rice, sweet corn and peas. Sprinkle with salt and turmeric. Add the chicken stock and stir
4. Close and secure the lid. Select the MANUAL setting and set the cooking time for 4 minutes at HIGH pressure.
5. When the timer beeps, use a Quick Release
6. Open the pot, if you like, you can add the butter, Serve.

Arborio Risotto

(Prep + Cook Time: 35 minutes **| Serves:** 5)

Ingredients:

- 1 ½ cups Arborio rice
- 1/3 cup brown sugar
- 2 apples, cored and sliced
- 1 cup apple juice
- 2 tablespoon butter
- 1 ½ teaspoon cinnamon powder
- 1/2 cup cherries, dried
- 3 cups milk
- Salt to taste

Directions:

1. Preheat the Instant Pot by selecting SAUTÉ. Once hot, add the butter and melt it
2. Add rice, stir and cook for 5 minutes.
3. Add sugar, apples, apple juice, milk, a pinch of salt and cinnamon, stir well
4. Close and secure the lid. Select the MANUAL setting and set the cooking time for 6 minutes at HIGH pressure.
5. Once timer goes off, allow to Naturally Release for 6 minutes, then release any remaining pressure.
6. Carefully unlock the lid, add cherries, stir well and close the lid. Leave aside for 5 more minutes. Serve

Mouthwatering Mexican Casserole

(Prep + Cook Time: 35 minutes **| Serves:** 5)

Ingredients:

- 2 cups uncooked brown rice
- 6-ounce tomato paste
- 1 cup soaked black beans
- 5 cups water
- 1 teaspoon garlic
- 2 teaspoon chili powder
- 2 teaspoon onion powder
- 1 teaspoon salt

Directions:

1. Put the dry beans in a bowl with enough water to cover them. Soak the beans for at least two hours and drain
2. Combine all of the ingredients in the Instant Pot and stir to mix
3. Close and secure the lid. Select MANUAL and cook at HIGH pressure for 28 minutes.
4. Once pressure cooking is complete, use a Quick Release
5. Carefully open the pot. Taste the dish and season more with salt if necessary, Serve.

Simple Mexican Rice

(Prep + Cook Time: 25 minutes **| Serves:** 5)

Ingredients:

- 1 cup salsa
- 1/4 cup onion, diced
- 2 cups long grain white rice
- 2 ⅓ cups chicken stock
- 1 tablespoon olive oil
- 1 teaspoon salt

Directions:

1. Select the SAUTÉ setting on the Instant Pot and heat the oil.
2. Add the onion and sauté for 2 - 3 minutes, until the onion is translucent
3. Add the rice and cook for 2 to 3 minutes.
4. Stir in the chicken stock, salsa and salt
5. Close and secure the lid. Select the MANUAL setting and set the cooking time for 10 minutes at HIGH pressure
6. When the timer goes off, let the pressure Release Naturally for 10 minutes, then release any remaining steam manually. Fluff the rice with the rice spatula or fork, Serve.

Pumpkin Risotto

(Prep + Cook Time: 20 minutes | **Serves:** 5)

Ingredients:
- 2-ounce extra virgin olive oil
- 2 cups Arborio rice
- 4 cups chicken stock
- 3/4 cup pumpkin puree
- 2 cloves garlic, minced
- 1 small yellow onion, chopped.
- 1/2 teaspoon cinnamon
- 1/2 cup heavy cream
- 1/2 teaspoon nutmeg
- 1/2 teaspoon ginger, grated
- 1 teaspoon thyme, chopped.
- Salt to taste

Directions:
1. Select the SAUTÉ setting on the Instant Pot, add and heat the oil.
2. Add the garlic and onion, stir and sauté for 1 - 2 minutes
3. Add the rice, chicken stock, pumpkin puree, thyme, nutmeg, ginger, cinnamon and stir well.
4. Close and secure the lid. Select MANUAL and cook at HIGH pressure for 10 minutes
5. When the timer goes off, use a Quick Release.
6. Open the lid, Add the heavy cream, salt and stir well, Serve.

Mushroom Risotto

(Prep + Cook Time: 30 minutes | **Serves:** 4)

Ingredients:
- 8-ounce mushrooms, sliced
- 2-ounce olive oil
- 4-ounce sherry vinegar
- 4-ounce heavy cream
- 2 tablespoon parmesan cheese, grated
- 1-ounce basil, finely chopped.
- 2 cloves garlic, crushed
- 1 yellow onion, chopped.
- 2 cups Arborio rice
- 4 cups chicken stock
- Salt to taste

Directions:
1. Select the SAUTÉ setting on the Instant Pot and heat the oil.
2. Add the garlic, onion and mushrooms, stir and sauté for 3 minutes
3. Add the rice, stock and vinegar, stir well.
4. Close and secure the lid. Select the MANUAL setting and set the cooking time for 10 minutes at HIGH pressure.
5. Once pressure cooking is complete, use a Quick Release
6. Open the lid, add the heavy cream and parmesan and stir. Add salt to taste. Top with basil and serve

Stocks and Sauces

Bone Broth Recipe

(Prep + Cook Time: 1 hour 45 minutes | **Serves:** 8

Ingredients:
- 2 - 3 pounds' bones (2 - 3 pounds' lamb, beef, pork, or non-oily fish, or 1 carcass of whole chicken)
- 3 carrots, cut into large chunks
- 2 stalks celery, cut into large chunks
- 1/2 onion
- Fresh herbs
- 1 - 2 tablespoon apple cider vinegar
- Water as needed
- 1 teaspoon sea salt

Directions:
1. Add the bones to the Instant Pot
2. Add all of the veggies, herbs, salt and vinegar.
3. Pour in the water to fill the pot 2/3 full.

4. Let it sit for 30 minutes (If you have enough time)
5. Close and lock the lid. Select the SOUP setting and set the cooking time for 120 minutes at LOW pressure.
6. Once cooking is complete, let the pressure Release Naturally for 15 minutes. Release any remaining steam manually.
7. Uncover the pot, Strain the broth and pour into jars. Store in the refrigerator or freeze

Notes: Before using lamb or beef bones, roast them in a preheated 350F oven for 30 minutes. Roasting the bones gives your broth a very rich depth

Cranberry Sauce Recipe

(Prep + Cook Time: 25 minutes | **Serves:** 6

Ingredients:

- 1-pound cranberries (fresh or frozen)
- 1 apple, cored and chopped.
- 10 strawberries, chopped.
- 1 teaspoon orange zest, grated
- 1 teaspoon lemon zest, grated
- 1/4 cup water
- 1 cinnamon stick
- 1 cup sugar
- Juice from 1 orange
- Juice from 1 lemon

Directions:

1. Combine all of the ingredients in the Instant Pot and stir to mix
2. Close and lock the lid. Select MANUAL and cook at HIGH pressure for 5 minutes.
3. When the timer beeps, use a Natural Release for 10 minutes
4. Uncover the pot, Serve chilled or at room temperature.

Mushroom Broth Recipe

(Prep + Cook Time: 25 minutes | **Serves:** 8

Ingredients:

- 4-ounce dried mushrooms, soaked and rinsed
- 1/2 cup celery, chopped.
- 1 onion, quartered
- 4 cloves garlic, crushed
- 4 bay leaves
- 8 cups water
- 1/2 cup carrots, chopped.
- Salt and ground black pepper to taste.

Directions:

1. Put all of the ingredients into the Instant Pot
2. Close and lock the lid. Select MANUAL and cook at HIGH pressure for 15 minutes.
3. Once timer goes off, use a quick release
4. Uncover the pot, Season with salt and pepper to taste.
5. Strain the broth and pour into jars. Store in the refrigerator or freeze

Pork Broth Recipe

(Prep + Cook Time: 1 hour 25 minutes | **Serves:** 8

Ingredients:

- 3 pounds' pork bones
- 3 large carrots, cut into large chunks
- 3 large stalks celery, cut into large chunks
- 1 bay leaf
- 2 cloves garlic, sliced
- 1 tablespoon apple cider vinegar
- 1 teaspoon whole peppercorns
- 8 cups water
- Salt to taste

Directions:

1. Dump all of the ingredients into the Instant Pot and give it a little stir to mix everything evenly
2. Close and lock the lid. Select MANUAL and cook at HIGH pressure for 60 minutes

3. Once cooking is complete, select Cancel and let Naturally Release for 10 minutes. Release any remaining steam manually.
4. Uncover the pot, Strain the broth and pour into jars. Store in the refrigerator or freeze

Notes: Before using pork bones and veggies, roast them in a preheated 350F oven for 30 minutes. Roasting the bones and veggies gives your broth a very rich depth.

Fish Stock Recipe

(Prep + Cook Time: 1 hour 10 minutes | Serves: 10

Ingredients:
- 2 salmon heads, large-sized, cut into quarters
- 1 cup carrots, roughly chopped.
- 1 cup celery, roughly chopped.
- 2 cloves garlic, sliced
- Handful fresh thyme, including stems
- 1 tablespoon olive oil
- 2 lemongrass stalks, roughly chopped.
- Water as needed

Directions:
1. Wash the fish heads and pat them dry.
2. Preheat the Instant Pot by selecting Sauté. Add and heat the oil.
3. Add the salmon heads and lightly sear the fish on both sides
4. Press the CANCEL key to stop the SAUTÉ function.
5. Put all of the ingredients into the Instant Pot and pour the water to cover mix.
6. Close and lock the lid. Select SOUP and cook at HIGH pressure for 45 minutes
7. When the timer beeps, let the pressure Release Naturally for 15 minutes and then release any remaining steam manually.
8. Open the lid, Strain the stock and pour into jars. Store in the refrigerator or freeze

Vegan Alfredo Sauce Recipe

(Prep + Cook Time: 20 minutes | Serves: 4)

Ingredients:
- 2 cups asparagus
- 6 cups vegetable broth
- 1/2 teaspoon salt
- 1 ½ tablespoon olive oil
- 10 cloves garlic, minced
- 3/4 cup raw cashews
- 6 cups cauliflower florets

Directions:
1. Select the SAUTÉ setting on the Instant Pot and heat the oil.
2. Add the garlic and sauté for 1 - 2 minutes, until fragrant
3. Add the cashews, cauliflower, asparagus and broth.
4. Press the CANCEL key to stop the SAUTÉ function.
5. Close and lock the lid. Select MANUAL and cook at HIGH pressure for 3 minutes
6. Once timer goes off, use a Quick Release.
7. Carefully unlock the lid, Transfer to a blender. Season with salt and blend until smooth. Serve with pasta or brow rice

Chili Sauce Recipe

(Prep + Cook Time: 30 minutes | Serves: 4)

Ingredients:
- 4 medium-sized Ancho chili peppers
- 2 tablespoon apple cider vinegar
- 2 cloves garlic, crushed
- 2 tablespoon heavy cream
- 1 ½ teaspoon sugar
- 1/2 teaspoon cumin, ground
- 1/2 teaspoon dried oregano, ground
- 1 ½ cups water
- 2 teaspoon kosher salt

Directions:

1. Cut the peppers in half and remove the stems and seeds. Chop into small pieces
2. Add the peppers, cumin, oregano, salt and sugar to the Instant Pot.
3. Pour in the water and stir well.
4. Close and lock the lid. Select MANUAL and cook at HIGH pressure for 8 minutes
5. When the timer goes off, let the pressure Release Naturally for 10 minutes, then release any remaining steam manually.
6. Open the lid, Transfer the mixture to a food processor. Add the vinegar, garlic and heavy cream. Pulse until smooth and creamy. Serve and enjoy

Vegetable Stock Recipe

(Prep + Cook Time: 55 minutes | **Serves:** 8

Ingredients:

- 4 carrots, cut into chunks
- 4 celery stalks, cut into chunks
- 4 thyme sprigs
- 2 teaspoon garlic, chopped.
- 2 green onions, sliced
- 8 cups water
- 2 bay leaves
- 6 parsley sprigs
- 10 whole black peppercorns
- 1 ½ teaspoon salt

Directions:

1. Put all of the ingredients, except salt, into the Instant Pot
2. Close and lock the lid. Select SOUP and cook at HIGH pressure for 30 minutes.
3. When the timer beeps, let the pressure Release Naturally for 15 minutes and then release any remaining steam manually
4. Open the lid, Season with salt to taste.
5. Strain the stock and pour into jars. Store in the refrigerator or freeze

Chicken Stock Recipe

(Prep + Cook Time: 1 hour 25 minutes | **Serves:** 8

Ingredients:

- 1 chicken carcass
- 2 large carrots, cut into chunks
- 12 whole pieces peppercorns
- 2 bay leaves
- 2 tablespoon apple cider vinegar
- 1 sprig thyme
- 10 cups water
- 1 onion, quartered
- Salt to taste

Directions:

1. Put all of the ingredients into the Instant Pot.
2. Close and lock the lid. Select MANUAL and cook at HIGH pressure for 60 minutes
3. When the timer goes off, let the pressure Release Naturally for 15 minutes and then release any remaining steam manually.
4. Open the lid, Season with salt to taste.
5. Strain the stock and pour into jars. Store in the refrigerator or freeze

Turkey Stock Recipe

(Prep + Cook Time: 1 hour 10 minutes | **Serves:** 6

Ingredients:

- 1 bag turkey giblet
- 1 teaspoon whole black peppercorns
- 1 carrot, cut into chunks
- 1 onion, quartered
- 1 bay leaf
- 6 cups water
- 1 stalk celery, cut in half

Directions:
1. Put all of the ingredients into the Instant Pot.
2. Close and lock the lid. Select MANUAL and cook at HIGH pressure for 45 minutes
3. When the timer goes off, let the pressure Release Naturally for 10 minutes and then release any remaining steam manually.
4. Open the lid, Strain the stock and pour into jars. Store in the refrigerator or freeze

Vanilla Caramel Sauce Recipe

(Prep + Cook Time: 25 minutes | **Serves:** 4)

Ingredients:
- 3 tablespoon coconut oil
- 1/3 cup condensed coconut milk
- 1 teaspoon vanilla extract
- 1 cup sugar
- 1/3 cup water

Directions:
1. To preheat the Instant Pot, select SAUTÉ
2. In the Instant Pot, combine the sugar and water.
3. Sauté the mixture for 12 minutes
4. Add the coconut oil, milk and vanilla, Stir well.
5. Cook, stirring occasionally, until the mixture is smooth.
6. Press the CANCEL key to stop the SAUTÉ function.
7. Transfer to a heatproof container. Let it cool and serve

Tabasco Sauce Recipe

(Prep + Cook Time: 25 minutes | Cups: 2

Ingredients:
- 18-ounce fresh hot peppers or any kind, stems removed, chopped.
- 1 ¾ cups apple cider
- 3 teaspoon smoked or plain salt

Directions:
1. Combine all of the ingredients in the Instant Pot.
2. Select MANUAL and cook at HIGH pressure for 1 minutes
3. Once timer goes off, allow to Naturally Release for 15 minutes and then release any remaining pressure manually.
4. Uncover the pot, using an immersion blender, puree the mixture
5. Pour into clean and sterilized bottles and refrigerate.

Tomato and Basil Sauce Recipe

(Prep + Cook Time: 45 minutes | **Serves:** 4)

Ingredients:
- 2 ½ pounds' Roma tomatoes, diced
- 1/2 cup chopped basil
- 1/4 cup vegetable broth
- 1 tablespoon olive oil
- 3 cloves garlic, minced
- Salt to taste

Directions:
1. Press the SAUTÉ button on the Instant Pot and heat the oil
2. Add the garlic and sauté for 1 minute. Add the tomatoes, basil and broth. Mix well
3. Press the CANCEL button to stop the SAUTE function, then select the MANUAL setting and set the cooking time for 10 minutes at HIGH pressure.
4. Once timer goes off, use a Quick Release. Carefully unlock the lid, Select SAUTÉ again and cook for 5 minutes more.
5. Press the CANCEL key to stop the SAUTÉ function.
6. Using an immersion blender, blend until smooth. Taste and season with salt if necessary and serve

White Sauce Recipe

(Prep + Cook Time: 15 minutes **| Serves:** 4)

Ingredients:

- 12-ounce cauliflower florets
- 2 tablespoon almond milk
- 1/2 cup water
- 1/4 teaspoon garlic salt
- 1/4 teaspoon pepper

Directions:

1. In the Instant Pot, combine the cauliflower florets, garlic salt, pepper and water
2. Close and lock the lid. Select MANUAL and cook at HIGH pressure for 3 minutes
3. When the timer goes off, use a Quick Release.
4. Carefully unlock the lid, Using an immersion blender, blend until smooth.
5. Pour in the almond milk and mix well and Serve

Herb Stock Recipe

(Prep + Cook Time: 25 minutes **| Serves:** 4)

Ingredients:

- 2 cloves garlic, crushed
- 1 teaspoon whole black peppercorns
- A handful of rosemary
- 3 bay leaves
- 4 cups water
- 2 sprigs parsley
- 1/2 teaspoon salt

Directions:

1. Put all of the ingredients, except salt, into the Instant Pot
2. Close and lock the lid. Select MANUAL and cook at HIGH pressure for 15 minutes.
3. When the timer beeps, let the pressure Release Naturally for 10 minutes and then release any remaining steam manually
4. Open the lid, Season with salt to taste.
5. Strain the stock and pour into jars. Store in the refrigerator or freeze

Cranberry Apple Sauce Recipe

(Prep + Cook Time: 30 minutes **| Serves:** 2)

Ingredients:

- 10-ounce cranberries, frozen or fresh, preferably organic
- 1/2 cup maple syrup or honey
- 1/4 cup lemon juice
- 1 - 2 apples, peeled, cored and then cut into chunks
- 1 teaspoon cinnamon
- 1/4 teaspoon sea salt

Directions:

1. Combine all of the ingredients in the Instant Pot.
2. Close and lock the lid. Select the MANUAL setting and set the cooking time for 1 minutes at HIGH pressure
3. Once cooking is complete, use a Natural Release for 15 minutes and then release any remaining pressure manually.
4. Open the lid, using a wooden spoon, mash the fruit a bit
5. Select Sauté and simmer for 1 to 2 minutes to evaporate some water, stirring occasionally.
6. Once the sauce begins to thicken, press the CANCEL key to stop the SAUTÉ function. Pour into clean jars and refrigerate

Chicken Feet Stock Recipe

(Prep + Cook Time: 1 hour 20 minutes | **Serves:** 8

Ingredients:
- 1 ½ pounds' chicken feet, cleaned and rinsed
- 2 carrots, cut into chunks
- 1 onion, quartered
- 2 stalks celery, cut in half
- 1 teaspoon black peppercorns
- 1 bay leaf
- 8 cups water

Directions:
1. Put all of the ingredients into the Instant Pot.
2. Close and lock the lid. Select MANUAL and cook at HIGH pressure for 60 minutes
3. When the timer goes off, let the pressure Release Naturally for 10 minutes and then release any remaining steam manually.
4. Open the lid, Strain the stock and pour into jars. Store in the refrigerator or freeze

Seafood Soup Stock Recipe

(Prep + Cook Time: 50 minutes | **Serves:** 8

Ingredients:
- Shells and heads from 1/2-pound prawns
- 4 carrots, cut into chunks
- 3 cloves garlic, sliced
- 2 bay leaves
- 4 onions, quartered
- 1 teaspoon whole black peppercorns
- 8 cups water

Directions:
1. Put all of the ingredients into the Instant Pot.
2. Close and lock the lid. Select MANUAL and cook at HIGH pressure for 30 minutes
3. When the timer beeps, let the pressure Release Naturally for 15 minutes and then release any remaining steam manually.
4. Open the lid, Strain the stock and pour into jars. Store in the refrigerator or freeze

Homemade Salsa with IP

(Prep + Cook Time: 50 minutes | **Serves:** 6

Ingredients:
- 6 cups fresh tomatoes, diced, peeled and seeded
- 2 yellow onions, diced
- 1 cup jalapeno peppers, seeded and chopped.
- 1/4 cup vinegar
- 1 ½ green bell peppers, diced
- 1 ½ tablespoon sugar
- 1 ½ cans (6 oz) tomato paste
- 1 tablespoon garlic powder
- 1/2 tablespoon kosher salt
- 1 tablespoon cayenne pepper

Directions:
1. Put all of the ingredients into the Instant Pot. Stir well to combine.
2. Select the MANUAL setting and set the cooking time for 30 minutes at HIGH pressure
3. Once cooking is complete, select Cancel and let Naturally Release for 10 minutes. Release any remaining steam manually.
4. Uncover the pot, Serve warm or cool

Mushroom Gravy Sauce Recipe

(**Prep + Cook Time:** 25 minutes | **Serves:** 8

Ingredients:
- 1/4 cup shallots, chopped.
- 2 cups beef broth
- 2 tablespoon flour
- 1/4 cup half and half
- 1/2 teaspoon ground black pepper
- 2 tablespoon butter
- 1 package button mushrooms, sliced
- Salt to taste

Directions:
1. Preheat the Instant Pot by selecting SAUTÉ.
2. Once hot, add the butter and melt it
3. Add the shallots and mushrooms. Cook until fragrant.
4. Whisk in the broth and flour. Whisk until smooth.
5. Simmer the mixture for 5 minutes.
6. Pour in half and half, stir well. Season with salt and pepper
7. Press the CANCEL button to reset the cooking program, then press the MANUAL button and set the cooking time for 3 minutes at HIGH pressure.
8. Once cooking is complete, let the pressure Release Naturally for 10 minutes. Release any remaining steam manually.
9. Uncover the pot, and Serve

Beef Bone Broth Recipe

(**Prep + Cook Time:** 1 hour 40 minutes | **Serves:** 10

Ingredients:
- 4 pounds' beef bones
- 2 carrots, cut into large chunks
- 1 onion, quartered
- 3 stalks celery, cut into large chunks
- 2 bay leaves
- 4 cloves garlic, minced
- 2 tablespoon black peppercorns
- 1 tablespoon apple cider vinegar
- 10 cups water

Directions:
1. Put all of the ingredients into the Instant Pot.
2. Close and lock the lid. Select MANUAL and cook at HIGH pressure for 1 hour 15 minutes
3. Once timer goes off, allow to Naturally Release for 15 minutes and then release any remaining pressure manually.
4. Uncover the pot, Strain the broth and pour into jars. Store in the refrigerator or freeze

Strawberry Applesauce Recipe

(**Prep + Cook Time:** 30 minutes | **Serves:** 6

Ingredients:
- 8 peeled apples, cored and sliced
- 3 cups strawberries, hulled and chopped.
- 2 tablespoon sugar
- 2 tablespoon lemon juice
- 1/4 teaspoon cinnamon powder

Directions:
1. Combine all of the ingredients in the Instant Pot and stir to mix.
2. Select MANUAL and cook at HIGH pressure for 5 minutes
3. Once cooking is complete, use a Natural Release for 15 minutes, then release any remaining pressure manually.
4. Open the lid, use a potato masher to mash the mixture and get the consistency you like

Bolognese Sauce Recipe

(Prep + Cook Time: 50 minutes | **Serves:** 4)

Ingredients:

- 1-pound ground beef
- 1 can pasta sauce
- 1 tablespoon sugar
- 1/4 teaspoon basil, dried
- 1/2 tablespoon unsalted butter
- 2 teaspoon garlic, minced
- 1 carrot, chopped.
- 1 stalk celery, chopped.
- 1/4 cup half and half cream
- 1/8 cup parsley, chopped.
- 1/2 teaspoon kosher salt
- 1/4 teaspoon ground black pepper

Directions:

1. To preheat the Instant Pot, select SAUTÉ. Once hot, add the butter and melt it.
2. Add the garlic and sauté for 30 seconds
3. Add the carrots and celery and sauté for 6 to 8 minutes, or until soft.
4. Add the ground beef and cook for another 4 to 5 minutes until browned, stirring occasionally
5. Add the pasta sauce, sugar, salt, pepper and basil, Stir well
6. Press the CANCEL button to stop the SAUTE function, then select the MANUAL setting and set the cooking time for 15 minutes at HIGH pressure
7. Once cooking is complete, let the pressure Release Naturally for 10 minutes. Release any remaining steam manually
8. Uncover the pot, Add the half and half to the pot. Stir to combine. Top with parsley and serve

Yogurt Recipes

Strawberry Yogurt.

(Prep + Cook Time: 20 minutes | **Serves:** 4)

Ingredients:

- 1 cup strawberry puree
- 4 capsules high-quality probiotic
- 1 tablespoon raw honey
- 1 teaspoon vanilla paste
- 2 tablespoon gelatin powder
- 2 cans full cream milk

Directions:

1. Pour the milk in instant pot
2. Lock the lid and select the yogurt button; then press the adjust button till the display states boil
3. When the Instant Pot beeps; turn off the pot, remove the lid and take out the metal bowl
4. Using a candy thermometer measure the temperature of the milk till it reaches 115 C
5. Once the milk is cooled below 115 C; empty the contents of probiotic capsules in the milk
6. Return the metal bowl to the pot; close the lid and seal it and press the yogurt button again
7. Use the (+) button to adjust the time to 14hours. When the Instant pot beeps; taste the yogurt to make sure it is tart
8. Transfer the yogurt to the blender or food processor, sprinkle gelatin powder and add remaining ingredients.
9. Blending the yogurt in a food blender until smooth.
10. Pour the yogurt into glasses or bowls and refrigerate the same for 2 - 3 hours.

Raspberry Yogurt.

(Prep + Cook Time: 20 minutes | **Serves:** 6)

Ingredients:

- 1 cup raspberry puree
- 4 capsules high-quality probiotic
- 2 tablespoon gelatin powder
- 1 teaspoon vanilla paste
- 1 tablespoon raw honey
- 2 cans full cream milk

Directions:

1. Pour the milk in instant pot.
2. Lock the lid and select the yogurt button; then press the adjust button till the display states boil
3. When the Instant Pot beeps; turn off the pot, remove the lid and take out the metal bowl
4. Using a candy thermometer measure the temperature of the milk till it reaches 115 C
5. Once the milk is cooled below 115 C; empty the contents of probiotic capsules in the milk.
6. Return the metal bowl to the pot; close the lid and seal it and press the yogurt button again.
7. Use the (+) button to adjust the time to 14hours. When the Instant pot beeps; taste the yogurt to make sure it is tart
8. Transfer the yogurt to the blender or food processor, sprinkle gelatin powder and add remaining ingredients.
9. Blending the yogurt in a food blender until smooth
10. Pour the yogurt into glasses or bowls and refrigerate the same for 2 - 3 hours.

Chocolate Yogurt.

(Prep + Cook Time: 20 minutes | **Serves:** 4)

Ingredients:

- 4 capsules high-quality probiotic
- 2 tablespoon cocoa powder
- 1 cup melted dark chocolate
- 1 tablespoon raw honey
- 2 tablespoon gelatin powder
- 2 cans full cream milk
- 1 teaspoon vanilla paste

Directions:

1. Pour the milk in instant pot. Add cocoa powder
2. Lock the lid and select the yogurt button; then press the adjust button until the display states boil
3. When the Instant Pot beeps; turn off the pot, remove the lid and take out the metal bowl
4. Using a candy thermometer measure the temperature of the milk till it reaches 115 C
5. Once the milk is cooled below 115 C; empty the contents of probiotic capsules in the milk
6. Return the metal bowl to the pot; close the lid and seal it and press the yogurt button again.
7. Use the (+) button to adjust the time to 14hours. When the Instant pot beeps; taste the yogurt to make sure it is tart.
8. Transfer the yogurt to the blender or food processor, sprinkle gelatin powder and add remaining ingredients.
9. Blending the yogurt in a food blender until smooth
10. Pour the yogurt into glasses or bowls and refrigerate the same for 2 - 3 hours.

Slow Cooked Fruity Yogurt.

(Prep + Cook Time: 12 hours | **Serves:** 4)

Ingredients:

- 5 ⅔ cups. milk; organic, reduced fat or whole
- 4 tablespoon yogurt culture; plain; divided
- 4 tablespoon dry milk powder; non-fat; divided
- 1 ½ cup. water; for the pot
- 4 tablespoon sugar; all natural; divided
- 2 cups. fresh fruit; chopped.

Equipment:

- 4 wide mouth pint jars

Directions:

1. Pour the water into the Instant Pot and then put a rack or a grate in the pot
2. Pour 1 and 1/3 cup. Milk into each jar and the cover the jar loosely with their lids. Put the jars onto the rack/ grate.
3. Set the Instant Pot to Pressure Cycle and set the timer to 2 minutes; this will heat the milk and kill any pathogens that might be in the milk
4. When the cycle is done; turn the steam valve to quick release the pressure
5. Open the pot lid and with a jar lifter, remove the jars from the pot. Put the jars into cool water and carefully remove the jar lids
6. Once the milk is below 100F; add 1 tablespoon yogurt culture, 1 tablespoon dry milk powder; and 1 tablespoon sugar into each jar; stir until well mixed.
7. Carefully add about 1/2 cup. of fresh fruits into each jar; do not over fill them and leave at least 1/ 8-inch clear from the top each jar. Return the jar lids back.
8. Check and make sure that there is still 1 ½ cup. of water in the bottom of the Instant Pot
9. Put the jars back onto the rack/ grate. Press the yogurt cycle and set the timer for 8 - 12 hours.
10. When the cycle is complete; put the jars in the refrigerator; this will cool them down and stop the cooking process.

Tips: Making the yogurt in jars enables you to make plain or different flavored yogurt at the same time

Vegan Soy Yogurt.

(Prep + Cook Time: 12 hours | **Serves:** 4)

Ingredients:
- 1 packet vegan yogurt culture
- 1-quart soy milk (use only made soybeans and water; no vitamins or sugar added.)
- Sweetener; if desired

Directions:
1. Pour the soymilk into a wide mouth; 1-quart Mason jar with lid or into multiple heatproof containers with a lids
2. Add the vegan yogurt culture. Close the lid and shake to mix. Remove the lid from the jar; you don't need it at this point
3. Put the Mason jar directly into the Instant Pot container. Close and lock the Instant Pot lid. You can leave the steam valve to "Sealing" or "Releasing"; it won't affect the cooking. Press the YOGURT button and the timer to 12 hours
4. When the timer beeps at the end of the cooking cycle, carefully remove the Mason jar from the pot, cover with its lid and refrigerate for at least 6 hours.
5. Sweeten and/ or flavor, if desired. This will keep for up to 6 days in the refrigerator

Tips: This thick, creamy, unsweetened, tart soy yogurt can be used as a sour cream substitute or in recipes. You can enjoy it topped with pears and cinnamons; with bananas, shredded coconut and pecans, with jam or sweetened with coconut sugar. You can also strain it overnight to make yogurt cheese.

Pumpkin Spice Yogurt.

(Prep + Cook Time: 20 minutes | **Serves:** 4)

Ingredients:
- 2 tablespoon gelatin powder
- 4 capsules high-quality probiotic
- 1 teaspoon vanilla paste
- 1 tablespoon raw honey
- 1 tablespoon pumpkin spice
- 2 cans full cream milk

Directions:
1. Pour the milk in instant pot.
2. Lock the lid and select the yogurt button; then press the adjust button till the display states boil.
3. When the Instant Pot beeps; turn off the pot, remove the lid and take out the metal bowl.
4. Using a candy thermometer measure the temperature of the milk till it reaches 115 C
5. Once the milk is cooled below 115 C; empty the contents of probiotic capsules in the milk
6. Return the metal bowl to the pot; close the lid and seal it and press the yogurt button again.
7. Use the (+) button to adjust the time to 14hours. When the Instant pot beeps; taste the yogurt to make sure it is tart.
8. Transfer the yogurt to the blender or food processor, sprinkle gelatin powder and add remaining ingredients
9. Blending the yogurt in a food blender until smooth
10. Pour the yogurt into glasses or bowls and refrigerate the same for 2 - 3 hours.

Mango Yogurt.

(Prep + Cook Time: 30 minutes | **Serves:** 4)

Ingredients:
- 2 cans full cream milk
- 2 tablespoon gelatine
- 1 teaspoon vanilla extract
- 4 capsules high-quality probiotic
- 1 tablespoon raw honey
- 1 cup mango puree or pulp

Directions:
1. Pour the milk in instant pot.
2. Lock the lid and select the yogurt button; then press the adjust button till the display states boil
3. When the Instant Pot beeps; turn off the pot, remove the lid and take out the metal bowl
4. Using a candy thermometer measure the temperature of the milk till it reaches 115 C
5. Once the milk is cooled below 115 C; empty the contents of probiotic capsules in the milk.
6. Stir in mango puree as well
7. Return the metal bowl to the pot, close the lid and seal it and press the yogurt button again
8. Use the (+) button to adjust the time to 14hours. When the Instant pot beeps; taste the yogurt to make sure it is tart.
9. Transfer the yogurt to the blender or food processor, sprinkle gelatin powder, add honey and vanilla extract
10. Blending the yogurt until smooth
11. Pour the yogurt into glasses or bowls and refrigerate the same for 2 - 3 hours

Passionfruit Yogurt.

(Prep + Cook Time: 20 minutes | **Serves:** 4)

Ingredients:
- 4 capsules high-quality probiotic
- 2 cans full cream milk
- 2 tablespoon gelatin powder
- 1 ½ cups passionfruit pulp
- 1 tablespoon raw honey
- 1 teaspoon vanilla paste

Directions:
1. Pour the milk in instant pot.
2. Lock the lid and select the yogurt button; then press the adjust button till the display states boil.
3. When the Instant Pot beeps; turn off the pot, remove the lid and take out the metal bowl
4. Using a candy thermometer measure the temperature of the milk till it reaches 115 C
5. Once the milk is cooled below 115 C; empty the contents of probiotic capsules in the milk
6. Return the metal bowl to the pot; close the lid and seal it and press the yogurt button again.
7. Use the (+) button to adjust the time to 14hours. When the Instant pot beeps; taste the yogurt to make sure it is tart.
8. Transfer the yogurt to the blender or food processor, sprinkle gelatin powder and add remaining ingredients, including pulp
9. Blending the yogurt in a food blender until smooth.
10. Pour the yogurt into glasses or bowls and refrigerate the same for 2 - 3 hours.

Kiwi Yogurt.

(Prep + Cook Time: 20 minutes | **Serves:** 4)

Ingredients:

- 4 capsules high-quality probiotic
- 1 teaspoon vanilla paste
- 3/4 cup kiwi puree
- 2 tablespoon gelatin powder
- 1 tablespoon raw honey
- 2 cans full cream milk

Directions:

1. Pour the milk in instant pot
2. Lock the lid and select the yogurt button; then press the adjust button till the display states boil.
3. When the Instant Pot beeps; turn off the pot, remove the lid and take out the metal bowl
4. Using a candy thermometer measure the temperature of the milk till it reaches 115 C
5. Once the milk is cooled below 115 C; empty the contents of probiotic capsules in the milk
6. Return the metal bowl to the pot; close the lid and seal it and press the yogurt button again
7. Use the (+) button to adjust the time to 14hours. When the Instant pot beeps; taste the yogurt to make sure it is tart.
8. Transfer the yogurt to the blender or food processor, sprinkle gelatin powder and add remaining ingredients.
9. Blending the yogurt in a food blender until smooth.
10. Pour the yogurt into glasses or bowls and refrigerate the same for 2 - 3 hours

White Chocolate Yogurt.

(Prep + Cook Time: 20 minutes | **Serves:** 4)

Ingredients:

- 1 cup melted white chocolate
- 2 tablespoon gelatin powder
- 1 tablespoon raw honey
- 2 cans full cream milk
- 4 capsules high-quality probiotic
- 1 teaspoon vanilla paste

Directions:

1. Pour the milk in instant pot.
2. Lock the lid and select the yogurt button; then press the adjust button till the display states boil
3. When the Instant Pot beeps; turn off the pot, remove the lid and take out the metal bowl
4. Using a candy thermometer measure the temperature of the milk till it reaches 115 C
5. Once the milk is cooled below 115 C; empty the contents of probiotic capsules in the milk
6. Return the metal bowl to the pot; close the lid and seal it and press the yogurt button again.
7. Use the (+) button to adjust the time to 14hours. When the Instant pot beeps; taste the yogurt to make sure it is tart.
8. Transfer the yogurt to the blender or food processor, sprinkle gelatin powder and add remaining ingredients, including white chocolate.
9. Blending the yogurt in a food blender until smooth
10. Pour the yogurt into glasses or bowls and refrigerate the same for 2 - 3 hours.

Blueberry Oats Yogurt.

(Prep + Cook Time: 20 minutes | **Serves:** 6)

Ingredients:
- 4 capsules high-quality probiotic
- 2 cans full cream milk
- 1/2 cup roasted oats
- 2 tablespoon gelatin powder
- 1 tablespoon raw honey
- 1 teaspoon vanilla paste
- 1 cup blueberry puree or pulp

Directions:
1. Pour the milk in instant pot.
2. Lock the lid and select the yogurt button; then press the adjust button till the display states boil.
3. When the Instant Pot beeps; turn off the pot, remove the lid and take out the metal bowl
4. Using a candy thermometer measure the temperature of the milk till it reaches 115 C
5. Once the milk is cooled below 115 C; empty the contents of probiotic capsules in the milk
6. Return the metal bowl to the pot; close the lid and seal it and press the yogurt button again
7. Use the (+) button to adjust the time to 14hours. When the Instant pot beeps; taste the yogurt to make sure it is tart
8. Transfer the yogurt to the blender or food processor, sprinkle gelatin powder and add remaining ingredients.
9. Blending the yogurt in a food blender until smooth.
10. Pour the yogurt into glasses or bowls and refrigerate the same for 2 - 3 hours.

Cinnamon Yogurt.

(Prep + Cook Time: 20 minutes | **Serves:** 6)

Ingredients:
- 2 cans full cream milk
- 1 teaspoon vanilla paste
- 2 tablespoon gelatin powder
- 4 capsules high-quality probiotic
- 1 tablespoon raw honey
- 2 teaspoon Ceylon cinnamon

Directions:
1. Pour the milk in instant pot.
2. Lock the lid and select the yogurt button; then press the adjust button till the display states boil.
3. When the Instant Pot beeps; turn off the pot, remove the lid and take out the metal bowl
4. Using a candy thermometer measure the temperature of the milk till it reaches 115 C
5. Once the milk is cooled below 115 C; empty the contents of probiotic capsules in the milk.
6. Return the metal bowl to the pot; close the lid and seal it and press the yogurt button again.
7. Use the (+) button to adjust the time to 14hours. When the Instant pot beeps; taste the yogurt to make sure it is tart
8. Transfer the yogurt to the blender or food processor, sprinkle gelatin powder and add remaining ingredients
9. Blending the yogurt in a food blender until smooth.
10. Pour the yogurt into glasses or bowls and refrigerate the same for 2 - 3 hours.

Vanilla Yogurt.

(Prep + Cook Time: 20 minutes | **Serves:** 4)

Ingredients:

- 3 teaspoon vanilla paste
- 2 tablespoon gelatin powder
- 1 tablespoon raw honey
- 4 capsules high-quality probiotic
- 2 cans full cream milk

Directions:

1. Pour the milk in instant pot.
2. Lock the lid and select the yogurt button; then press the adjust button till the display states boil
3. When the Instant Pot beeps; turn off the pot, remove the lid and take out the metal bowl.
4. Using a candy thermometer measure the temperature of the milk till it reaches 115 C.
5. Once the milk is cooled below 115 C; empty the contents of probiotic capsules in the milk.
6. Return the metal bowl to the pot; close the lid and seal it and press the yogurt button again.
7. Use the (+) button to adjust the time to 14hours. When the Instant pot beeps; taste the yogurt to make sure it is tart
8. Transfer the yogurt to the blender or food processor, sprinkle gelatin powder and add remaining ingredients
9. Blending the yogurt in a food blender until smooth
10. Pour the yogurt into glasses or bowls and refrigerate the same for 2 - 3 hours

Dessert Recipes

Maple Crème Brulee.

(Prep + Cook Time: 1 hour 10 minutes | **Serves:** 2 - 3)

Ingredients:

- 1 ⅓ cups heavy whipping cream, warm
- 1/2 teaspoon maple extract
- 1 cup water
- 3 large egg yolks
- 1 ½ teaspoon sugar
- 1/4 teaspoon ground cinnamon
- 1/2 cup brown sugar

Directions:

1. Pour the water into the Instant Pot and set a steam rack in the pot
2. In a medium bowl, whisk together egg yolks, cinnamon and sugar until combined
3. Add the warm cream and stir well. Add the maple extract, stir
4. Divide the mixture between the ramekins and sprinkle sugar for the topping
5. Place the ramekins on the steam rack. Close and lock the lid
6. Select the STEAM setting and set the cooking time for 30 minutes
7. Once cooking is complete, use a Natural Release for 10 minutes, then release any remaining pressure manually. Open the lid
8. Let the ramekins cool and then refrigerate them for 10 to 15 minutes then Serve

Easy Baked Plums

(Prep + Cook Time: 45 minutes | **Serves:** 4-5)

Ingredients:

- 1 ½ pounds' fresh plums, pitted and halved
- 1-star anise
- 3 cardamom pods
- 1 teaspoon ground cinnamon
- 1 ½ cups water
- 2 tablespoon honey
- 1 teaspoon vanilla extract
- 4 cloves

Directions:

1. Put the plums into the Instant Pot
2. Add the water, honey, vanilla, cloves, anise, cardamom and cinnamon
3. Close and lock the lid. Select MANUAL and cook at HIGH pressure for 15 minutes
4. Once cooking is complete, let the pressure Release Naturally for 10 minutes. Release any remaining steam manually. Uncover the pot
5. Transfer the plums to a serving bowl.
6. Select the SAUTÉ setting on the Instant Pot on high heat
7. Reduce the remaining liquid by half. Serve or store the plums with the sauce

Coconut Yogurt Recipe

(Prep + Cook Time: 8 hours 30 minutes | **Serves:** 4)

Ingredients:

- 3 cans (14-ounce each) coconut milk
- 1 tablespoon maple syrup
- 2 tablespoon gelatin
- 4 capsules probiotics

Directions:

1. Remove the top cream from the coconut milk and add to the Instant Pot
2. Select the YOGURT and press ADJUST setting and bring the milk to a boil
3. Press the CANCEL key to stop the YOGURT function.
4. Let the milk cool to 100 F (use a thermometer).

5. When the temperature drops to 100 F, open the probiotics capsules and add to the milk. Stir until combined
6. Close and lock the lid. Select the YOGURT setting and set the cooking time for 8 hours
7. Once cooking is complete, let the pressure Release Naturally. Uncover the pot
8. Add the maple syrup and gelatin and gently stir well.
9. Pour equally into the jars. Let it cool completely and refrigerate for 1 to 2 hours before serving

Cranberry Stuffed Apples

(Prep + Cook Time: 30 minutes | **Serves:** 6

Ingredients:
- 5 medium apples, cored
- 1/3 cup fresh cranberries, chopped.
- 1/4 cup brown sugar
- 1/4 teaspoon cinnamon powder
- 1/2 cup water
- 2 tablespoon walnuts, chopped.
- 1/8 teaspoon ground nutmeg

Directions:
1. In a bowl; combine the walnuts, nutmeg, cranberries, sugar and cinnamon
2. Stuff each apple with the mixture.
3. Pour the water in the Instant Pot and put the apples in it
4. Add the leftover filling to the pot. Close and lock the lid.
5. Select the MANUAL setting and set the cooking time for 5 minutes at HIGH pressure
6. Once cooking is complete, use a Natural Release for 10 minutes, then release any remaining pressure manually
7. Open the lid, Serve and Enjoy

Chocolate Brownies

(Prep + Cook Time: 55 minutes | **Serves:** 10-12

Ingredients:
- 4 tablespoon unsweetened cocoa powder
- 6 tablespoon unsalted butter
- 3/4 cup all-purpose flour
- 1 cup sugar
- 1/4 teaspoon salt
- 2 large eggs, beaten
- 1/4 cup chopped walnuts
- 3/4 tablespoon baking powder
- 2 cups water

Directions:
1. Preheat a small pan on the stove, add and melt the butter
2. Remove from the stove and add the cocoa powder, mix well
3. In a bowl; combine the flour, baking powder, sugar and salt
4. Add the eggs and walnuts, stir. Add the cocoa mix, stir.
5. Grease a 7- to 8-inch baking pan and add the batter.
6. Cover the pan tightly with aluminum foil.
7. Pour the water into the Instant Pot and set a steam rack in the pot
8. Put the pan on the rack. Close and lock the lid.
9. Select MANUAL and cook at HIGH pressure for 35 minutes.
10. When the timer beeps, use a Natural Release for 10 minutes
11. Uncover the pot, Allow the brownies cool and serve

Delicious Chocolate Muffins

(Prep + Cook Time: 35 minutes | **Serves:** 6

Ingredients:

- 1/4 cup sweetened cocoa powder
- 1/4 cup coconut oil, melted
- 1 cup flaxseed meal
- 1/2 cup pumpkin puree
- 1 ½ cups water

Directions:

1. In a medium bowl, whisk together the coconut oil, pumpkin puree, cocoa powder and flaxseed meal until combined
2. Divide the mixture between 6 muffin cups.
3. Add the water to the Instant Pot and place a steam rack on top
4. Put the muffin cups on the rack. Close and lock the lid.
5. Select the MANUAL setting and set the cooking time for 18 minutes at HIGH pressure
6. Once timer goes off, use a Quick Release.
7. Carefully unlock the lid, Serve warm or chilled

Chocolate and Almond Candy

(Prep + Cook Time: 35 minutes | **Serves:** 4-5)

Ingredients:

- 14-ounce condensed coconut milk
- 1 cup almonds, chopped.
- 12-ounce dark chocolate chips
- 2 cups water

Directions:

1. In a baking pan that can fit into the pot, combine the chocolate chips and coconut milk
2. Cover the pan tightly with aluminum foil.
3. Pour the water into the Instant Pot and set a steam rack in the pot
4. Place the pan on the rack. Close and lock the lid.
5. Select MANUAL and cook at HIGH pressure for 3 minutes.
6. When time is up, do a Quick Release. Carefully unlock the lid,
7. Add the almonds and mix well
8. Line a sheet pan with a parchment paper. With a tablespoon, drop the candy onto the paper.
9. Slip the pan into the freezer for about 10 to 20 minutes and Serve

IP Chocolate Cake

(Prep + Cook Time: 55 minutes | **Serves:** 6-7)

Ingredients:

- 1 ½ cups all-purpose flour
- 4 large eggs, beaten
- 1/2 cup unsalted butter, melted
- 3/4 cup heavy cream
- 1 teaspoon vanilla extract
- 1/4 teaspoon baking powder
- 2/3 cup cocoa powder, unsweetened
- 3/4 cup stevia sweetener
- 1/4 cup protein powder, chocolate or vanilla flavor
- 1/4 teaspoon salt

Directions:

1. In a large bowl, combine the flour, baking powder, cocoa powder, stevia sweetener, protein powder and salt. Mix well. Add the eggs, butter, cream and vanilla. Stir to combine.
2. Pour the mixture into a 7- to 8-inch baking pan.
3. Add the water to the Instant Pot and place a steam rack. Place the pan on the steam rack. Close and lock the lid.
4. Select MANUAL and cook at HIGH pressure for 30 minutes
5. When the timer beeps, use a Natural Release for 10 minutes.
6. Uncover the pot, Let the cake cool for a few minutes and serve

Cranberry Pudding

(**Prep + Cook Time:** 50 minutes | **Serves:** 6

Ingredients:

- 3 large eggs, beaten
- 3 cups bread cubes
- 1 teaspoon vanilla extract
- 1 cup water
- 1/3 cup dried cranberries
- 1/2 cup sugar, granulated
- 2 cups milk
- 1/3 cup pecans, chopped.

Directions:

1. Prepare the Instant Pot by adding the water to the pot and placing the steam rack in it
2. In a bowl; whisk together the eggs, sugar and milk until combined.
3. Add the vanilla, stir
4. Grease a baking dish that can fit into the pot and add the cranberries and bread cubes.
5. Pour the egg mixture in the baking dish. Cover tightly with tin aluminum foil
6. Place the dish on the steam rack. Close and lock the lid.
7. Select the STEAM setting and set the cooking time for 25 minutes
8. When the timer beeps, use a Natural Release for 10 minutes. Open the pot
9. Uncover the baking dish and sprinkle with pecans. Serve or cover and chill up to 24 hours

Banana Cake Recipe

(**Prep + Cook Time:** 1 hour 10 minutes | **Serves:** 6-7)

Ingredients:

- 3 bananas, peeled and mashed
- 1 stick butter, soft
- 2 cups all-purpose flour
- 1 cup water
- 8-ounce sugar
- 3 medium eggs, beaten
- 1 teaspoon baking powder
- 1 teaspoon cinnamon
- 1 teaspoon nutmeg
- 1/4 teaspoon kosher salt

Directions:

1. In a bowl; whisk together butter, sugar and eggs until combined
2. Add the bananas, cinnamon, nutmeg and salt. Mix well.
3. Stir in the flour and baking powder.
4. Grease a 7- to 8-inch baking pan with butter. Pour the batter in the pan and cover with foil
5. Pour the water into the Instant Pot and set a steam rack in the pot
6. Place the baking pan on the rack. Close and lock the lid.
7. Select the MANUAL setting and set the cooking time for 50 minutes at HIGH pressure.
8. Once timer goes off, use a Quick Release
9. Carefully unlock the lid, Let the cake cool for a few minutes and serve

Stuffed Peaches.

(**Prep + Cook Time:** 25 minutes | **Serves:** 6

Ingredients:

- 5-6 medium peaches, cored
- 2 tablespoon butter
- 2-ounce cup sugar
- 1/4 cup flour
- 2-ounce teaspoon pure almond extract
- 1/2 teaspoon ground cinnamon
- 1 cup water
- 1/8 teaspoon sea salt

Directions:

1. In a bowl; combine the butter, salt, sugar, flour, almond extract and cinnamon.
2. Stuff each peach with the mixture
3. Prepare the Instant Pot by adding the water to the pot and placing the steamer basket in it.
4. Carefully put the peaches in the basket
5. Add the leftover filling to the pot. Close and lock the lid.

6. Select MANUAL and cook at HIGH pressure for 3 minutes
7. Once timer goes off, use a Quick Release.
8. Carefully unlock the lid, allow to cool for 10-12 minutes and serve

Pear and Caramel Pudding

(Prep + Cook Time: 55 minutes | **Serves:** 6

Ingredients:
- 4 medium pears, peeled and cubed
- 1 ½ teaspoon baking powder
- 1/2 cup pecans, chopped.
- 1/8 teaspoon ground cloves
- 1/2 teaspoon ground cinnamon
- 1 cup water
- 1 cup flour
- 3/4 cup brown sugar
- 1/4 cup butter, soft
- 3/4 cup boiling water
- 1/2 cup milk
- 1/2 cup sugar
- 1/4 teaspoon salt

Directions:
1. Prepare the Instant Pot by adding the water to the pot and placing the steam rack in it
2. In a baking dish that can fit into the pot, combine the flour, pears, baking powder, milk, sugar, salt, pecans, cloves and cinnamon
3. In a bowl; whisk together the butter, sugar and boiling water until combined.
4. Pour this mixture into the baking dish, don't stir. Place the dish on the steam rack
5. Close and lock the lid. Select MANUAL and cook at HIGH pressure for 35 minutes
6. When the timer goes off, use a Quick Release. Carefully unlock the lid, Let the pudding cool and then refrigerate before serving

Fruit Salad Jam Recipe

(Prep + Cook Time: 30 minutes | **Serves:** 2 - 3)

Ingredients:
- 1 cup blueberries
- 1 medium orange, peeled
- 1 medium apple, diced
- 1 teaspoon lemon zest
- 1/2 teaspoon cinnamon
- 1 ½ cups water
- 1 cup sugar

Directions:
1. In the Instant Pot, combine the blueberries, orange, apple, sugar, lemon zest, cinnamon and water.
2. Close and lock the lid. Select MANUAL and cook at HIGH pressure for 10 minutes
3. Once cooking is complete, let the pressure Release Naturally for 10 minutes. Release any remaining steam manually. Uncover the pot
4. Select Sauté and simmer the sauce until thickened.
5. Let it cool and then serve

Cheesecake Recipe

(Prep + Cook Time: 55 minutes | **Serves:** 6

Ingredients:
- 3 cups cream cheese, room temperature
- 3 large eggs, beaten
- 1/2 tablespoon vanilla extract
- 1 cup white sugar

Directions:
1. Pour the water into the Instant Pot and set a steam rack in the pot
2. In a medium bowl, combine the eggs, sugar, cream cheese and vanilla
3. Pour the mixture into a baking dish that can fit into the pot
4. Cover the pan tightly with aluminum foil.
5. Put the dish on the rack. Secure the lid.

6. Select MANUAL and cook at HIGH pressure for 30 minutes
7. When the timer goes off, let the pressure Release Naturally for 10 minutes, then release any remaining steam manually
8. Open the lid. Let the cheesecake cool for a few minutes and serve.

Instant Rice Pudding

(Prep + Cook Time: 40 minutes | **Serves:** 6

Ingredients:
- 1 cup basmati rice
- 1 teaspoon vanilla extract
- 3/4 cup heavy cream
- 1 ¼ cups water
- 2 cups milk
- 1/4 cup maple syrup
- A pinch of salt

Directions:
1. Rinse the rice well.
2. In the Instant Pot, combine the water, milk, rice, maple syrup and salt. Stir
3. Close and lock the lid. Select the PORRIDGE setting and set the cooking time for 20 minutes
4. Once cooking is complete, select CANCEL and let Naturally Release for 10 minutes. Release any remaining steam manually
5. Uncover the pot, Add the vanilla and cream. Mix well.
6. Serve warm with such toppings; dates, raisins, berry jam, chocolate chips, nuts, cinnamon, or butter

Brown Rice Pudding with Dates

(Prep + Cook Time: 1 hour 15 minutes | **Serves:** 6

Ingredients:
- 8-ounce brown rice
- 1/2 cup dates, pitted and chopped.
- 1/2 cup water
- 1 stick cinnamon
- 8-ounce pumpkin puree
- 1 teaspoon pumpkin spice
- 1/2 cup maple syrup
- 1 teaspoon vanilla extract
- 3 cups almond milk
- A pinch of salt

Directions:
1. Pour the boiling water over rice and wait for 10 minutes. Rinse
2. Add the water and milk to the Instant Pot.
3. Select SAUTÉ and cook the liquid until boiled.
4. Add the rice, dates, salt and cinnamon. Secure the lid.
5. Select the MANUAL setting and set the cooking time for 10 minutes at HIGH pressure
6. When the timer beeps, use a Natural Release for 15 minutes. Uncover the pot
7. Add the pumpkin puree, pumpkin spice and maple syrup, stir.
8. Select SAUTÉ and cook the mixture until thickened. Press the CANCEL key
9. Remove the cinnamon stick and add the vanilla, stir.
10. Transfer the pudding to a serving bowl and let it cool for 30 minutes. Serve and enjoy

Banana Bread

(Prep + Cook Time: 1 hour 10 minutes | **Serves:** 6-7)

Ingredients:

- 4 medium bananas, mashed
- 2 large eggs, beaten
- 4-ounce butter, room temperature
- 2 cups all-purpose flour
- 1 teaspoon baking powder
- 1 tablespoon vanilla extract
- 1/2 cup sugar
- 1 cup water

Directions:

1. In a bowl; whisk together the eggs, sugar and butter until combined
2. Add the bananas and vanilla, stir.
3. In another bowl, combine the flour and baking powder.
4. Pour the egg mixture into the flour mix. Stir until the batter is smooth
5. Grease a 7 to 8-inch baking pan with butter. Pour the batter in the pan.
6. Prepare the Instant Pot by adding the water to the pot and placing the steam rack in it.
7. Put the pan on the rack. Close and lock the lid.
8. Select MANUAL and cook at HIGH pressure for 45 minutes
9. When the timer beeps, use a Natural Release for 10 minutes. Uncover the pot. Let the bread cool for a few minutes and serve

Vanilla Cake Recipe

(Prep + Cook Time: 60 minutes | **Serves:** 6-7)

Ingredients:

- 1 ½ cups all-purpose flour
- 1/2 cup unsalted butter, melted
- 3/4 cup stevia sweetener
- 3/4 cup heavy cream
- 2 teaspoon baking powder
- 1/2 tablespoon vanilla extract
- 1 cup water
- 4 large eggs, beaten
- 1/4 teaspoon salt

Directions:

1. Prepare the Instant Pot by adding the water to the pot and placing the steam rack in it.
2. In a bowl; whisk together butter, stevia sweetener and eggs until combined
3. Stir in the flour, heavy cream, baking powder, vanilla extract and salt. Stir the mixture until just smooth.
4. Grease a 7- to 8-inch baking pan with butter. Pour the batter in the pan and cover with foil
5. Place the pan on the rack. Close and lock the lid.
6. Select the MANUAL setting and set the cooking time for 40 minutes at HIGH pressure
7. Once cooking is complete, let the pressure Release Naturally for 10 minutes. Release any remaining steam manually
8. Uncover the pot. Let the cake cool for a few minutes and serve

Lemon Marmalade Recipe

(Prep + Cook Time: 30 minutes | **Serves:** 4-5 jars)

Ingredients:

- 1-pound lemons, quartered, deseeded and sliced with a mandolin
- 1/2 cup water
- 2 pounds' sugar

Directions:

1. Add the lemons and water to the Instant Pot.
2. Close and lock the lid. Select MANUAL and cook at HIGH pressure for 10 minutes
3. When the timer beeps, use a Natural Release for 10 minutes. Uncover the pot
4. Add the sugar and stir for 2 minutes until the sugar melts
5. Select SAUTÉ and bring to a boil, cook for 5 minutes.
6. Transfer the mixture into clean or sterilized jars. Serve chilled or store in the refrigerator

Molten Lava Cake Recipe

(Prep + Cook Time: 35 minutes | **Serves:** 1 - 2

Ingredients:

- 1 teaspoon vanilla extract
- 1/2 cup semi-sweet chocolate chips
- 4 tablespoon butter, soft
- 2 cups water
- 2 tablespoon flour
- 1/4 cup powdered sugar
- 1 egg, beaten

Directions:

1. Prepare the Instant Pot by adding the water to the pot and placing the steam rack in it
2. Prepare and grease the ramekin with butter.
3. In a small bowl, whisk together the egg and vanilla.
4. Preheat a small pan on the stove, add and melt the chocolate with butter
5. Remove from the stove and let it cool for about 30 seconds.
6. Add the egg mix, flour and sugar to the chocolate mixture, stir to combine
7. Fill the ramekin halfway-full. Place on the rack. Close and lock the lid
8. Select the MANUAL setting and set the cooking time for 7 minutes at HIGH pressure
9. Once cooking is complete, select CANCEL and use a Natural Release for 10 minutes. Serve and enjoy

Egg Custard

(Prep + Cook Time: 35 minutes | **Serves:** 6

Ingredients:

- 6 big eggs, beaten
- 1/4 teaspoon cinnamon
- 1 teaspoon vanilla extract
- 4 cups milk
- 1 ½ cups water
- 3/4 cup sugar
- A pinch of salt

Directions:

1. In a bowl; whisk together the eggs, sugar, salt, vanilla and milk, until combined.
2. Pour the mixture into six ramekins and cover with foil.
3. Poke some holes in the foil
4. Add the water to the Instant Pot and place a steam rack in it
5. Place the ramekins on the rack. Close and lock the lid.
6. Select MANUAL and cook at HIGH pressure for 7 minutes
7. Once cooking is complete, use a Natural Release for 10 minutes, then release any remaining pressure manually. Open the lid
8. Remove the ramekins from the pot and let them cool for 3 minutes, Sprinkle the dish with cinnamon and serve

Choco Berry Mug Cake

(Prep + Cook Time: 30 minutes | **Serves:** 2)

Ingredients:

- 1/2 cup berries of choice (blueberries, strawberries, raspberries)
- 1/2 teaspoon vanilla
- 1/3 cup almond flour
- 1 egg, beaten
- 1 tablespoon maple syrup
- 1 ½ tablespoon chocolate chips
- Salt to taste

Directions:

1. In a small bowl, combine the flour, egg, maple syrup, chocolate chips, berries, vanilla and salt. Mix well
2. Pour the mixture in a mug that can fit into the pot
3. Cover the mug tightly with aluminum foil.
4. Prepare the Instant Pot by adding the water to the pot and placing the steam rack in it
5. Put the mug on the steam rack. Close and lock the lid.

6. Select MANUAL and cook at HIGH pressure for 10 minutes
7. When the timer goes off, use a Quick Release.
8. Carefully unlock the lid, Let the cake cool for a few minutes and serve

Raspberry Curd Recipe

(Prep + Cook Time: 30 minutes | **Serves:** 6-7)

Ingredients:
- 18-ounce raspberries
- 3 egg yolks
- 3 tablespoon butter
- 1 ½ cups sugar
- 3 tablespoon lemon juice

Directions:
1. In the Instant Pot, combine the raspberries, sugar and lemon juice
2. Close and lock the lid. Select the MANUAL setting and set the cooking time for 2 minutes at HIGH pressure.
3. When the timer goes off, let the pressure Release Naturally for 5 minutes, then release any remaining steam manually. Open the lid
4. Use the mesh strainer to puree the raspberries and remove the seeds
5. In a bowl; whisk egg yolks and combine with the raspberries puree
6. Return the mixture to the pot. Select SAUTÉ and bring the mixture to a boil, stirring constantly
7. Press the CANCEL key to stop the SAUTÉ function.
8. Add the butter and stir to combine. Serve chilled and enjoy

IP Stewed Pears

(Prep + Cook Time: 40 minutes | **Serves:** 4-5)

Ingredients:
- 3 cups red wine
- 1 bay leaf
- 16-ounce brown sugar
- 6 pears, peeled, leave the stems
- 1 teaspoon ginger powder
- 4 cloves
- 1 teaspoon ground cinnamon

Directions:
1. In the Instant Pot, combine the red wine, ginger, cloves, cinnamon, bay leaf and sugar.
2. Stir until the sugar has dissolved
3. Put the pears into the pot. Close and lock the lid.
4. Select the MANUAL setting and set the cooking time for 4 minutes at HIGH pressure
5. When the timer goes off, let the pressure Release Naturally for 10 minutes, then release any remaining steam manually. Open the lid
6. Transfer the pears to a serving plate. Remove the bay leaf.
7. Select SAUTÉ and cook for 4 to 5 minutes to reduce the liquid. Serve the pears with this sauce

Chocolate Custard

(Prep + Cook Time: 60 minutes | **Serves:** 4-5)

Ingredients:
- 13-ounce dark chocolate, chopped.
- 6 whisked egg yolks
- 1 cup whole milk
- 1 cup fresh cream
- 1 teaspoon vanilla extract
- 1/2 cup sugar
- 4 cups water

Directions:
1. In a saucepan, combine and simmer the milk, cream, vanilla and sugar, until sugar has dissolved.
2. Add the chocolate and remove the saucepan off the heat
3. When the chocolate has melted, slowly stir in the whisked egg yolks.

4. Pour the mixture into a 6- to 7-inch baking pan.
5. Prepare the Instant Pot by adding the water to the pot and placing the steam rack in it
6. Place the pan on the rack. Close and lock the lid.
7. Select the MANUAL setting and set the cooking time for 30 minutes at HIGH pressure
8. Once cooking is complete, let the pressure Release Naturally for 10 minutes. Release any remaining steam manually
9. Uncover the pot, serve warm or chilled

Cherry Compote.

(Prep + Cook Time: 25 minutes | **Serves:** 8

Ingredients:
- 3 cups cherries, fresh or frozen
- 1 ½ tablespoon maple syrup
- 1 cup apples, peeled and diced
- 1 tablespoon coconut oil
- 3/4 cup water
- 2 tablespoon cornstarch
- A pinch of salt

Directions:
1. In the Instant Pot, combine the cherries, apples, coconut oil, water, maple syrup and salt.
2. Close and lock the lid. Select MANUAL and cook at HIGH pressure for 4 minutes
3. Once timer goes off, use a Quick Release. Carefully unlock the lid
4. Stir well. Select the SAUTÉ setting on the Instant Pot.
5. Add the cornstarch and stirring occasionally, bring the mixture to a boil
6. Press the CANCEL key to stop the SAUTÉ function.
7. Let the compote cool for 10 minutes. Serve and enjoy

Raspberry Jam Recipe

(Prep + Cook Time: 30 minutes | **Serves:** 6-7)

Ingredients:
- 4 cups raspberries (fresh or frozen)
- 3 tablespoon lemon juice
- 1 cup sugar or 2/3 cup light honey
- 1 ½ tablespoon water
- 1 ½ tablespoon cornstarch

Directions:
1. In the Instant Pot, combine the raspberries, sugar and lemon, Stir well.
2. Close and lock the lid. Select MANUAL and cook at HIGH pressure for 3 minutes
3. Once cooking is complete, let the pressure Release Naturally for 10 minutes. Release any remaining steam manually. Uncover the pot
4. In a cup, whisk together the cornstarch and water until combined
5. Pour this mixture in the pot and stir. Let the jam cool and use up within a week, or freeze for later

Easy Sweet Roasted Pecans

(Prep + Cook Time: 35 minutes | **Serves:** 2 - 3)

Ingredients:
- 3 cups pecan halves
- 1/2 cup water
- 1/4 cup white sugar
- 1/4 cup brown sugar
- 1/3 teaspoon nutmeg
- 1/3 tablespoon cinnamon
- 1/3 tablespoon vanilla extract
- 1/2 cup maple syrup
- 1/3 teaspoon salt

Directions:
1. Preheat the Instant Pot by selecting SAUTÉ.
2. In the Instant Pot, combine the pecans, nutmeg, cinnamon, vanilla, maple syrup and salt.
3. Stirring constantly, cook for 7-10 minutes, until the pecans are tender

4. Press the CANCEL key to stop the SAUTÉ function.
5. Pour in the water.
6. Close and lock the lid. Select MANUAL and cook at HIGH pressure for 10 minutes
7. Once timer goes off, use a Quick Release. Carefully unlock the lid,
8. Preheat the oven to broil at 375 F
9. Pour the pecans mixture onto a baking sheet and bake for 5 minutes then flip and cook for another 5 minutes.
10. Transfer the pecans to the bowl and let them cool for 10 minutes. Add sugar and mix well then Serve

Chocolate Pudding Recipe

(Prep + Cook Time: 45 minutes | **Serves:** 4-5)

Ingredients:
- 6-ounce bittersweet chocolate slivers
- 5 egg yolks
- 1/4 teaspoon cinnamon
- 1/4 cup brown sugar
- 1 ½ cups water
- 1 ½ cups whipping cream
- 1/2 cup milk
- 2 teaspoon vanilla extract
- Dash of salt

Directions:
1. Prepare the Instant Pot by adding the water to the pot and placing the steam rack in it
2. In a saucepan, combine the cream and milk and bring to a simmer.
3. Remove from heat. Add the chocolate. Stir until the chocolate is melted
4. In a bowl; whisk together the egg yolks, vanilla extract, salt, cinnamon and sugar until combined
5. Stirring constantly, add hot chocolate to yolk mixture.
6. Pour the mixture in a baking pan that can fit into the pot. Cover the pan tightly with aluminum foil
7. Place the pan on the rack. Close and lock the lid.
8. Select MANUAL and cook at LOW pressure for 20 minutes
9. When the timer goes off, let the pressure Release Naturally for 5 minutes, then release any remaining steam manually. Open the lid
10. Remove the pan from the pot. Let it cool to room temperature, cover and chill at least 4 hours or up to 2 days. Serve and Serve

Cinnamon Apple Cake

(Prep + Cook Time: 1 hour 15 minutes | **Serves:** 6-7)

Ingredients:
- 1/2 tablespoon ground cinnamon
- 1/2 tablespoon baking powder
- 1/2 cup vegetable oil
- 1/2 teaspoon vanilla extract
- Powdered sugar
- 1 cup water
- 2 ½ cups apples, peeled, cored and diced
- 1/2 cup + 3 tablespoon sugar
- 3 eggs, beaten
- 3 tablespoon orange juice
- 1 cup flour
- 1/4 teaspoon kosher salt

Directions:
1. Prepare the Instant Pot by adding the water to the pot and placing the steam rack in it
2. In a bowl; mix the apple pieces, 3 tablespoons sugar and cinnamon
3. In a large bowl, combine the flour, salt and baking powder
4. In another bowl, whisk together the eggs, sugar, orange juice, oil and vanilla until combined.
5. Stirring, slowly pour the egg mixture into the flour mix, Stir well
6. Grease a 7- to 8-inch baking pan. Add half of batter to the pan. Layer half of the apples on the batter.
7. Then add the remaining batter and layer the remaining half apples
8. Cover with foil and place the pan on the steam rack.
9. Select MANUAL and cook at HIGH pressure for 50 minutes

10. When the timer goes off, let the pressure Release Naturally for 10 minutes, then release any remaining steam manually
11. Open the lid, Let the cake cool for a few minutes and top with powdered sugar and serve

Awesome Mango Cake

(Prep + Cook Time: 60 minutes | **Serves:** 6-7)

Ingredients:

- 1 teaspoon mango syrup
- 1 ¼ cups flour
- 1/4 teaspoon baking soda
- 1 teaspoon baking powder
- 1 cup water
- 1 tablespoon lemon juice
- 1/2 cup sugar
- 3/4 cup milk
- 1/4 cup coconut oil
- 1/8 teaspoon salt

Directions:

1. Pour the water into the Instant Pot and set a steam rack in the pot
2. Grease a baking dish that can fit into the pot. Add the sugar, milk and oil and stir until sugar melts.
3. Add the mango syrup and stir
4. Add the flour, baking soda, baking powder and salt. Stir to combine.
5. Add the lemon juice and stir
6. Pour the mixture into the baking dish.
7. Place the dish on the rack. Close and lock the lid.
8. Select the MANUAL setting and set the cooking time for 35 minutes at HIGH pressure
9. Once cooking is complete, select CANCEL and let Naturally Release for 10 minutes. Release any remaining steam manually
10. Uncover the pot, Let the cake cool for 10 minutes and serve

Chocolate Fondue Delight

(Prep + Cook Time: 25 minutes | **Serves:** 3-5)

Ingredients:

- One 100 g bar dark chocolate 70-85%, cut into large chunks
- 1 teaspoon amaretto liqueur
- 1/2 cup heavy cream
- 1 tablespoon sugar
- 2 cups water

Directions:

1. Divide the chocolate, sugar, amaretto liqueur and heavy cream between 3 ramekins
2. Pour the water into the Instant Pot and set a steam rack in the pot.
3. Place the ramekins on the rack. Close and lock the lid.
4. Select MANUAL and cook at HIGH pressure for 3 minutes
5. When cooking is complete, let the pressure Release Naturally for 10 minutes. Release any remaining steam manually. Uncover the pot.
6. Remove the ramekins from the pot
7. Using a fork quickly stir the contents of the ramekins vigorously for about 1 minute, until the texture is smooth and thick. Serve with fresh fruit or bread pieces

IP Baked Apples

(Prep + Cook Time: 40 minutes | **Serves:** 6)

Ingredients:
- 6 medium apples, cored
- 1/2 cup white sugar
- 1-ounce raisins
- 1 cup red wine
- 1 teaspoon cinnamon powder

Directions:
1. Add the apples to the Instant Pot.
2. Season with cinnamon, sugar, raisins and red wine. Close and lock the lid
3. Select MANUAL and cook at HIGH pressure for 10 minutes
4. When the timer goes off, let the pressure Release Naturally for 10 minutes, then release any remaining steam manually. Open the lid
5. Transfer the apples to a serving plate, Pour the remaining liquid over the apples and serve

Sweet Coconut Tapioca

(Prep + Cook Time: 30 minutes | **Serves:** 6-7)

Ingredients:
- 1 cup cashew nuts, toasted
- 16-inch lemongrass, diced
- 1 cup pearl tapioca, rinsed
- 5 cups coconut milk
- 2 teaspoon ginger, grated
- 4 egg yolks
- 1 cup sugar
- 1/2 teaspoon salt

Directions:
1. In the Instant Pot, combine the tapioca and coconut milk
2. Add the ginger and lemongrass, stir. Close and lock the lid.
3. Select the RICE setting and set the cooking time for 6 minutes
4. When the timer beeps, use a Natural Release for 10 minutes. Uncover the pot.
5. In a bowl; whisk together the egg yolks, sugar and salt until combined
6. Select the SAUTÉ setting on the Instant Pot and add the egg mixture
7. Simmer until the mixture has thickened. Sprinkle with toasted cashew nuts and serve

Delightful Quiche

(Prep + Cook Time: 45 minutes | **Serves:** 2)

Ingredients:
- 1/4 cup milk
- 3 large eggs
- 1 cup water
- 1 tablespoon chives, chopped.
- 1/2 cup cheddar cheese, shredded
- Cooking spray
- Salt and ground black pepper to taste

Directions:
1. In a medium bowl, whisk together eggs, milk, salt, pepper and chives until combined
2. Grease a 7- to 8-inch baking pan with cooking spray. Add the cheese to the pan.
3. Pour the egg mixture into the pan and spread evenly.
4. Pour the water into the Instant Pot and set a steam rack in the pot
5. Place the pan on the rack. Close and lock the lid.
6. Select the MANUAL setting and set the cooking time for 30 minutes at HIGH pressure
7. Once timer goes off, use a Quick Release. Carefully unlock the lid and Serve

Blueberries Yogurt Recipe

(Prep + Cook Time: 30 minutes | **Serves:** 4)

Ingredients:

- 2 cups blueberries
- 2 cups drained low-fat yogurt
- 1 tablespoon pistachios, shelled and diced
- 1/4 cup sugar
- 1/2 teaspoon balsamic vinegar
- 1 tablespoon lime juice

Directions:

1. In the Instant Pot, combine the sugar, blueberries, vinegar and lime juice
2. Close and lock the lid. Select MANUAL and cook at HIGH pressure for 10 minutes
3. When the timer beeps, use a Natural Release for 10 minutes. Uncover the pot
4. Prepare the yogurt jars. Pour 1/4 cup of yogurt into each jars
5. Then add 2 tablespoon of blueberry sauce into jars.
6. Make another layer of yogurt and top with blueberry sauce again
7. Sprinkle with pistachios at the end. Refrigerate until ready to serve